TRAGIC HEROES

THE BURNEY BROTHERS OF HAY AT WAR

Hugh Purcell

Margaret Percy

For Christopher Burney's children, Juliette Paton and Peter Burney, for James Munro Mackenzie, the late Andrew Adams and his wife Val, for Cynthia Comyn and Lecky Thyne

TRAGIC HEROES

THE BURNEY BROTHERS OF HAY AT WAR

HUGH PURCELL AND MARGARET PERCY

Our gratitude to Y Lolfa:
to Lefi Gruffudd, Commissioning Editor;
our patient text editor Eirian Jones;
and Alan Thomas who designed the cover and image layout.

First impression: 2022

© Copyright Hugh Purcell & Margaret Percy and Y Lolfa Cyf., 2022

Cover design: Y Lolfa
Surcouf image: Department of Defence archives,
Marine Nationale, Vincennes
Drawing of Buchenwald: © Auguste Favier family

ISBN: 978 1 80099 185 9

Published and printed in Wales
on paper from well-maintained forests by
Y Lolfa Cyf., Talybont, Ceredigion SY24 5HE
website www.ylolfa.com
e-mail ylolfa@ylolfa.com
tel 01970 832 304
fax 832 782

PREFACE

THE BURNEY BROTHERS of Hay on Wye are forgotten. At least Lieutenant Roger Burney has his name on the Second World War memorial, but the best our guide to Hay's 'war heroes' could answer when we asked about Christopher Burney was to say, 'wasn't he some sort of spy?'

The fact is the Burney brothers had remarkable wars. Roger has his place in history not least because Benjamin Britten dedicated his *War Requiem* to him. Christopher deserves to have his place in any anthology of Second World War literature because his two books, *Solitary Confinement* and *Dungeon Democracy*, were regarded as classics. As evidence, the celebrated writer Rebecca West called the latter 'the most important book to appear for twenty-five years', and the politician and diarist Harold Nicholson wrote of the former, 'I beg you to read this remarkable book. None who read it will ever forget it'.

For the record

Christopher Burney (1917–1980) was parachuted into France in 1942 as an SOE agent. He was captured after a few months, tortured by the Gestapo, and endured eighteen months solitary confinement in Fresnes gaol. He was transported to Buchenwald Concentration Camp where he survived for fifteen months, led the non-communist resistance and was one of only four Britons to emerge at the end of the war. He wrote *Dungeon Democracy* and *Solitary Confinement* about his experiences but was gradually overcome by post-traumatic stress which contributed to his premature death in 1980.

Roger Burney (1919–1942), his younger brother, was at the start of the war a scholar, singer, painter, and pacifist who became a friend of Peter Pears and Benjamin Britten. Depressed by German atrocities he joined the Royal Navy and was Liaison Officer on the Free French submarine *Surcouf*. The mysterious sinking of this unique vessel with all hands in 1942 was the greatest submarine disaster of all time (so says the *Guinness Book of Records*) and until recently its cause was wrongly attributed. Our researches give the most likely reason for the disaster. The *War Requiem* is dedicated to Roger Burney.

We cannot begin to tell the story of Christopher without introducing a third character. She is Julia, whom Christopher married in 1946 after a miraculous reunion and with an intensity of passion, only for it to end, Julia wrote, *when eventually the result of Nazi barbarity caught us, many years later, in its wicked net.* After his death she wrote a hundred-page memoir of all the things she knew about him and felt about him from her understanding of him. Without this memoir no biography of Christopher would be possible, as will become apparent. Here is a flavour, taken from our text, with Julia's writing in italics. It captures well the romance overlaying tragedy that was part of the Second World War for so many.

'On the morning of 16 April 1945 Miss Julia Burrell, a secretary, was at her desk in the Secret Intelligence Service (MI6) headquarters in Westminster when the phone rang. It was Christopher. In a daze she agreed to meet him that lunchtime at St James's Park Tube station.

Almost three years before, in May 1942, Christopher Burney had disappeared without trace. Julia assumed he had parachuted into France as an agent for SOE (the Special Operations Executive) but since then, nothing, nothing at all. They had been in love, she was still in love, and she remembered over and over again the poem he had given her:

But give me time
And understand
And wait for me.

But time had almost run out and that weekend Julia Burrell was planning to introduce to her parents in Scotland another man who wanted to marry her.

When at last we did meet, we stood in front of each other and exchanged a perfunctory kiss. I did not notice he was wearing a strange assortment of clothes; an army battledress top, thin grey flannel trousers over which were pulled home-made wellington boots. His head had been shaved, but long enough ago to have grown a moleskin skullcap of short hair. His face was as bloated and as white as a dandelion puff. I noticed none of this; I only knew I was in his element and that I was in Heaven.
'Where have you been,' I asked, breaking a long silence.
'It will take time to tell.' Pause.
'Are you married?'
'No.'

Attached to the memoir is a ten-page 'Letter from Buchenwald', written by Christopher in January 1945 when the weather was searingly cold, and he was at the end of his tether. It must be the most revealing letter he ever wrote and therefore precious to a biographer. It was intended for Julia, and she found it in his concentration camp clothes sometime after he returned home.

We found another bundle of letters in the Burney files the family lent us. These were the five love letters that Julia wrote to Christopher spanning the three years of his disappearance. They are a mystery. Are they originals that Julia had second thoughts about posting to the PO Box in Wimpole Street Christopher had given as his address? Are they originals returned by SOE after the war? Are they copies of letters that Julia sent? It is hard to tell, but Christopher never received them, and Julia never knew that he had not. This adds to the pathos of undiminishing love for Christopher but decreasing confidence that he was still alive.

Before we tell the Burney biographies, we need to place the two brothers in the context of the border countryside around Hay which meant so much to them, and we must trace, briefly, the Burney family lineage.

Herefordshire Roots

Headstones to Christopher and Julia stand side by side in the Burney family plot in Kenchester churchyard, six miles north-west of Hereford. Behind them is the headstone of Joan, Christopher and Roger's older sister, and on the back of that is the memorial to Roger 'lost at sea with all hands while serving aboard the *Surcouf*. The graveyard is sorely in need of care, but several other Burney family graves are visible above the undergrowth and rabbit holes; those of their parents, 'Jack' and Dorothy Burney, their grandparents, Arthur and Annette Burney, the first of the family to make Herefordshire their home in the late nineteenth century. Several aunts, uncles and cousins are recorded too.

The church of St Michael is late twelfth-century early Gothic, without a tower but with a Welsh slate roof borne up on stout wooden trusses. Amid the interior gloom are two armorial windows recessed deep in the chancel walls either side of the altar. Each depicts a Burney 'knight at arms': Geoffrey Asteley Burney of the Royal Flying Corps, killed over France in 1916, and Arthur George Burney, the first of the Herefordshire line who died in 1924; in his hand are the scales of justice, for he was a barrister. The morning sun shines through stained glass layered with cobwebs. The effect is of beauty, peace, and awe that this simple building has been worshipped in for a thousand years.

When Christopher was in solitary confinement in Fresnes prison in 1942/3, he remembered childhood attendance at morning service in St Michael's, anticipating a Sunday lunch of roast beef and Yorkshire pudding at The Weir:

> I found myself in a daydream walking back from the old church in Herefordshire where we used to be taken every Sunday in the holidays. The fields had their August warmth and yellowness, the hopyards stood like orderly jungles waiting for the pickers, there were blackberries in the hedges and thirsty bullocks waiting in the shade. Across the stile and through the gate was lunch.

The Weir is a large Georgian house on the bank of the River Wye, with walled garden, an arboretum, a boathouse, and the site of a Roman villa. Christopher and Roger's Burney grandparents had moved there after their marriage in 1881, wanting to raise a family far from the consanguinity of the Home Counties. They had wished to buy this beautiful house (now a nursing home) and its garden (now in the care of the National Trust) but, failing that, settled in as tenants with their five children and extended family. They left when Grandfather Arthur died in the mid-1920s, but their Herefordshire home meant so much to the family that when Arthur's granddaughter Joan died, getting on for a century later in 2002, the wake was held at The Weir. Within a few years of leaving the old house, the Burneys had set up home in Hay on Wye on the Welsh border.

Hay in the 1930s was a market town with a railway, where once a week farmers descended from the hills with their animals and walked them to auction through the narrow streets. Hay is a major crossing point on the Wye and dominated by its castle, one of a chain in the border country – Abergavenny, Crickhowell, Tretower and Brecon – marking the Norman line of invasion and subsequent defence from Welsh armies. Whether Hay is in England or Wales is still disputed but the border is just east of Hay along Offa's Dyke, so-called because King Offa of Mercia fortified his frontier in the eighth century. The appeal of Hay is its surrounding landscapes rather than the town, from the broad flowing River Wye to the Black Mountains. Perhaps for this reason it has long attracted a rich culture of writers and artists, not least the Revd Francis Kilvert, of diary fame in the mid-nineteenth century; and more recently, the Hay Literary Festival. Just up the hill from the festival campus, Oakfield House is where the Burney brothers grew up from 1933 onwards. Before moving forward though, we must trace the family back through two centuries of the all-important Burney lineage.

The Burney Heritage

Christopher probably admired his immediate family predecessors more than Roger because they were fighting men. Their father, known as Jack, was Colonel Arthur Edward Cave Burney of the Royal Artillery, twice decorated for bravery at Gallipoli with a DSO and MC, who subsequently entered Jerusalem with General Allenby in 1917. Here he encountered Christopher's hero, the Arabist and guerrilla fighter T E Lawrence. During his children's early years, he was based on the North-West Frontier of India with his family. His wife Dorothy, née Norton, was also from a Royal Artillery family. Jack's uncle was Brigadier-General Herbert Burney, who spent most of his life fighting wars in Africa and India. His two sons, George and Gilbert, were in the care of their uncle Arthur, so formed part of the extended Burney family at The Weir during the holidays, though they were a generation older than Christopher and Roger. George Talbot Burney became a Brigadier General with the 51st Highland Division and died a Prisoner of War in 1940. Gilbert was killed in the Great War in 1915 and is buried near Bethune in Belgium.

Roger, on the other hand, may well have felt a closer affinity with the illustrious eighteenth and nineteenth-century Burneys who were writers, artists, and musicians. Best known among them was the famous satirical novelist and playwright Frances 'Fanny' Burney, known after she married as Madame d'Arblay, whose portrait by a cousin hangs in the National Gallery in London. Her brother Charles Burney DD, was a classicist, schoolmaster and a direct ancestor of Christopher and Roger. Charles's and Fanny's father was the celebrated musician and composer, Charles Burney FRS (1726–1814), an active member of Samuel Johnson's literary 'club' in London. Reynolds's portrait of him also hangs in the National Gallery.

The arts and the martial arts are united in the Burney family crest that shows a lyre on the sleeve of the crest above a helmet – the union of music with the martial arts, whether intentional or not. The Latin motto beneath is 'Omne Bonum Desuper', 'all good from above'.

Christopher insisted that he was Scottish not English, and when he was living alone in Normandy in the 1960s the villagers called him 'l'écossais'. He was right to do so because Charles Burney FRS was the son of James MacBurney, a land agent in Shropshire who dropped the 'Mac' at the time of the Jacobite rebellion. His ancestors had come south from Scotland at the time of James I.

Christopher and Roger's earliest and happiest memories were of India. They were born in Fleet, in Hampshire, but soon went out with their sister Joan and mother Dorothy to join Jack in his Adjutant's bungalow on Peshawar Road, Rawalpindi, with hot season stays in Thandiani hill station. For six years they had a charmed childhood, educated by private tutors and enjoying all the outdoor life on offer in the Indian foothills. They came back on monsoon leave once or twice to The Weir, then to Mantley Chase, Gloucestershire, where their widowed Grandmama Annette lived for several years. Their happy Indian existence ended in 1926 when their parents returned their children to England and enrolled them in boarding school: Joan was twelve, Christopher nine and Roger seven. Jack and Dorothy returned to India leaving the children miserable at school and, according to Christopher, miserable in the holidays too with Grandmama Annette.

In 1930 Jack and Dorothy returned to England for good. Jack had suffered long-term pulmonary decline, so he was invalided out of active service and appointed Commandant of the Royal School of Artillery at Larkhill on Salisbury Plain. The children continued to board, now more happily as the boys had been moved to Bilton Grange prep school where the headmaster, John Fawcus, was quite probably the only teacher Christopher ever liked. Holidays were at the family's army home at Windyridge, Larkhill.

Disaster struck at Easter 1931. It was 1 April, the first day of the holidays: Jack complained of exhaustion and was pleaded with to go on a family outing to a local point-to-point race. When they got home, they all were at the tea table when Jack unexpectedly collapsed: a fatal heart attack. He was forty-eight. If it was a terrible shock for Dorothy, it was horrific for their children, who adored their father. A month later, Dorothy had to move out of married quarters on a paltry pension, with three children to educate.

Rescue came from an unlikely knight in shining armour. Wilfred Young was Jack's first cousin once removed, in his sixties and living with unmarried sisters in London. By all accounts he was a crusty old colonel who had served in India with Hodson's Horse; he had married in India many years before, but his wife died young. Moved by affection as well as duty, he bought a house for Dorothy's orphaned family in the border country they loved and so exchanged London for Hay on Wye. Dorothy, who had been 'camping out' with various

Burney connections in the area, was relieved to accept the arrangement.

'God exists' in the Black Mountains

In 1933 this unlikely family arrived at Oakfield; 'Uncle Wilf', his 'housekeeper' and three unsettled children. Shortly afterwards Wilfred and Dorothy discreetly went off to France and got married, for appearances sake. That offended Christopher, though it was clearly no more than a marriage of convenience, as Dorothy assured Julia years later. 'Uncle Wilf', a background figure, died in 1942 but Dorothy, known by all as 'Ma', took up her favourite place in the kitchen by the Aga cooker and large pine table and lived there for thirty years.

Oakfield is a large Grade II listed Regency house up a secluded track off the Brecon Road, surrounded by pasture. It looks north across the Wye Valley, and over the wooded hill behind Hay Bluff stands sentinel in the Black Mountains.

In his years of solitary confinement, Buchenwald and after, the walk behind the house up to Hay Bluff played a huge part in Christopher's imagination. It became a symbol to him, a symbol Julia wrote of 'all that was secret and good and eternal': but also, in Buchenwald, a 'via dolorosa' that symbolised his despair. Those few of us who know the walk well, for our family cottage is just up the hill from Oakfield, will readily recognise that the walk is steeped in history that lingers in the air; lodges in the imagination.

On the ridge over Oakfield, sheep shelter under hawthorn trees bent over by the wind. Here was an Iron Age camp, there a long cairn standing minus its stone roof; archaeology has uncovered human use going back many hundreds of years, no doubt drovers sheltering for the night: on the ridge on a windy autumn afternoon one can sense them, centuries of the heavy huff and breath of cattle, the light quick patter of sheep, moving east towards London.

Then the walk descends a track to Penywrlodd Estate, the

house originally built by one of Cromwell's generals in the seventeenth century, before continuing downhill through pasture to Cilonw brook. Following the brook down the valley is a path to Llanigon village with its medieval motte and Norman church; scrambling up by the brook the path leads to 'a little wooded valley with a waterfall you can sometimes hear but not see, which disappears behind the shoulder of a low foothill', as Christopher described it to Julia. The side of the valley is steep, the wood dark and the path uncertain, but the sound of a waterfall gives direction. As Julia wrote, it is a place of seclusion and secrets; easier to retrace steps and follow the scarcely used lane up to the top from Penywrlodd.

Scrambling up the brook, or following it on the lane above, steeply up through woodland, the track leads to a T-junction; turn right past Dan y Capel and Hill Farm, working sheep farms still, and over a cattle grid onto a high plateau. Inescapably the eye is drawn across the open vista to Hay Bluff and Lord Hereford's Knob (Twmpa), guardians of the Gospel Pass leading to the ruins of the Augustinian Priory of Llanthony.

Hay Bluff is the red sandstone northern escarpment of the Black Mountains. On a dull day it appears as a dark-hued wedge silhouetted against the grey sky; on a bright day its steep green slopes invite a gentle climb to the summit at 670 metres. The weather predominates: on a summer's day picnickers sit on soft grass while children fly kites or slither down the Bluff; in winter, as Christopher discovered, 'the high plateau is swept by the bitterest of all winds which tore off what protection I had and cut through me'. Benign or savage, the weather is controlling.

There is a personal but timeless quality to the walk that can be deeply affecting. Perhaps it is that view from the top of further ridges over secluded valleys with softer fields down to the ever flowing Wye. One may say, as Christopher Burney certainly did, 'God exists'. In 'Letter from Buchenwald' the walk no longer symbolises his way into the future with Julia but a via dolorosa when 'the death of despair gnawed at my heart': but his belief in God did not leave him.

Now we leave the 'we' of joint authorship and move to the 'I', for Hugh has written the biography of Christopher Burney and Margaret the biography of Roger that follows. For thanks and acknowledgements to all those who helped us over two years, please read the Chapter Notes.

PART I

CHRISTOPHER BURNEY

CONTENTS

CHAPTER 1

THE MAKING OF A REBEL

CHRISTOPHER WAS FIFTEEN when the family moved to Oakfield. According to his sister Joan he told neighbours that he did not really belong to this dull family because he was by birth a prince of royal Russian blood: a fantasy that he would re-enact when he changed identity during the war years. He resented his stepfather and Wilf found him impossible to deal with. The neighbours would have seen a slim boy of medium height with a long face, rather foxy looking perhaps, grey eyes and dark straight hair. They may have been put off by his arrogant manner and independent spirit, but admired his liking for tough adventures. His nickname was 'Chucha'.[1]

A few months after witnessing the death of his father at Easter 1931, he began his secondary education at Wellington College. He had intended to go to Eton but now the money was not available. Not surprisingly, he was unhappy. 'He doesn't look awfully fit, though he says he is all right', wrote his housemaster at Picton House, Sumner Scott, to John Fawcus, the headmaster of Christopher's previous school, Bilton Grange. 'He looks white, as if all the cares in the world were upon him. Is this habitual with him?' It was certainly understandable: the Burney family had not only lost their father but also their breadwinner, though Dorothy's anxieties about paying school fees were mitigated by Wellington giving

Christopher an Exhibition. 'Habitual' or not, the next few years of Christopher's life were unhappy.

He was soon at war with authority over his future and after two years or so he ceased to work, culminating in him running away from Wellington. He then wandered around Europe, 'miserably', according to his mother, before moving from job to job in London. Had Christopher received strong paternal guidance he may well have stayed at school, progressed to Oxford or Cambridge and then fought a more conventional war than being dropped into France as a secret agent. This is conjecture, of course, but Julia may well have agreed. She wrote that he had a very close relationship with his father and that the loss of his guiding hand had *disastrous results in his early years*. Christopher's personality was emerging. He was becoming restless, argumentative, and arrogant, determined to have his way.

Out of Bounds

How much was Christopher failed by Wellington? It is easy to blame a narrow, conservative public school intended for the sons of army officers and senior civil servants and that is some way justified. However, Wellington was also strongly affected by the climate of the times for revolution was in the air. The growing tensions in society over communism, fascism and democracy were reaching the public schools and nowhere was this more true than at Wellington. The originators of protest at the school were the Romilly brothers, Giles and Esmond, whose Wellington years almost exactly coincided with those of Christopher and Roger. While at school they published *Out of Bounds*, a socialist, anti-war and anti-conformist magazine that was distributed in public schools by fervent supporters, where it sometimes led to riots. Christopher disliked the Romillys and he was certainly not a pacifist, but he shared their dislike of the 'ancien régime' and the unfairness of society. He was restless for change too.[2]

21

No copy of the magazine *Out of Bounds* exists in either the Wellington College library or the British Library, so we must turn to the Romillys' book with the same title that was published in 1935. What depressed Giles Romilly, who wrote the first half of *Out of Bounds*, was the drab conformity of the school, even by public school standards. This must have depressed Christopher too, for there was no space at Wellington for free spirits. Life was centred on the 'dormitory' (the House, like Picton) where forty junior boys ate and slept, regimented according to their year of entry. Socialising outside your year was frowned on and outside your dormitory was forbidden, Giles said, so the peer group of boys was limited to no more than seven or eight, the same faces, habits, voices year after year at meals, at games, at night. A boy's only privacy was his 'room', a small cubicle, bed, chair, and desk.

New entrants to dormitories were chosen according to 'the right type to maintain the tone', so wrote Giles. In his dormitory, boys who liked team games, the Officer Training Corps and were all-round 'toughs' were preferred. This accounted for the 'remarkable homogeneity of most dormitories, mopping up individuality'. Loyalty to the dormitory came first and being 'anti-social' was a damning indictment. Esmond Romilly's biographer called this conformity 'a doctrine of suppression'.

Wellington was no different from other public schools then and for the next twenty-five years in maintaining among the boys a quasi-feudal system of hierarchy, with 'prefects' at the top and 'fags' at the bottom, the former using the latter as personal servants and reinforcing their authority by beating; but that was usual. What was conspicuous at Wellington according to the writer T C Worsley, who taught at Wellington when the Burney and Romilly brothers were there, was the indifference to culture and the arts. It was 'philistine to a degree almost unimaginable in a great school, in every possible way... thirty, forty, fifty years behind the times'.

Giles's description of the dormitory library is good

evidence of this. It was popular because it was the only place to meet indoors outside the dormitory but that was its only recommendation. It was a dreary room decorated with busts of eminent Victorians, the shelves bearing leather-covered books and bound copies of *The Illustrated London News*. No book had been added since about 1900, wrote Giles, unless it was written by an Old Wellingtonian: 'Everywhere books were missing or had lost their labels.'

Esmond Romilly was taught 'politics' twice a week by a Mr Debrett:

> The master who took these classes was a member of an organisation known as the 'English Mistery', which went in for extreme right-wing Toryism – 'the restoration of the function of royalty in the body politic' and 'the enlightened rule of the aristocracy'. He waged a relentless struggle against intellectuals.

The conservatism of Wellington was increased by it being a school for the military. Over 700 Wellingtonians had been killed in the Great War fighting to preserve British society, so their families, by and large, were in no mood to encourage radical change.

A counterculture did exist, just about, centred on the right for free speech. Giles Romilly's housemaster reluctantly had to accept it: 'You're entitled to your opinions of course, but remember, no propaganda – this is a military school. You must play the game, play the game.' As ever, the Debating Society was regarded as a verbal playing field where this game was played. The motions debated during these years show that the forces of liberalism were not altogether lost. 'Patriotism is the last refuge of a scoundrel' was carried by twenty-eight votes to sixteen while, 'This house is in favour of the present system of party government' was won by sixteen votes to twelve. However, co-education at Wellington was still a long way away: 'In the opinion of this house the political freedom of women is a sign of a civilised society' was a motion that sank towards the bottom, twenty-nine votes to nine.

The university entry boys, the 'intellectuals', were not without cultural outlets as Roger Burney would come to appreciate; a choir, play-reading group, film society, music, but the verdict of a later Master of Wellington, Graham Stainforth, must stand: 'Wellington was brutal and tough… except in patches. It was narrow, rigid and somewhat philistine.'

That makes the protest of the Romilly boys even more remarkable. Both were sincere socialists and above all anti-war. On Remembrance Day, 11 November 1933, just before Christopher absconded, the Romilly brothers and about thirty others, including a teacher, wore British Anti-War Movement badges below their poppies. This led to fights breaking out between 'toughs' and 'intellectuals'. The hostility became more emotional when the anti-war lobby inserted pacifist propaganda into hymn books at the page to be opened for the sacred hymn 'O, Valiant Hearts'. This is sung to pay homage to the 'fallen' just before the two minutes' silence:

O valiant hearts who to your glory came
Through dust of conflict and through battle flame;
Tranquil you lie, your knightly virtue proved,
Your memory hallowed in the land you loved.

Proudly you gathered, rank on rank, to war
As who had heard God's message from afar;
All you had hoped for, all you had, you gave,
To save mankind—yourselves you scorned to save.

This sacrilege almost led to expulsion and a personal apology to Mr Debrett for 'spoiling his Armistice service', wrote Giles.

Christopher must have hated this. His family was steeped in service in the armed forces, and he was determined to follow that calling. Many a Sunday in the holidays he sat in the family church of St Michael, Kenchester, looking at the stained-glass armorial windows recently installed to two Burney knights at arms. One of these was G A Burney (Christopher's cousin), bearing the banner of St George. He was killed in action over France on 7 July 1916 while in the Royal Flying Corps.

The Armistice demonstration was just the beginning of Romilly protest. During the winter holiday of 1933/4 they spent their time distributing copies of the Communist Party *Daily Worker* and hanging around the Parton bookshop in west London, a meeting place for radical intellectuals. These activities gave them the idea to start a magazine for rebellious public schoolboys called *Out of Bounds ("Against Reaction in Public Schools")*. They issued a manifesto and announced the first edition for March 1934. Then the storm broke. The *Daily Mail* announced in bold type: **Red Menace in Public Schools, Moscow Attempts to Corrupt Boys.**

The press was excited by Esmond Romilly's signature at the end of the manifesto because he was the nephew of Sir Winston Churchill. The rebellious statesman said he found the episode 'amusing'. The school was excited too, divided into factions stacked against the Romillys. 'Bitter indignation exists at Wellington College', announced the *Daily Mail*. Sympathetic Wellingtonians offered the brothers a bodyguard of twenty-five supporters. The Headmaster, F B Malim, was visited by the Special Branch and consequently told the brothers to abandon their activities. Running away was the only option, Esmond decided, and this he did on 8 February.

Breaking Out

Christopher had absconded the previous November, but his reasons were more personal. Soon after he had joined the school as a late entrant aged fourteen, he had started arguing with his housemaster and then headmaster about his future. According to his mother, 'ever since he was seven or eight, he was set on going into the Indian Army with a view later of joining the Secret Service'. He was not dissuaded by his stepfather Wilf, despite a warning letter:

> I know your intention is to join the Indian Army in order to serve in the Gurkhas... You know that a Constitution is to be given to India. India will be governed by Indians and goodness knows how this will affect Europeans – safe to say it will not be to their advantage. Indian officers will gradually replace British officers. I can only tell you that none of my Brother Officers are sending their sons into the Indian Army which they would have done under normal conditions.

Christopher wanted to follow in his father's footsteps by taking the quickest route possible into the army, which meant entering the Royal Military Academy at Woolwich known as 'the Shop' for the training of commissioned officers in the Royal Artillery and Royal Engineers. Wellington teachers, however, were soon aware of Christopher's aptitude for Greek and Latin, and this pointed to a classical education at Oxford or Cambridge which was then regarded as the height of scholastic attainment. On 8 November 1931 Christopher wrote home:

> Dear Mummy,
> My tutor swears you told the Master that I was going to continue classics. He also says he knows a general in India who entered the Army through the Varsity, but I don't care if he knows fifteen generals, he can't deny that Woolwich or Sandhurst are the only good ways. He says he is writing to you but for Heaven's sake don't listen to his hidebound arguments. All he wants is honour and glory for the school. Nevertheless, I know who could give advice: Brigadier Anstey because he was here [Wellington] and would know what is best.

Dorothy Burney wrote to Brigadier Edgar Anstey, a family

friend serving in India, and he replied on 30 December 1931, having given the matter weighty consideration:

> My dear Dorothy,
> I have consulted the Adjutant General in India, General Sir Norman McMullen, and Major General Karslake, and they both say – University.
>   Firstly, it is not true that by going to university he will lose seniority with the Shop cadets. The Varsity candidates for the Army are given a two-year ante date to bring them into line in order to encourage boys to go to the University as it is believed that the training and experience there are of value to them as Officers.
>   The strongest arguments are these: it gives him longer in which to make up his mind: it is a form of insurance in case he wants to leave the army as it should help towards other employment: and it may be that he will disclose capabilities or talents of such a high order that he would be wasted in the Army.

These were arguments that Christopher did not want to hear but the disagreement lay dormant until the summer of 1932 when, after just one year at Wellington College, he passed his School Certificate with six credits, including Latin and Greek. He was obviously very bright, 'a born Greek scholar' said the Master, Frederick Malim, who insisted he should enter the Classical Sixth Form with Oxford or Cambridge in mind. Christopher resisted. He said he wanted to study modern languages, as they were far more useful for his chosen career. His Housemaster, Sumner Scott, wrote to Dorothy:

> He seems obsessed with the commercial view of education that it consists not in training your brain so that it can be put, like a steam engine, to any kind of work (I think this is Huxley's definition) but in amassing information or techniques that he

will actively use in life after school. This is the same view that maintains that we ought to be teaching stenography, book-keeping, shorthand etc.

Christopher gave in and agreed to specialise in Classics, although he was still determined to leave school for Woolwich or Sandhurst and then the Army as soon as he could. His headmaster reluctantly agreed with this, though he persisted with pushing the classics. He wrote to Sumner Scott on 6 August 1932:

> My dear Scott,
> Why should not Burney go on doing Classics? They are first rate scoring subjects for Sandhurst.
> Yours sincerely
> F B Malim

Christopher's heart was not in it and his work suffered. Sumner Scott wrote to his mother on 7 November:

> I think he has been doing very little work indeed. I am greatly perplexed as to his future. It is essential for his own brain that it should not be allowed to 'tick over'. He is a danger to himself, and I can't have a prefect, which Christopher could well be in two years' time, who is a bad worker and a bad example to others. I have been having another talk with the Master about him.

The Master then issued a threat, through the Picton Housemaster, that Christopher 'cannot possibly continue to hold his Exhibition if he does not work really hard'. This was interpreted by Dorothy Burney that if Christopher did not continue with Classics, he would have to leave Wellington when he was sixteen; and Christopher's reaction was that he was not allowed to argue because the College paid for him and, therefore, he had no independence. 'Boy, you are here on charity, you will do what you are told', is how he put it to Julia years later. He found this insulting.

His mother wrote: 'I told him that he must go on with Classics until he left school. He agreed but he was very restless and unhappy and unruly, though he did get into the Classical Sixth when he was sixteen.' Then, in October 1933, he suffered a nasty accident which Dorothy thought significantly affected his attitude to school: 'He was knocked out at boxing and fell on the back of his head so that he was unconscious for some time and in the sanatorium for about a week.'

Was this the last straw? Christopher had had enough. Obstinate, independent, resentful that Wellington was against him, 'in November he walked out of college early one morning and disappeared' – Dorothy.

Christopher and a fellow truant, the 'Games Captain' was how Christopher described him, hitch-hiked to London from where he phoned his sister Joan. She was unsympathetic, so he 'disappeared', as his mother said and it was only a week or two later when she appealed through the agony column of *The Times*, 'Come home, all is forgiven,' or words to that effect, that he reappeared, again using Joan as intermediary.

He refused to go back to school, although the Master said he would overlook Christopher absconding. Dorothy still thought his boxing accident had turned him from 'quite a normal and peaceful boy into someone absolutely without thought for the consequences of his acts', so she took him to a 'Brain Specialist', Mr Mappother. He suggested sending Christopher to a private tutor in London to study modern languages and thence to university, but the Burneys could not afford it.

Instead, Dorothy asked his former prep school headmaster at Bilton Grange, John Fawcus, to have Christopher to stay for a few weeks to assess what best to do. This he did. The outcome was not happy. Although Christopher had respected him more than other teachers, the feeling was not now reciprocated. Fawcus wrote to Dorothy on 18 March 1934:

He is passing through the stage of 'laying down the law' on all subjects, advancing immature views that all bear traces of a revolt against the accepted order of things. If only he were more tractable, more sympathetic, more tolerant, it would be so much easier to help him. In his present blind conceit (forgive the expression with regard to your son), he does not make friends nor inspire confidence that here is a boy we can help.

The headmaster understood what motivated Christopher throughout his young life and what often offended the company he was in:

He is obsessed with a restless spirit of adventure, the call of the East, and feels a strong urge to some sort of activity which will satisfy his craving. I understand that he may get an interview at the Foreign Office with a view to a post in the Intelligence Department, but he may not stand a chance. He sets too high a value on his own powers. His attitude of super-self-assurance has sorely tried the patience of those here who try to help him.

His practical suggestion to Dorothy was to send Christopher to France or Germany to learn a foreign language and 'to learn a lot about life of which he is presently lamentably ignorant'. This Dorothy did and May 1934 finds Christopher, still only sixteen, in Grenoble living with a family and studying international law at the university on a six-month course. He was consumed with the need for adventure, for money to support it and for a knowledge of foreign languages which he saw, with prescience, as essential for the life he wanted to lead.

Footloose in Europe

Dorothy Burney wrote a single-page account of Christopher's next year. It is a confused story – sometimes contradicted by what he told Julia later – of an increasingly unhappy and desperate teenager and a mother unable to cope with him.

His studies in Grenoble lasted for just one lecture and then he walked out. He was at a loose end. Wellington was alarmed. A teacher who knew Grenoble wrote, 'Not yet seventeen he will be exposed to every form of temptation'. He was right. Christopher got into debt, did not turn up for a meeting with Joan in Italy because, 'he had lent all his money to a friend to keep him out of prison', and returned home before Christmas 'miserable and restless'.

Dorothy Burney then decided to send him to Santander to learn Spanish. He lasted for two weeks living with a family, then sent her a request for more money and disappeared. Eventually he turned up in Grenoble again and this was too much for Dorothy. As he was legally under-age, she contacted the British Consul. He found Christopher living with an American girl, older than he was, who was teaching in a girls' school and this he reported to Mrs Burney. She went out to Grenoble and confronted the two, receiving mixed messages. 'She seemed a nice Lady', Dorothy wrote, 'she says she does not love him and is not living with him.' Young Christopher saw the relationship differently: 'They were absolutely in love, and she was begging him to stay with her.' The outcome was that Christopher was sent back to Santander. More misery. Christopher wrote that he was still absolutely in love and if the girl asked, he would walk the 600 miles to be with her again. In fact, Christopher had had enough. Year one of his first year of freedom, as described by Mrs Burney, ended sadly:

> He wrote a letter saying he would like to come home and get
> a job as things hadn't gone as he had hoped. He came home
> looking very ill and I'm sure wants thoroughly overhauling. He
> has been smoking much too much and has been treated to too
> many drinks.

Year two, 1935–6, was more promising.

First, using his newly acquired fluency in French, he went to Paris. Possibly he stayed with Jacque Foure, the brother of his American girlfriend in Grenoble, who was there, training to be a dentist. There is no evidence of this, but Jacque Foure was to play a significant part in his life, both during and after the coming war. Christopher hung around the Café de Flore that Julia described as *a sort of overflow* in the famous Pigalle area for get-togethers of Picasso, Scott Fitzgerald, Ernest Hemingway and other writers. Christopher recalled the occasion of his meeting with Hemingway in an interview in 1973: 'I got to know everybody in the Café Flore. Hemingway once took my drink, so I protested. "Do you want to make a thing of it?" he asked but passed out before we could go outside to fight.'

After the war Christopher returned to the Pigalle and introduced Julia to some of the artistic clientele. She wrote: *They included Chick Henshaw, an American journalist who bobbed in and out of our lives, and Ernestine Evans who was the first American reporter allowed to work in Russia after the Revolution.* Significantly, Christopher also met Russian émigrés and acquired useful spoken Russian.

Christopher returned to Oakfield in early summer 1936. Despite the unhappiness of kicking his heels in Europe for two years as an unworldly teenager with little money, he could now speak French and had learned a smattering of Spanish and Russian. Christopher's languages would save his life in the war looming ever nearer. His second ambition at Wellington College was about to be achieved too, for on 6 June 1936 he was commissioned into the South Wales Borderers (SWB) as a 2nd Lieutenant Supplementary Reserve Officer, so he achieved an officer rank of sorts not much later than had he entered Woolwich or Sandhurst straight from Wellington.

The SWB was based in nearby Brecon where a museum commemorates its famous history, notably the Zulu War of

1879 where the 1st Battalion was wiped out in the massacre of Isandlwana, but a small force of the 2nd Battalion redeemed the honour of the regiment by fighting off the victorious Zulus at the Defence of Rorke's Drift, after which eleven Victoria Crosses were awarded.

The Supplementary Reserve, initially known as the Special Reserve, was set up to maintain a reservoir of trained manpower in case of war. Reservists like Christopher enlisted for six years and were required to undergo six months of basic training on recruitment and a further three to four weeks training every year. During training Christopher realised that one of his jobs was to translate from Welsh what his soldiers were saying: many were Welsh speakers from the mining villages of the nearby Valleys.

His civilian life over the next three years was as unstable and volatile as before. He claimed that he was offered $500 to fly for General Franco in the Spanish Civil War but turned down the offer. More plausible is what he told Julia:

> There were periods when he homed back to Oakfield. He was briefly on Fleet Street, and as a cub reporter covered Crufts; that glimmer of a career ended when, in his words, he threw a telephone directory at a sub-editor. He unsuccessfully tried his hand as a door-to-door salesman of ladies' stockings but honesty, he said, inhibited salesmanship. His demented mother thought he might benefit from a spell on the psychiatrist's couch, but when he arrived for his appointment at the address she had given him, he found he was on the doorstep of a taxidermist [This became one of his best jokes]. His behaviour in those days was that of a fine colt without a bridle, and I am sure that if he had the guiding hand of his father, or even if Ma had been dependent on him for money and not the other way round, his life might have run a different course.

About this time Dorothy invited to stay at Oakfield a young German Jewish refugee, Lotte Katz, to work as a help around the house. She did not stay very long but kept in touch with Dorothy in the years ahead. In old age she remembered the two Burney brothers; Roger was kind and treated her as an equal but Christopher was a snob who regarded her as a servant.

On 3 September 1939 Prime Minister Neville Chamberlain declared war on Nazi Germany. For Julia Burrell, aged nineteen and living with her family at Nether Auchendrane on the banks of the River Doon in Ayrshire, it was an unforgettable experience:

> *Big Ben chimed and the Prime Minister, in his stagey sepulchral voice, announced that we were now at war with Germany. Mummy, the most self-possessed of people, burst into tears and startled us by saying that if ever there was a moment in our lives, now was the time to get down on our knees and pray.*

Fighting the Germans

On 29 April 1940, Lieutenant Christopher Burney of the 2nd Battalion, South Wales Borderers, disembarked from a converted liner at Haakvik, south of Narvik, inside the Arctic Circle in Norway. The 2nd Battalion claimed the distinction of being the first battalion of the regiment to go into action. More than that, the Narvik campaign was the first British Army engagement in Europe in the Second World War, for although in September 1939 Britain had declared war on Germany for invading Poland, she did not send troops to defend Poland; nor did the British Expeditionary Force go into action in the Battle for France until early May, some weeks after the battle for Narvik began.[3]

German forces had invaded Norway earlier in April. One objective was to capture Narvik because it was the port through which iron ore from Sweden was exported, vital for Germany's armaments. Further, Hitler saw Narvik as a potential naval base, particularly important as it was ice-free in the winter months when much of the Baltic Sea was frozen over. German warships steamed up the Norwegian coast and landed troops that soon captured the port. The British Government saw the strategic value of Narvik too; it could be the base for opening up the Baltic for the Allies. So, the British Navy retaliated and moved a mixed force of British, French and Polish forces to retake the port.

The 2nd Battalion SWB disembarked at Haakvik on 29 April and was ordered to the Ankenes Peninsula only two miles south of Narvik, but by this time an assault on the port had been abandoned. Instead, in atrocious weather and strung out over an eight-mile front, the Battalion was reduced to skirmishing with German troops until 15 May when it was ordered to withdraw to HMS *Effingham* with the intention of defending the new airfield at Bodø, one hundred miles to the south. Typical of the doomed campaign, the *Effingham* struck a rock and had to be abandoned with the loss of all the 2nd Battalion kit, though no lives. Not long after the re-equipped SWB arrived at Bodø the Norwegian campaign was abandoned and the 2nd Battalion embarked for home on 5 June. An inglorious campaign, but what of Lieutenant Burney?

The only mention in the *War Diary*, that source on which historians depend for detailed knowledge of a battalion at war, is that he was kept at headquarters early in the campaign, and in the list of 'Officers Taking the Field' it says, 'Lieut. Burney 5%'. Was he only in action for a small amount of the campaign? Was he ill or injured in a skiing accident like another officer similarly labelled? We shall not know. The only tangible reminder of Burney in Norway was an ankle-length khaki cloak which Julia thought was *wonderfully romantic and marvellously Beau Geste*. In an interview in the 1970s Burney said he spent the campaign 'swanning around'.

The Norwegian campaign was inglorious, but was it a disaster?

In fact, the Royal Navy won a significant victory by sinking or putting out of action no fewer than fifteen German destroyers and heavy cruisers and one small battleship, thereby discouraging the German invasion of Britain later that summer. The Allied army, however, lost heavily. A combination of over hasty preparations and lack of equipment, the failure of air and artillery support and atrocious weather resulted in its inability to stop German troops taking Narvik. The Allied forces did not dislodge them until the end of May, by which time they were ordered to withdraw from Norway in order to defend France. Norway was forced to surrender on 10 June, and King Haakon VII escaped to Britain on a British destroyer. For the British Army it was not a morale boosting campaign to begin the fight against fascism, and worse was to come.

For Christopher Burney the campaign was another chapter of frustration, so he must have leapt at the chance of joining the new Special Service Brigade, known as the 'Commandos'. Formed that autumn by order of Prime Minister Churchill to 'develop a reign of terror down the enemy coast', it was a dramatic call that appealed to young Burney whose role model at the time was the guerrilla fighter in the Arabian desert T E Lawrence. There were soon twelve units of 450 commandos each, and Burney's was the twelfth because it was formed in Londonderry where the 2nd Battalion SWB had been based before the Narvik campaign. Significantly for Christopher, when he was captured two years later, although the Commandos were seconded from their former regiments they remained on the roll, so he could claim with truth when he was captured for spying that he was an officer with the South Wales Borderers. In fact, he is one of the select few from the Second World War on its Roll of Honour.

Among soldiers of the old school, former officers of the Great War, the Commandos had a bad reputation, as did guerrilla war itself. They were thought to be ill-disciplined, unethical, up to 'dirty tricks'. The very name was suspect because it came from the guerrilla bands of Boer soldiers who had outsmarted the British Army in South Africa forty years before. The Commandos were thought to attract desperados, reckless men yearning for adventure at any cost.

One of these, of course, was Christopher, who achieved notoriety early on during training at Aldergrove airport in Northern Ireland. A popular indoor game among commandos was a form of 'Russian roulette', when lights were turned out in the large hall where officers were billeted, and live rounds shot carelessly at invisible targets – 'but Chris always aimed', one officer told Julia.

Finding Love

In the late summer of 1941, 12 Commando arrived for more training in Ayr. Soon began the most romantic but ultimately tragic affair between Julia and Christopher:

> One evening, lying in bed with inner-ear trouble and listening on my wireless to Carol Gibbons playing all the popular dance tunes at London's Savoy, Anne [her sister] came into my room to give me the latest bulletin on social life in Ayr. She sat on my bed and told me the rendezvous that evening had been at the Station Hotel and then she told me the names of all who had been in her party. As she got up to leave, she said casually, 'Oh, and by the way, I saw somebody, and I know you'll have a big affair with him. I only hope I'm not around when it happens.' She left, and alone once more I dreamed, listening to Carol Gibbons and wishing I was at the Savoy, dancing.[4]

Shortly afterwards Anne introduced the two at a local pub:

> It was a dingy bar, blue with cigarette smoke and the sour taste of beer where before the war well brought up young girls would no more have thought of entering than we would have pushed into a lavatory marked 'Gents'.
> I remember after Anne's build-up that I did not see a shower of shooting stars; instead, I saw a medium-sized beige-coloured

37

man. He was untidy and more smoke seemed to hang around him than elsewhere. He was politely aloof... He seemed bored and arrogant, and the more he kept up that attitude the more I longed to please.

Eventually the ice cracked when the general conversation turned to the exciting news that Russia had joined the Allies. Christopher seized the initiative announcing, to the disbelief of many, that he spoke Russian, and with subtle innuendo implied he had an inner knowledge of the country. A second lieutenant and twenty-three years old, he was brighter and better informed than many, but his bumptious interruptions were not an endearing quality to his fellow officers. He irritated, but as he was amusing company he was good-naturedly tolerated.

Christopher's former headmaster at Bilton Grange, John Fawcus, would have recognised him from this description.

Julia was fascinated by the Burney boots, just as she would be when he returned from the war nearly four years later. They were his show-off badge of individuality:

They came halfway up the inside of his trouser leg, like short wellington boots in leather, and they had spongy rubber soles. He wore them all the time, even for dancing. I thought they might have come from his Russian travels, and he implied they had, but modesty prevented him from admitting it. Later he told me the boots had been made by Lobb in Paris and that it was in Paris that he had learnt a bit of Russian.

Somebody, happy to score off Chris, wondered not without malice what he would wear out of uniform. 'Oh,' he said with an aplomb that made everybody laugh, 'the nattier shades of fawn and grey'.

Christopher must have seen that he was being *flittered and flirted with* by a tall, slim and elegant young lady with a heart-shaped face and deep-set eyes below dark hair. She had the upbringing of her class:

*We were screened from the realities of life and also from
education; riding, dancing, a little French and piano playing,
basic manners and an ability 'to make the best of yourself',
more than this might frighten off the young men who might
ask for our hands in marriage. We believed in True Love and
were shocked by sex because it had no place in happy ever after
romance; but kissing was just so much fun. We must have been
the sillies of all time.*

Five years of war would rip apart the screen and show a
nightmare of life few of us can conceive. On 4 January 1945,
amidst the inhumanity of Buchenwald Concentration Camp,
Christopher wrote of a deeper vision of Julia, a picture shaped
by longing and remembering during two and a half years of
solitary confinement and living hell:

I can see now more in my love than I could before. I
realised that I loved more than your body or the things you
said, and I could even define it down to something in your
eyes and mouth that I couldn't describe for anything, but
I felt was a sort of secret touchstone of cleanness and a
sense of nobility. And now I realise that was so and I see a
lot more. I know I can only find that in someone who has
something in their blood which comes from heather and
horses and clean west winds. This sounds silly. I can't tell
you what I mean any more than I could before, but I know
that I love home with all my heart, and you seem so much a
part of it.

The romance between Julia and Christopher in 1941
was intense. He made up for his lack of social skills and his
ineptitude at dancing with irresistible romancing:

*Looking back, I associate those first few weeks of knowing
Christopher with the chill of late summer and early autumn.
I can remember sitting in our rose garden on a late summer*

*evening with the smell of burning leaves only just masking
the scent of the roses, and Christopher quoting from Omar
Khayyam, 'I sometimes think that never blows so red the rose
as where some buried Caesar bled'. When he learnt that I had
never heard of the Rubáiyát, he sent me a slim volume a few
days later. In my garden today I have a deep red rose called 'The
Knight'.*

*There were long drawn-out dinners in dismal wartime
surroundings in Ayr, but he generated such excitement that I
was only aware of him. His hero was Lawrence of Arabia and
when he recited the poem at the front of the 'Seven Pillars' I
knew it was for us, although we knew Lawrence was writing of
Arabia:*

*I loved you, so I drew these tides of men into my hands,
And wrote my will across the sky in stars
To earn you Freedom, the seven pillared worthy house,
That your eyes might be shining for me,
When we came.*

Julia Burrell was one of three daughters of a wealthy
family that had made its money out of shipping. Her father,
Gordon, was one of nine children of William Burrell, a ship
owner, and Gordon's brother, another William, became the
benefactor of the international Burrell Collection of art and
antiquities in Glasgow. They lived in what later owners called
'the Scots semi-baronial mansion' of Nether Auchendrane,
three miles outside Ayr. It had been built as a medieval tower
house with a turret reached by a winding stone staircase
offering glimpses of the River Doon below, *timeless, and
soothing and flowing endlessly to the sea,* according to Julia.
Around the house were acres of manicured lawns and paths,
and a long drive along which Christopher would tramp,
invited or uninvited.

The Commandos were not popular. 'One doesn't know
much about these chaps,' Christopher's landlord commented
after looking at his flowing cloak and generally flamboyant

behaviour. At the country club it was reported that Christopher had been seen marching at the head of his troop around Ayr's highways and byways singing 'The Red Flag' and chanting, 'Good old Joe [Stalin]'. Julia's father muttered darkly, 'That Burney chap looks to me like a Turk', which could be an accurate assessment as 'Turk' was current slang for 'Irish' but was more likely a term of mild abuse as it was the Turks who defeated the Royal Navy at the Dardanelles in 1915–16 and Julia's father had served in the Navy. This disapproval did not deter Julia and there was scarcely a day when they did not meet.

Under what Julia called Christopher's *braggadocio* she brought out his thoughtful side; his dream of a free Europe and his socialist ideals for redistributing resources. Typical of the upper-class British male at this time, Christopher did not show his feelings, perhaps tried to repress them, but with Julia it was different. He wrote her tender, revealing letters of his love, about his image of her that he would carry through the war:

> When I met you, darling, I had confidence outside, on my face, but inside I was quietly growing empty. I still had fever burning inside me, but they were hot dying embers and there was no more fuel for them.
>
> Then you smiled and fanned me gently and you brought me back to the things I love; horses and flowers and cleanness and the quiet things that make me happy.
>
> Even now, alone, I can't say clearly what you have done. The only thing I'm afraid of is losing you. I can't help that.

That reads like a goodbye letter. Julia realised that despite her love Christopher was restless, and longed to go on a Commando raid for which he had been trained. He was fit and frustrated. What she did not know was that he had taken an initiative:

One evening he said he thought he had found another means of getting into action, and a week or two later he went to London for interviews. He returned full of excitement and secrecy and with great hope.

CHAPTER 2

THE SHORT LIFE OF A SECRET AGENT

LATE IN 1941 Christopher Burney was at one of his 12 Commando parties in Ayrshire when the Brigadier called him over: 'Ever jumped out of an aeroplane, my boy? I've a feeling you're going to.' Burney told this story after the war and added that he had 'submitted a paper on how to liberate France from within' to an organisation in London. There is no evidence of this paper, but it was true to character. He was obsessed with Lawrence of Arabia, he yearned for adventure, and he was never shy of airing his views. Moreover, he knew to whom he should submit it. Brigadier Colin Gubbins was Director of Operations and Training at the so-called Special Operations Executive and had been for the last year. Gubbins was fascinated by irregular warfare, indeed he had written secret manuals on the subject like *The Art of Guerrilla Warfare,* and he had a hand in setting up the commando units after the Narvik raid: hence his probable acquaintance with Burney.

SOE – The Special Operations Executive

What was SOE? It was set up in July 1940 after Hugh Dalton, the Minister of Economic Warfare, had proposed:

We have to organise movements in enemy-occupied territory
comparable to the Sinn Féin movement in Ireland, to the
Chinese guerrillas now operating against Japan and – one
might as well admit it – to the organisations the Nazis
themselves have developed. These movements must use many
different methods, including industrial and military sabotage,
labour agitation and strikes, continuous propaganda, terrorist
acts, boycotts, and riots.

What is needed is a new organisation to inspire, control
and assist the nationals of the oppressed countries who must
themselves be participants. We need absolute secrecy and
fanatical enthusiasm. Such an organisation should be entirely
independent of the War Office machine.

Dalton's paper reached Prime Minister Churchill and it was
on his authority later in July 1940 that a most secret paper
ordered, 'a new organisation shall be established forthwith
to co-ordinate all action, by way of subversion and sabotage,
against the enemy overseas. This organisation will be known
as the Special Operations Executive.' Dalton was to be the
chairman and Churchill's brief to him was simple: 'And now
set Europe a-blaze.'

Nazi-occupied France was only one country where SOE
was active, but it was F Section that Burney was to join.
Such was the complexity of command and acronyms that
characterised SOE that F section was separate from RF
section: that consisted mostly of French nationals working
covertly in France answerable to the government-in-exile led
by General Charles de Gaulle in London. One of its agents who
became famous after the war was 'Tommy' Yeo-Thomas who
used the code name *White Rabbit;* his relations with F Section
were strained. RF Section caused problems for F Section
because it forced SOE to recruit primarily British agents who
nevertheless spoke French and had lived in France.[1]

Burney was just the type that F Section was looking for.
He was trained as a commando; he spoke French and he had

lived in France albeit briefly. He was an individual with an independent spirit that set him apart and he placed making war against Germany over his own safety. The SOE Recruiting Officer, Selwyn Jepson, found his man in Burney:

> I often came on a personality's desire to prove itself – to discover if it could function effectively in situations of greater demand than it normally met. In short, 'to overcome'. Then there were the adventurous ones; simpler, more extrovert who didn't doubt their capabilities in this direction and would enjoy exercising them.

Burney was a mixture of the two, depending on his mood.

SOE was a 'cloak-and-dagger' organisation, characterised by daring and risk-taking. 'Setting Europe a-blaze' was not a game of course, although in these early days some recruits regarded it as such. It was a matter of life or death, for agents were told that their chance of survival was no more than evens. In fact, twenty-five per cent of the 450 or so who landed in France never came back. So there was constant fear, suspicion, treachery, and tragedy too. This was the organisation Christopher Burney was to join while it was still in its infancy, a period of jumping into the dark, literally and metaphorically. The Head of F section, Major Maurice Buckmaster, said, 'There is no rule book because there are no rules.' In 1942 there was still a desperate shortage of resources as well as experience, and more than a little incompetence, as Burney was to discover to his cost.

There have been many accounts of SOE, and I do not intend to add to them except where my story relates to Christopher Burney, but I share with countless others a fascination with the organisation. Surely, no-one who has visited the airfield at RAF Tempsford (near the A1 in Bedfordshire), from where the SOE agents took off for France, can forget it? There is a barn still standing where they gathered for final briefing and checking. This is a hallowed place where messages and personal memorials are left. An annual service is still held. Is it my imagination or can one feel the atmosphere of excitement and dread that lay heavy in the air on that eve of departure?[2]

Christopher Burney becomes a Secret Agent

Early in January 1942 in Ayrshire, Julia was telephoned by Christopher. As a result of his interviews, he had been ordered to report the next day in London. They had dinner together and then went for a soulful walk:

> *I felt physically and emotionally exhausted. Then he told me he could tell me nothing about his future, but that he would send me a post-box number to write to; and, he added, I should not worry if I did not get immediate replies.*
>
> *'I love you', he said, and the intensity of his feelings together with a sudden instinctive fear for his safety threw me into a panic. 'Perhaps we better not be in touch until the end of the war.' After a pause Christopher said, 'If that is what you want.' I could not bear the sight of his sad white face; I turned and started to walk home, crying all the way.*

Julia, now aged twenty-two and therefore required by war regulations to get a job, packed her bags and followed Christopher to London. Through a family connection she joined 'Passport Control' as a secretary. This was a cover for MI6 where she first learned about SOE, though she still did not know that Christopher might work for it. Apparently SOE had a bad reputation:

> *MI6's job was to collect information from occupied territories by means of secret agents who did their work without recourse to violence. SOE, on the other hand, liberally equipped with guns and dynamite, blasted and blew their way through our territory as well as their own, often wrecking many of our well-laid plans and, worse, imperilling our sources.*

Christopher probably stayed at a hotel near 6 Orchard Court, the F section base, which is in Portman Square, a short walk from SOE headquarters in Baker Street. He used to meet Julia before and after work (despite her earlier protestations) and was careful never to tell her where he was staying. He chafed against his inactivity. He wrote to her, 'I've nothing to do now and am waiting for the clogged machinery of war to get moving again.' In fact, it is probable that he spent three weeks at Wanborough Manor near Guildford at an induction school called STS5. This was to weed out mostly civilian recruits through a demanding but elementary course in field skills like map reading, handling explosives and weapons training. The acronym 'SOE' was never mentioned. In the evenings the supervision continued. Conversational French was compulsory and, so it is said, flirtatious women were on hand at the local pub to detect any lack of moral fibre. Recruits were allowed to write and receive personal, though censored, letters via a PO Box in Wimpole Street. Christopher wrote to Julia in this way, composing a poem for her which, with hindsight of the tragedies that would shortly befall him, has a sad resonance:

You touched me where resistance ends
In depth and abyss yet unknown,
You came into my darkest days
When I was frightened and alone.

It was just so,
But now
That you will lead me further still
To richer fullness and to fuller sound
I hesitate like one who had not found
Not yet
The answer to all that which was before.
Just one step more
And I will cross the threshold to all that
Which is to be.

But give me time
And understand
And wait for me.

Then it was back to London and romantic evening meals at Chez Josef in Soho. He wanted to take her to *one of the palaces* but, Julia writes, *the Ritz was out of bounds, for he had been chucked out of the bar one evening when he started making threatening gestures with his revolver, pointing it at a man who was making it clear he fancied him.* One morning he failed to arrive on her doorstep, and she guessed he was *off on a job.* A few weeks later he was waiting for her outside her office:

His beige skin was turned golden brown. His green eyes were as bright as emeralds. The glamorous sun-tan Christopher returned with was the result of being at sea. I do not think he had landed in France; I think he had been at sea reconnoitring coasts and perhaps undergoing tests.

Where had Christopher been? Most probably he had spent three weeks at the SOE paramilitary training camp at Arisaig (STS23), based at Meoble Lodge on the remote west Inverness coast. It is in an area known as the Rough Bounds, wilderness country then closed to the public and best reached by boat. None of the recruits there could have any excuse for not knowing what was in store for them. Training included 'silent killing', practical demolition work and living off the land. Boat work and advanced raiding parties from the sea were also on the agenda. It was a tough, competitive course that took no hostages. Then came parachute training at Ringway Airfield outside Manchester, course STS51; four drops were necessary, the final one being at night.

In the absence of Burney's personal file[3], we may only assume that he was given this standard SOE training and, another assumption, that he acquitted himself well. It is salutary to read the report in Violette Szabo's file, later one of the heroines of SOE:

> A quiet, physically tough, self-willed girl of average intelligence. Out for excitement and adventure but not entirely frivolous. Has plenty of confidence in herself and gets on well with others. Not easily rattled. In a limited capacity not calling for much intelligence and responsibility and not too boring she could probably do a useful job, possibly as courier.
>
> Although I am absolutely sure that she has not the faintest idea of what is going on the other side, she does not seem to bother to find out in the least, which in my opinion is a very bad sign. She does not seem to realise the implications of her work; she lacks foresight and has a fatalistic mind.
>
> She is very anxious to carry on with her training but I'm afraid it is not with the intention of improving her knowledge but simply because she enjoys the course and the spirit of competition and being very fit – the physical side of the training.

Those who know how Violette Szabo was captured may find this report all too true.

When Christopher returned he no longer wore the familiar khaki battledress but instead a new set of clothes that startled Julia. For her this was too obvious a sign of a change of identity:

> *His new suit was straight Damon Runyon, light navy-blue with broad white stripes and huge loose shoulders. Friends were quick putting two and two together, softly whistling the 'Marseillaise'. In his new suit he was also very conspicuous to those who did not know him, for every able-bodied male at this stage of the war was in uniform. When I asked him why such an abrupt change from Savile Row, he said that his office told him to wear it so that when the time came it would look worn.*

With the new suit came a new name, the code name *Caesar*, sometimes with its French spelling of *César*. This led to a thoughtless mistake by the desk-bound in Orchard Court. Burney was down at Oakfield in Hay on Wye visiting his mother, perhaps for the last time.

Christopher came back to London in a rage. One day the phone had rung and his mother had answered it. The voice at the other end had asked to speak to Caesar.

'I think you must have the wrong number. This is Hay on Wye...'

'I know,' said the caller, 'and I would like to speak to Caesar.'

'But there is no-one here called Caesar' said his mother.

The voice at the other end then said irritably, 'Then can I speak to Christopher Burney.'

After she had put the phone down, his mother said, 'What a strange friend. She said she wanted to speak to Caesar.'

Christopher's office had blown his cover and given away his pseudonym in one brief phone call.

Most likely, some of the girls in the Hay telephone exchange had been listening to this rare phone call from London.

Above the clatter of cups and many an aghast, 'Well, whatever next', the puzzle of Mr Christopher and Caesar (just imagine, pronounced the French way) would be generously shared, security thrown to the four winds.

One more course was required for SOE recruits, a 'finishing school' in the New Forest at a country house near Beaulieu. This must have been the most useful of all for Christopher because the training was in clandestine techniques and security; how to spot a follower, how to contact by pre-arranged password, how to look natural. The saying went, 'he that has a secret should not only hide it but hide that he has it to hide'. Then there were the mind mantras, drummed in: Be self-reliant!

Be aggressive! Be inured to disappointment! Be patient, but ready to pounce!

Christopher Burney was given the identity of *Christophe Brunet*, a young man of private means with a French father and an American mother, who had lived most of his life in America. This was supposed to account for his sharp suit and his Grenoble accent. He was given an identity card, a food card, and a demobilisation card, which all young men who had fought for the French Army before surrender were given. He was also given a gun, probably a Colt .32 revolver, which was easy to conceal, and offered a suicide pill, a tiny rubber ball of potassium cyanide that would kill in forty-five seconds when bitten into. He accepted the first and rejected the second. Contrary to one report that he was tall with blond hair, *Brunet* (Burney) was five foot ten inches with dark hair and medium weight. A photo taken at the time, possibly for his identity card, shows a thin, long face below a full head of hair, swept back.

He was given his assignment. He was to drop into Normandy by parachute and make his way to Caen. Here he was to make contact with *Cavelier*, real name Noël Fernand Raoul Burdeyron, who had been parachuted into France the previous July to set up a resistance 'circuit' (as these groups were called) in western Normandy. *Cavelier* had quickly joined up with one of the very first SOE agents, Pierre de Vomécourt (code name *Lucas*), who had arrived by parachute two months earlier and was working from Paris with great effectiveness setting up a circuit called AUTOGIRO, the first big F section circuit in northern France. *César's* role was to become *Cavelier's* assistant and report back on the condition of AUTOGIRO. For this purpose, he was to make contact in June in Le Mans with a WT (Wireless Transmitter) operator who had the equipment necessary to send back information and receive further instructions.

César's mission in the broad sense was based on a directive

SOE received on 13 May 1942. This envisaged, rather vaguely, 'a large-scale descent on Western Europe in the Spring of 1943' which would be preceded by air and coastal raids for the rest of 1942. Christopher told Julia after the war that his brief was to expect one of these coastal raids soon after his arrival and render assistance. (Caen is near the coast.) SOE's job, as Gubbins put it, was that 'when invasion came, we would have men there to attack and cut communications and generally hinder German action. This would be of real benefit at the critical moment, even if the Germans were only held up for forty-eight hours.'

We now know that the SOE directive of 13 May 1942, envisaging 'a large-scale descent on Western Europe in the Spring of 1943', was either wishful thinking or make-believe, to appease the Russians who blamed the western Allies for lack of offensive ambition. No 'large-scale descent' took place, of course, though the Allied amphibious raid on Dieppe, in August 1942, was certainly a small-scale – and disastrous – forerunner.

SOE's Early Days, 1941–2

What did *César* know about AUTOGIRO before he was parachuted in? He would have known the history of F Section to date. The first agent had been dropped into France only a year earlier, on 5/6 May 1941. He was George Bégué, alias *George Noble*, and he brought with him a precious transmitter in a portable suitcase. This could transmit and receive morse code but it required a seventy-foot aerial. He teamed up with Pierre de Vomécourt, established himself at Châteauroux in the Indre region of central France which was still under the control of the Vichy regime, and got to work. That June the first two containers of supplies were dropped successfully onto Pierre's brother Phillipe de Vomécourt's chateau estate near Limoges. Morale was high and Pierre de Vomécourt claimed he could get 10,000 French resisters to aid an Allied landing. It all seemed easy but 'the dark ages' of 1942 were soon to come when F Section seemed to fall apart.

Bégué soon realised the effectiveness of the German wireless interception service, so he proposed a novel way of sending messages in code. This became the BBC's 'personal messages' programme, broadcast nightly on the BBC's foreign programme over powerful transmitters. The first message, 'Lisette is well', was broadcast that September. Underneath such banal messages, normally only three to eight words in length, were coded signals about the date and place of drops or the movements of agents, and so on. The messages became increasingly cryptic – 'In my aunt's garden there are three beehives,' followed by 'Gaston is going to eat honey'– partly because Buckmaster was a crossword whizz who loved composing them. These 'personal messages' became an attractive part of SOE's work all over occupied Europe.[4]

That September of 1941, another WT operator and set arrived by parachute in a party of six SOE agents. George Bloch (*Draughtsman*) was appropriated by Pierre de Vomécourt and went into hiding in Le Mans. Then came disaster. The next month Bégué was captured by Vichy police and, although he escaped over the Pyrenees and served for the rest of the war alongside Buckmaster as SOE's signals officer, it meant that F Section lost its most effective WT operator. In November Bloch was captured and shot in Le Mans, soon after he had arranged a small supply drop for AUTOGIRO. That left AUTOGIRO without any WT communications.

This dearth of WT was little short of catastrophic. How else could agents in the field communicate with SOE headquarters? How could they be organised? *César* must have known about it, but did he realise the implications? Buckmaster wrote in his *History of F Section*, 'without radio communications an organiser is powerless and almost totally ineffective anyway over a long period'. It led Gubbins to rule at the end of 1942 that F Section operatives should work in threes, an agent, a

WT operator with set, and an assistant: but for *César* this was in a future of which he had no part.

So F Section was left with no means of exchanging messages with London except, as neither the Germans suspected nor the British could have anticipated, through the American diplomatic bag in Lyons in Vichy France. The F Section base in Lyons was a face-saver. It was set up by the first female SOE agent in France, the American Virginia Hall, codenamed *Marie*. She had arrived from Spain in August 1941 and registered openly as an accredited correspondent for the *New York Post*. Her secret role was known to the USA vice-consul in Lyons who took her messages in the diplomatic bag to Berne, the Swiss capital, from where the military attaché at the USA Embassy phoned them through to London. Replies and sometimes money would be sent back to *Marie, c/o Lion*, the code name of the Lyons vice-consul. This was a reliable if slow channel of communication and it was how, eventually, *César's* capture was known in London.[5]

Red haired but nevertheless cool headed, *Marie* was aggressive but cautious and she survived for fourteen months without arrest. As a courier she arranged contacts, passed on escapers and, most important for F Section, got messages out and distributed incoming messages when they arrived through the diplomatic bag. Her flat became a rendezvous for Allied servicemen on the run and for agents like *César* who regarded her as a lifeline in the summer of 1942. She lasted until November when she was forced to escape to Spain over the Pyrenees, trekking fifty miles in forty-eight hours despite a wooden foot she called Cuthbert, the result of a shooting accident years before.

While *César* was waiting for his mission, that March 1942 he met in London Pierre de Vomécourt, alias *Lucien*, who had returned by sea for an SOE briefing. He had brought with him his assistant, Mathilde Carré, whom, incredibly, he knew to be a double agent working for the Nazis. This is the extraordinary back story.

Lucien, frustrated at not being able to send messages, had met her through her lawyer at a café in Paris on Boxing Day in 1941. She told him she was an ardent 'resistant' and she could get messages transmitted through a Polish resistance group in Paris called INTERALLIE. She was the mistress of its leader, she said. *Lucien* and SOE were desperate for wireless communication so they accepted this offer. These transmissions seemed to work for a while, but in fact *Victoire*, as SOE called her or, more appropriately, *La Chatte* (The Cat), was also having an affair with Sergeant Hugo Bleicher who worked for German Intelligence, the *Abwehr*, and she was telling him F Section secrets. As a result, several of the early members of AUTOGIRO were arrested and others, like de Vomécourt, were allowed to carry on in the hope that more secrets would be divulged over the bedclothes.

De Vomécourt was tipped off. With great cool he decided not to kill her but to turn her into a triple agent and, apparently, she agreed to this, perhaps because she was his mistress too. *La Chatte* was known for her voracious sexual appetite. The first step was to get them both to London. *Victoire* persuaded Bleicher that they should be allowed to return without capture. Not knowing that she had been turned, Bleicher assumed *Victoire* could observe how the SOE pick-ups were conducted, and when in London how the clandestine system operated. On returning to France, he supposed, de Vomécourt could be trailed and then captured. Preposterous as it may seem, Bleicher and his bosses fell for it and on 27 February 1942 the two arrived in London. This was all too much for Gubbins. *Victoire* was arrested and spent the rest of the war in Holloway gaol.

Did *César* know this? What must he have thought of the rackety secret organisation he had joined? As a restless agent desperate for adventure, who was brought up on the tales of

John Buchan and then Lawrence of Arabia, he was probably prepared for anything.

At about this time, March 1942, Christopher must have been told of the probable death of his brother, Roger, in the *Surcouf* submarine disaster. What effect this had on his willingness to fight a highly risky war we do not know.

Lucien, after a thorough debriefing, was dropped back onto his brother's estate near Limoges on 1 April. He was alone because no WT operator was ready to go with him. He carried a new codename, *Sylvian*, and his pursuers were distracted by a broadcast from INTERALLIE that he would not be dropped until the next full moon. De Vomécourt set about reviving AUTOGIRO, but without arms or WT this was hard going.

Christopher took with him to France a list of AUTOGIRO members to contact. This was a highly dangerous, amateurish, thing to do. He was also given a photograph of himself in case he needed a new identity card; the words 'for CÉSAR' were written on the back. He stated this in one of his debriefings after the war under the heading 'Criticisms', from which it is reasonable to deduce that he did not take this photograph with him to France (More on this in Notes for Chapter Six).

SOE had the reckless habit of giving agents information on paper to take with them. In October 1941 a party of four agents had arrived in the Vichy Zone of France, all carrying a document with the address and map of an SOE safe house in Marseilles. One of the agents was captured soon after arrival, and the location was a safe house no longer. This gave rise to a mysterious and damaging incident. A WT operator G C Turck, codenamed *Christophe*, summoned many agents in the Vichy Zone to meet at the safe house in Marseilles to co-ordinate activities. At least five were arrested on arrival by the Gestapo. How much did Turck know in advance? Did he lead the others into the trap? Burney got to know Turck in Buchenwald, and gave supportive evidence to SOE after the war about his bravery there and on the transport train from Compiègne. In the end Turck was awarded a Military Cross, so the suspicion that he had given away the address of a safe house was presumably wrong. SOE had a lot to learn in these early days.

César in Enemy France

By the end of April 1942 Julia knew that Christopher was shortly going to France. He said he would be away for three to six months and that she should not try and find out about him. If friends asked, he had 'gone to India', a fib that probably fooled nobody. He gave her his box number for letters. She said she would marry him on his return, despite her father's disapproval of commandos.

> *April became almost May, and at the end of an evening together*
> *Christopher quoted the end of his poem:*
> *'But give me time*
> *And understand*
> *And wait for me.'*
> *When he said goodnight, I knew it was goodbye.*

The goodbyes were protracted, for several times over the next month Christopher turned up by surprise after a final kiss the day before. *'What happened?' I asked. 'The moon' was his cryptic reply.*

When he finally failed to appear one day at the end of the month, Julia wrote that after all the anti-climax her *emotions were blunted.* She did not realise she would neither see nor hear nor know anything about him for nearly three years.

César did not drop alone. His companion was Charles Grover-Williams, code name *Sebastien*. In the 1930s he had been a glamorous racing driver, winner of both the French and Belgian Grand Prix, and husband of a beautiful model. He had lived in Monte Carlo before the war and spoke excellent

French. His mission was to go to Paris, recruit his racing driver friends including former world champion Robert Benoist, and set up a 'circuit' there based on Benoist's secluded estate south of Paris.[6]

The two assembled on 30 May, probably at the secret SOE airfield at RAF Tempsford, and climbed into a twin-engine Whitley bomber with a range of 500 miles. (Contrary to supposition, Lysander light aircraft were used for set-downs and pick-ups, but could not drop passengers from the air). *César* and *Sebastien* were required to jump through a hole in the floor on a fixed line, and if the drop was from 500 feet or so on a still night, they would meet up with the ground in only fifteen seconds, the parachute silk collapsing around them. *Christophe Brunet*, alias *César*, alias Christopher Burney, takes up the story in a paper he submitted on 26 April 1945 before his first debriefing:

> I took off with Sebastien Williams and some pigeons during heavy rain on the night of 30/1 June [*sic*] 1942. [Homing pigeons were sometimes carried on RAF bombers to send back messages.] The pilot lost his way and it was about 1.30am when he finally found his spot and ordered us to jump. I jumped first and landed straight and soft near a horse. I was followed by Williams with a separate suitcase and we found both safely. One suitcase was difficult to find and should have had some sort of illumination. We stacked our landing gear under fairly deep water in a ditch. We needed to do this in a hurry because the plane made a second circuit over us at the same altitude, and we landed only one hundred yards from a farm.[7]

They had landed as arranged near the village of La Flèche in the Pays de Loire, just south of the River Sarthe. There was no-one to meet them. They were on their own in German occupied France at night. The first move was to walk to La Flèche from where there was a bus service to Le Mans and thence a train to Paris. They were nearly surprised by a patrol, so they hid in a field and took some brandy after which, wrote Burney, 'we felt brave enough to continue on our way'. At least they knew where they were going. F Section was so weak on detailed maps of France that it was said to rely on pre-war Michelin holiday guides from a London travel agency. In La Flèche they had to wait all morning for a bus which must have made them conspicuous and was another mistake, Burney admitted in his debriefing. Why had they not memorised the times of buses before they left? They arrived in Paris in the early evening and Williams left to meet his own contact. *Christophe Brunet* signed in at a hotel near the Gare Montparnasse and caught a train to Caen the next morning.

Caen was then an historic university town dominated by its castle and two abbeys. A third abbey (now a ruin), the Abbeye aux Dames, housed the Hospice St Louis, a charitable institution for the aged, infirm and orphans. Here *César* met a contact called Alice Dubois, although her real name was probably Madame Terrien, as that is how Burney later referred to her. But *César*'s first call was at *Cavelier*'s address and now, for the first time, he sensed trouble:

I went to the apartment of *Cavelier* and found that it was empty and also that a rather obvious looking man was lounging around the house opposite. The order of discovery was in fact reversed for obvious reasons. I went to a hotel for the night and in the morning visited my contact [Alice Dubois at the Hospice St Louis]. She was extremely helpful and gave me food tickets; but she said she had not heard from *Cavelier* for more than a month. Then she gave me an address he most frequently used in Paris. I stayed in Caen for three days.

César must have felt increasingly anxious. He looked out of place in this provincial Normandy town with his sharp suit, and his French/Swiss accent was conspicuous too. People shied away from him and were reluctant to talk. *Cavelier*, he discovered, had blown up a train on which German soldiers were going on leave and the Germans had exacted reprisals. He said in his second debriefing that he also heard *Cavelier* might have been arrested. He met Alice Dubois once more in a church and she gave him the address in Paris where *Cavelier* often stayed. He then returned to Paris.

Here he checked in at *Cavelier's* hotel, the Grand Hôtel du Havre in the 8th Arrondissement, a popular hotel for tourists near the Arc de Triomphe, with short-stay guests coming and going. The manager had not seen *Cavelier*:

> She implied she thought some ill had befallen him... Thence to Le Mans to keep my RV with the assigned WT. I found neither *Cavelier* in Paris nor the WT in Le Mans. I then met Williams [*Sebastien*] by pre-arrangement in Paris and, after fixing a further RV with him, returned to Caen. *Cavelier* was still absent.

César must have realised that AUTOGIRO had at least gone to ground. The official historian of SOE, M D R Foot, put it this way: 'AUTOGIRO, like a headless chicken, did not die instantly, for an agent left to join it (Burney) when there was nothing left to join.' In retrospect, *César* should have aborted his mission at this early stage and crossed over into Vichy France to liaise with *Marie* in Lyons: but out of determination or foolhardiness he stayed on.

Meanwhile, Julia wrote Christopher her first letter, in time for his birthday on 16 June. It is written in pencil on a scrappy piece of paper. Is it a copy? Did she decide not to send it? Or was it returned at the end of the war from the Box Office in Wimpole Street?

> *Darling Heart,*
> *I love you my dearest love, and I am sure that in the end my eyes will be shinning* [sic] *for you when you come. And you will come. Thank you for all the lovely times we have had together*

and especially for our last evening. I loved you a hundred times for the things you said and how you said them. I shall remember it every hour of every day. I'll celebrate your birthday, but it will be anything but a celebration.

> *All my love darling*
> *Good luck and be happy,*
> *Julia*

In July, a WT operator did turn up in Paris after *Sebastien* had sent his wife down to Lyons to ask *Marie* (Virginia Hall) for help. Probably this was *Georges*, real name Marcel Clech, a former Breton taxi driver who had arrived in Lyons after landing by submarine on the Riviera that April. At last, a rendezvous worked! *César* must have been mighty relieved, but he was soon let down once again. *Georges* did not have the wireless transmitter set with him and he was 'an indiscreet chatterbox', so Burney told Julia after the war. *Sebastien* (Williams) sent him back to the unoccupied zone.

César was beginning to feel 'a little windy' and now only just averted disaster:

> On one early return from Le Mans, standing near the door of a crowded railway carriage, I put my briefcase with most of my money and a few books near the door, and a neighbour mistaking an early platform for the Gare Montparnasse opened the door and let it fall out. It was found by a railway employee and returned to the lost property office, but I hesitated to claim it directly. A friend of mine, Dr Jacque Foure, got me through to some important man on the SNCF and through him I was given the case directly. The story for all concerned but my friend was that I was an emigrated Lorrain [Lorraine was now part of Germany] who was trying to place some out-smuggled money in French concerns.

Jacque Foure was the brother of the girl Christopher had lived with in Grenoble several years before and now he was a dentist practising in Paris. After the scare on the train Burney left most of his money, over one million francs, in Foure's safekeeping. He was the first of *César's* recruits to the Resistance, anticipating an Allied invasion in 1943.

After the failure of the RV with *Georges* in July, *César* was living on borrowed time. Now he considered crossing the line into Vichy France at Chateauroux, making his way to Lyons to brief London through *Marie,* and then carrying on as an SOE agent under a change of disguise. However, he stayed on longer, hoping to recruit resisters to aid the expected invasion, but without AUTOGIRO as a circuit for them to join, this was hopeless.

This is what had happened to AUTOGIRO, although *César,* of course, did not know it. Its revival was tragically short-lived. Pierre de Vomécourt was back in Paris in April 1942, with the new codename of *Sylvian.* Lacking a WT operator, his only means of communicating to London was through Virginia Hall, but his messenger to her was arrested in the third week in April by a routine German army patrol. Papers found on him were handed to Bleicher and he recognised *Sylvian's* handwriting. Motivated no doubt by revenge as well as duty, he tracked de Vomécourt to the flat where he was living and arrested him the next day, 25 April, at a café rendezvous. Burdeyron was captured on 9 May, and the remaining members of AUTOGIRO followed into the net.

In one way they were fortunate. Perhaps because of de Vomécourt's status as a member of the French nobility they were all tried by court martial in Paris and treated as prisoners of war. De Vomécourt and Burdeyron spent the rest of the war in Colditz prison. At the end of the war it turned out that the AUTOGIRO circuit comprised about a quarter of all F Section agents who had been captured and survived. Burney was not known for bitterness, but he refers in *Solitary Confinement* to the man he was sent to meet who was arrested before he even arrived and who was then treated as a prisoner of war 'without any repercussions from my quarter', while he ended up in Buchenwald Concentration Camp.

Sitting at her desk in London Julia feared the worst too:

One of the secretaries from the French Section came on a visit and announced that every single member of SOE in northern France had been captured. I tried to look indifferent, but I felt stunned, telling myself frantically that Christopher was too newly arrived in France, that he would be too insignificant to attract attention (even in that suit), and finally there was a good possibility that the girl from the French Section was exaggerating.

Although I was still learning my job, I knew enough about the workings of the office to have sent for Christopher's file. I could have read it and returned it without anyone being any the wiser, but I remembered in time that he said I must not, on any account, try to find out about him. He added darkly, 'For you never know'. It took a great deal of self-restraint, but I kept my promise.

Perhaps she did not want to know the worst; that would have been human nature after all.

Capture by the Gestapo

On 28 June, *César* was given a fright that should have served as a warning sign. What happened comes from the report on his first debriefing:

Source [Burney] states that on 20 June he had gone to the Mairie (town hall) of the 8th Arrondissement to change his food tickets. He remembers he was attended to by a woman he describes as being about 5ft 4ins in height, very heavy and fat, very light yellow hair, and so far as Source can remember a very small mouth. She was, Source states, a very unattractive woman. In order to get new tickets, Source had to hand to her his food card and 'certificat de domicile' stating the hotel he was staying in as he was 'de passage'. [He gave the name of his hotel as the Hôtel Paris-Londres where he did stay, having selected it at random.] He remembers that, after looking at him and at the card, the woman said, 'Excuse me for a few minutes. I have something I have to do but I shall be back quickly.' She left Source waiting for some ten minutes. She then came back and changed the card quite normally. Source, in view of what he was told under interrogation, thinks that it must have been this woman who denounced him.

By mid-August *César* had had enough. His careful attempts to enlist support had met with blank faces or anti-British sentiments, an uncooperative attitude he did not forget. It was time to head for the Loire. He was staying at a hotel in the 8th Arrondissment 'somewhere between the Avenue des Ternes and the Avenue de la Grande Armée' where he made plans for his departure. He collected a set of clothes from Jacque Foure to wear instead of 'that ridiculous suit' and he gave him his pistol. He arranged an RV with *Sebastien* at a nearby café for the next day to tell him his plans, and finally he replied to a letter from Madame Terrien in Caen; both letters, suitably coded so that neither could be identified, were in his room. Perhaps they discussed his plan to leave for Vichy France; but it was too late:

I was arrested at 6 a.m. on August 15th, 1942. Two plain-clothes men entered my room while I was in bed. I was searched naked and then handed clothes after they had been searched. Unfortunately, owing to rafles [round-ups] which had been taking place during the last two nights in the quartier [neighbourhood], I had dumped my pistol and was unable to do anything about it. I was vaguely mishandled while the men searched the room and my belongings, and they then sent for the manageress, paid my bill, and marched me off. I was handcuffed.

I was driven to the Rue des Saussaies [Number 11 was

Gestapo Headquarters] and led up to the top floor. I was photographed, had my finger and palm prints taken and then led back for interrogation by the same two men who had arrested me, one of whom was addressed as 'Bischof'. The interrogation was banal and brutal and appeared to reach no conclusion. At 4 in the afternoon, still as Christof Brunet, I was driven to Fresnes [prison]. There my braces and shoelaces were taken off me and I was consigned, under the name of Arschloch [Asshole], to cell 449.

Further proof that the woman at the Mairie of the 8th Arrondissement, where he had been on 20 June to change his food tickets, had denounced him came after capture, from *César*'s German interrogators. They told him that she had spotted a flaw in his food card. They also said that the Gestapo had been looking for him 'from the end of June'. Why had they taken six weeks to find him? He supposed that his resistance activities had been minimal, so his arrest was not a matter of urgency. The flaw in *César*'s papers should not cause surprise. Not only did SOE give its agents too much paper, but the essential papers were sometimes wrong. It was not unknown for ration cards to give a non-existent address or to be stamped with the wrong date.

Why was *César* sent to join AUTOGIRO?

Several questions need to be answered and Burney must have asked them over and over again during his three years of captivity. Did F Section know that AUTOGIRO had been 'blown' before they dropped him into France? If so, why did they do it? And why did they do it without telling him? Julia gives his answer:

> When he returned to London in 1945, he told me he discovered SOE knew all those AUTOGIRO contacts had been picked up before he left on his mission. The many postponements of his

departure, which had given me those unexpected and rapturous extra evenings together, had nothing to do with the moon, but rather with his bosses, who were unable to make up their minds whether to tell him he was being sent into France 'blind', or to drop him there in ignorance, but armed with the list of names they knew the Germans had arrested. They decided in the end to do the latter.

Why did they drop him at all? Christopher's view, writes Julia, was that after the collapse of AUTOGIRO, F Section was left without a single circuit operating in German-occupied France. This would have displeased Churchill who took a keen interest in SOE, the organisation he had initiated with the order to 'set Europe ablaze', so Burney was a sort of sacrificial lamb to prove F Section was still active. Further, writes Julia, Christopher presumed that the 'irresponsible lunacy' of sending him off with a list of AUTOGIRO members they knew to be already captured was because F Section did not dare tell him he was being dropped in enemy territory with no back-up in case he refused to go.

The truth is surely more nuanced. Virginia Hall, as always well informed, did not send word through until *near the end of May* that AUTOGIRO had been blown. Presumably this was the first SOE knew about it, only a day or so before Burney's drop; and even then SOE might not have been certain of the extent of the collapse. Burney said in his debriefing that his orders were to discover what 'misfortune had befallen *Cavelier* since news had not been received of him', so there was just a chance he was still at liberty. It is possible that when Burney left England, SOE was not sure of the fate of AUTOGIRO.

In his official history, *SOE in France*, Foot wrote that F Section was 'hedging its bets against the probability that de Vomécourt's circuit was already in trouble' by sending in Williams to set up a new circuit in Paris. So, Burney was dropped in to find out more, just on the slight chance that something could be salvaged. It was high risk, it might have been dishonest, but those were the chances that SOE took. To SOE, sacrifices were simply the necessary price of a bigger prize. Gubbins noted in a memo about this time:

Strategically, France is by far the most important country in the western Theatre of War. I think that SOE should regard this theatre as one in which the suffering of heavy casualties is inevitable. But it will yield the highest possible dividends.

In the SOE *War Diary* for July–September 1942, there are one hundred or so pages of F Section activity but just one mention of *César*. On 2 September *Marie* cabled that her courier had reported *Caesar* [*sic*] had been arrested. London answered that they were distressed by the news and asked if they could do anything. Later *Marie* said she had no news of *Caesar*. Could he, she asked, be an RF Section agent?' Such was the lack of impact that Christopher Burney had made in France that Virginia Hall, so well informed, did not know he was in F Section of SOE.

There is an unhappy postscript to this account of Burney with SOE. In his 'Letter from Buchenwald', written in January 1945 when he was profoundly depressed by hunger and cold and the horrors of a concentration camp, he wrote about SOE:

Although I had led a wild and useless life from the age of 16…
I had not lost that gift of success and could have applied it to anything worthwhile. But even this last expression of energy of crusading in France [SOE] was half-killed in England by officialdom and given the coup de grâce in France when I found that the French on the whole did not want to put themselves in any danger of their lives or their pockets, and that the method to which I had submitted in England was a snare and a delusion which cost huge numbers of lives and that unnecessarily.

CHAPTER 3

INTERROGATION AND SOLITARY CONFINEMENT

I had no idea where I was. I only realised that it was a prison, bleak and uncompromising, boding not temporary detention, but an irrevocable end. Where men wait powerless and destitute on 'the crowded, arid margins of existence'.[1]

CÉSAR WAS IN Fresnes gaol on the southern outskirts of Paris. During the war it was used for the incarceration of SOE agents, Resistance fighters and Allied airmen, several of whom Christopher Burney would meet up with in Buchenwald, though he had no idea they had been languishing alongside him for months. Built in the late nineteenth century in the shape of the letter E, three four-storey cellblocks connected at right angles with a central corridor and prisoners were exercised in the small courtyards that lay between. The prison was surrounded by a wall with observation towers and its various buildings were linked by long underground tunnels.

The cells were much like they were in other prisons at that time, but there were dungeons too, 'cellules de force' where prisoners survived in the semi-dark and without beds of any kind, having to sleep on a floor clammy with fungus. *César* would be confined in Fresnes gaol, alone, for the next 526 days and nights.

The door slammed behind me with a crash, the double lock bolted with two heavy clicks, and I was alone... At first I was overshadowed by sheer bewilderment at the finality of these two clicks. I felt that the last thing but one in my life had happened and that all that remained was for the lock to click twice more, and I would be taken out on my last journey...

Light came from a high window on the end wall with opaque panes, firmly locked, and bars on the outside. Above it was a skylight that opened when pulled thirty degrees backwards into the cell. Through the frosted, opaque panes, only the vague shadow of another building was visible but in the gap over the open skylight was an oblong of blue sky.

César looked round the cell. It measured about ten feet long, or five short paces, and five feet wide. Along one wall was a bed, similar to a school or army bed, but hinged to the wall. On it was a thin straw mattress and two dirty blankets. As he would soon discover, the bed was excruciatingly uncomfortable but nevertheless reassuring:

> The broad latticework of iron laths, which took the place of springs, was unique and almost supernatural in its torment... Yet this bed retained a quality of bed-ness which summoned my associations with all the beds I had ever known. In it my fears, joys, sorrows, and relief were those of bed, not to be found in haystacks or ditches or on the floor, but common to every bed from canopy to canvas.

Opposite the bed was a wooden table hinged to the wall with a stool chained to it and in the corner was a dirty earthenware toilet with a tap. On closer inspection he saw that the walls were filthy but decorated with pencil work, scrawled sketches, signatures, and the counting of days by pencil strokes, the longest line amounting to fifty-six. In the door was a peephole through which 'a cold blue eye, like slimy glass' would watch him. The effect on *César* of this initial inventory was dispiriting:

> There was an obscenity in this calculated degradation of a human dwelling-place which chilled the heart. There was no filth, generally no vermin: only the diabolic essence of perversion and the smugly spruce technology of a stockyard.

Waiting for Interrogation

When *César* was kicked into Cell 449 and called 'Arschloch' ['Arsehole'] he was still *Christophe Brunet*, but he knew this cover identity would soon be discovered. He had given his birthplace as Sancerre, and this could easily be checked. There would be another interrogation, and unless he confessed he would be tortured and whatever the outcome he would be shot. Each time he heard footsteps outside his cell he assumed he was being taken to his execution. He tried to visualise it:

> Imagine a bare plot of ground with a wall around it; see yourself standing against the wall, with soldiers in front of you, aiming their rifles at you. Imagine the flashes and the sudden start, and the pain of bullets ploughing through you. Only so far can you imagine. Death has retreated like the rainbow's end. And if you go further with the scene, and see the body lying crumpled before the wall, you are using a playwright's licence. For this body is not yours, but another: unable to imagine the feelings of your own self after dying, you have skilfully substituted an impersonal dummy for your body. You can imagine the simple physical perishing of someone else, but you can only track your own death to the threshold of its lair, where it lies hidden from you.
>
> For death, as a word, is a limitless negation. It means life with a minus sign *ad infinitum* and is therefore irrational.

César extended this detachment to apply to the interrogation he dreaded, but he was prepared to die, and he accepted that his life was unimportant. He said in a BBC radio discussion in 1954 on torture: 'Unless you accept the fact that you are prepared to die you haven't a hope of withstanding any interrogation. You've got to realise your life could be wiped out and what does it matter? What more can they do to you?' This negation of himself made it easier to imagine he was somebody else: 'You've got to stand back from the situation and say: This isn't happening to me. It's happening to somebody else who is not in my care. All his background and feelings and everything else are totally unknown to me.'

For Christopher Burney this was more than a theoretical statement. Over the next three years he was to show extraordinary self-discipline leading to a detachment from the horrors of his life that his peers called 'serene' and the concentration camp psychology called 'camp autism' – a necessary condition for survival.

César was brought no food for the first three days. While he tried to cope with hunger, claustrophobia, and the guilt of capture, he plotted the next interrogation he knew was coming. Fatalistic he was, but life was too precious to throw away. Unknown to him he had a week to devise a plan. He knew his *Christophe Brunet* paperwork would not bear examination and therefore he needed to dictate the lines of interrogation with a convincing story that would, at best, take him to a prisoner of war camp and, at worst, somehow save him from further torture and death.

First, he identified the 'targets', as he called them in his debriefing report after the war, that had at all costs to remain hidden. They were 'the organisation of SOE, *Sebastien* (Williams), *Cavelier* (Noël Fernand Raoul Burdeyron), and my own Caen contact (Madame Terrien)', to which list he should have added, as he does in *Solitary Confinement*, his new accomplice Dr Jacques Foure. He revealed in *Solitary Confinement* that he had been briefed for three missions

71

before finally leaving London, so he had a lot to hide. Then came the summons:

> On the morning of the fourth Tuesday a sergeant burst into my room as I was trying to wash under the tap. I asked weakly where I was going. *Tribunal.* This laconic answer brought me back to my senses as I had taken for granted that I was bound straight for the place of execution.

Torture

César was locked in a police van and taken to the S.S. counter-intelligence headquarters at 84 Avenue Foch. Once again, he was taken to the top floor and met by Bischof and his accomplice who had arrested him, the 'little man' and the 'big man'. He was shown a newspaper that announced the recent failure of the Dieppe raid, an amphibious landing of 6,000 mainly Canadian troops intended to capture the port and hold it for a short while as a morale booster and practice for a larger Allied invasion:

> 'You may well be disappointed,' said Bischof, 'it is a pity you were caught before you could carry out your orders. The invasion you were supposed to help has failed and you are here.'
> A few minutes later an officer came in dressed in the uniform of a major in the Gestapo. He was dark and wiry, more Latin than German, with a ruthless, wolfish face... Suddenly he strode across the room and struck me in the face with a swing of his open hand roaring, *'Wie heißt du?'* [What's your name?]
> I looked at him as calmly as I could and replied 'Brunet'.
> He came in again savagely, hitting and kicking and swelling with fury as I parried or avoided his blows. Then the big man came and held me from behind while the little one [Bischof] put a pair of rigid handcuffs on my wrists. Then the major attacked again, nastily now and without anger...

The beating-up went on for some hours, all over his body including his testicles, until *César* knew that 'coherent thought was slipping away. I emitted a sound of defeat'. Now was the time to use his first cover story in the guise of confession extracted under extreme duress, as indeed it was. It was a mixture of what was true and could be checked and what was false but could not be checked.

He revealed his true name, rank, and number in the South Wales Borderers. He recounted his actions until April 1940 but then, instead of going to Narvik he joined the 51st Highland Division in northern France as an interpreter, working for his cousin Brigadier General George Talbot Burney of the Gordon Highlanders. With the rest of the 51st Highlanders, claimed *César*, he was captured before Dunkirk at Saint-Valery-en-Caux but managed to escape and made his way to the south of France before heading for the Pyrenees. This story sounded plausible and would be hard to disprove because, as *César* knew, General Burney had died as a prisoner of war and the story of the escape to the south of France came from a friend who had done just that.

How to account for the next two years without compromising any innocent French persons was more difficult, but Burney told his story; he had always expressed his views with confidence, whether based on fact or fiction. It ended with him wandering around Normandy trying to find a boat which would take him across the Channel. However vague the details, he thought he had an answer for everything. He signed his statement:

My three judges appeared a little taken aback.

'I hope that was the truth,' said Bischof doubtfully. 'Your signature as an officer is your honour, and if you have signed nothing but lies you will find we refuse you any respect.' The lift took me down again and another Black Maria bumped me back to Fresnes. The sergeant of the top floor, summoned to escort me to my cell, stared at me and muttered '*Aber du lieber mann!*' ['But you dear man!']

For the next few days Burney 'lived in a mad exaltation of confidence', imagining life in a prisoner of war camp with no work to do and an endless supply of food parcels. He thought his interrogators may well have given him the benefit of the doubt, so when after another three weeks he was taken back to 84 Avenue Foch he was not anxious. He should have been. His guard took him to another office and another interrogator, a young man who offered him a soft handshake and spoke perfect French. He was probably Ernst Vogt, a Swiss-German civilian attached to the office as senior interrogator:

> I studied him, found a high-domed brow and rather humorous un-German eyes, and foresaw truly that I had entered the intelligent phase in the cycle of interrogation.
>
> 'So... you say you are a prisoner of war? I will tell you at once that some people believe your story. But I'm afraid I don't.'

Whereas in his first interrogation Burney had been purposefully vague, this time he was forced to provide detail. Where had he changed out of uniform after his escape from capture at Saint-Valerie-en-Caux? The German produced a large-scale map and held a particular section in front of Burney in such a way that he could not unfold it and get his bearings. Burney pretended to recognise sites on the map but not the farm he was asked to identify. Disaster! His interrogator unfolded the map to its full extent and showed triumphantly that Burney had recognised sites many miles away from where he said he had been captured. He left the room as if to show distaste for what was to happen next.

According to Burney's post-war debriefing, his guard then produced a *nerf-de-boeuf* (slang for a cosh named after a bull's penis which in former times had been used as a truncheon) and beat him up badly. Once again, Burney feared the worst and realised he had to resort to his ultimate fallback cover story.

This time he told the truth up until 1941, giving his account of the Narvik expedition and 12 Commando. Then, however, he began his lie, with confessions perilously near the truth. He was, he said, summoned to meet an officer at the War Office (wrong building and wrong name supplied) where he was told to take a message and money to a man in Caen in German-occupied Normandy. For this purpose, he was given parachute training near Manchester (where he had practised drops with SOE, but he gave the location of a different airfield) and dropped into the nearby French countryside (true). He could not describe his contact in Caen because they had not met (true), but then he was caught off-guard. He was shown Burdeyron's photo. Unnerved by this he nevertheless had the presence of mind to shake his head and move to another mugshot of a man with his face bandaged: 'That might be him, though it's very hard to tell.' What was the message he was asked to deliver? Practised by now in the SOE personal messages of BBC radio, he came up with 'Forget the Cherbourg line and go and find Yves.' Of course, he had no idea what this meant or who Yves was. This may have sounded plausible, but Burney was beginning to lose confidence.

Worse followed. His interrogator produced the letter he had written to Madame Terrien and left in his hotel room the night before capture. It was, of course, addressed to a mythical person at an agreed accommodation address, but this line of questioning was also dangerously close to the truth and his uncovering as a spy. He had the presence of mind to describe Madame Terrien as looking like his sister, very different from the real Madame Terrien, and he quoted several passwords they had agreed in advance that, if they were ever used, would reveal that *Christophe Brunet* had been captured. This semi-fiction seemed to be accepted and was written down on a typewriter. The interrogator did not refer to Madame Terrien or *Sebastien* or Jacque Foure, but Burney worried until the end of the war whether he had given away any of his three 'targets' while semi-conscious under a *nerf de bœuf*. Then the interrogator changed the subject, but the worst was over:

> It was late in the afternoon when he finally rang a bell and told an orderly to bring me a meal. It was a good meal of braised heart, which I remembered for many years. When I had finished it, my interrogator drove me back to Fresnes in his own car. He talked little on the way, and of trivialities, but when we arrived at the entrance of the prison and a guard came to take me, he held out his hand for a second time. 'Goodbye,' he said, 'I don't believe a word you've told me.'

Unable to prove that *Christophe Brunet* was Christopher Burney the spy, and probably aware that his few weeks in France were of little consequence, the Gestapo did not shoot him but left him in Fresnes to rot.

Julia wrote in her memoir:

> *After six months had passed and he had not appeared, I did become very anxious. Every evening when I returned to the Hammonds'* [with whom she was staying in London] *I expected to find him there waiting for me. When the telephone rang and someone called, 'It's for you', I would rush with a pounding heart hoping to hear Christopher's voice, and when it turned out to be a casual friend, I could be polite only with difficulty. On days off when I heard a taxi engine idling outside, I could not resist looking to see if he was there, paying it off. Each small disappointment would herald a black depression.*

Solitary Confinement

The historian and politician Harold Nicholson began his review of *Solitary Confinement* with the question that explains why the book was so important when it was first published in 1952:

> How would you or I behave if, for a year and a half, we were locked up alone in a cell measuring ten foot by five, suffering always from cold and starvation, expecting every morning to be summoned to death or torture? No question is more pertinent if we wish to probe our own character.

Burney was satisfied that his account in *Solitary Confinement* was objective and reasonably accurate. There were difficulties. Apart from the impossibility of precise recall, there was the problem, on the one hand, of describing an experience that few of us have endured and, on the other hand, of overstating the hardships so as to distort the truth. He wrote: 'The experience of unpleasantness is as exaggerated in the second-hand reading as it is dimmed in the first-hand remembering; imagination can be fired more readily than memory.' Of one point he was sure: it was impossible to tell the whole story because, as he puts it in a memorable phrase, 'there was so much total emptiness between the actions as to make it resemble an astronomer's description of the universe'.

'I soon learned,' Burney began his book, 'that variety is not the spice but the very stuff of life. We need the constant wavelets of sensation, actions and emotions lapping on the shore of our consciousness, to keep even isolation in the ocean of reality.' The trouble was that his senses were severely limited.

First his sight: all he could see was his cell with its filthy walls, an opaque window with a tantalising crack of sky above it through a skylight, his door with spy hole, bed, table and stool, toilet; 'because I could see no change or movement, I was as good as blind'. He should have qualified this by describing the changing light entering his room, at no time of day more important than when he was timing his supper:

> In summer I waited until the sun was behind the other building and no longer shone into my cell; later in the year, till sunset, judging the moment by the colour of the clouds in the tiny patch of sky I could see; and finally, when winter came on, till dark, scrupulously estimating the fine degrees of twilight and even reckoning with the moon and the brightness of the stars to make sure I was not too early.

There was an electric light, but this was controlled from outside the cell by the sentry and only turned on for spying.

Burney's senses of smell and taste became acute but, apart from picking the minute oats out of his bread and noticing the differing tastes, he had little to exercise them. His hearing was his best-nourished sense, he writes, but even then he had to be satisfied with the shouts of German guards and the rumbling of the food trolleys. Loneliness is made bearable by the right kind of sound, a caring kind of sound, said Burney in a BBC TV interview about *Silence* in 1963: 'During the day there are a lot of noises going on that remind you that you are alive. At night and at weekends you get nearly total silence. This is the worst thing that can happen to you.' He described graphically in 'Letter from Buchenwald' the awfulness of weekends in Fresnes:

> Saturday and Sunday were very bad. One always had hopes that there would be some extra meal as long as the guards were there, but at weekends they went off, and before going they went around the cells banging the key in the locks. The noise of that always brought a sinking feeling, and the ensuing silence made one acutely and hopelessly conscious of the time to be passed. Unable to see outside or even to hear things

happening outside, one felt all the more the bareness of the cell and the loneliness.

Such was the regularity of noise that he expected sounds to be recognisable; any break with the pattern and he became confused: 'There was a cracked bell outside the prison which chimed wrong. Something out of focus makes nonsense of life. It is worse than silence.' Such was his solitude that he found speech difficult and attempts to shout or sing out loud were soon banned by the guard. 'So you see,' Burney concludes in *Silence*, 'outside influences practically ceased to affect me and I became the playground for those which my own nature provided.' He had no books or paper to read, at least for the first year, and no pencil to write or draw.

At the start of his imprisonment, he envisaged bleakly that the fourteen hours of daylight could only be filled by aimless movements of his body or the meandering thoughts of his mind. As the months went by, he experienced the maddening tedium, the incipient hysteria, the emptiness and despair that only protracted solitary confinement can induce. At times he thought he was going mad, that his mind was parting from reality as in schizophrenia, and at other times he tried to go mad as reality was too awful to bear. A way out was suicide, but for Burney this was out of the question. Another way out was the firing squad which Burney thought was inevitable, and this gave him a dread sort of perspective.

Hunger

Burney's constant companion was hunger. Yet, he writes, such was the poverty of his existence that in one way hunger was probably better than food:

> Hunger lowers the whole vitality. Thought grows more abstract, sex goes to sleep, and a sort of balance with the empty environment is attained, with only a single giant

79

appetite to disturb it. All the pressures and strainings of the body are, as it were, collected together in the stomach, where they are more safely, if no less painfully, controllable.

The event of the day was the clattering of the trolley at midday, carrying tubs of a thin soup, mostly cabbage and water, though it improved during Burney's incarceration. He would stand at the hatch offering his *gamelle* or mess tin for the guard to pour in a ladle's worth. Burney would separate out the food from the liquid and slowly digest both. Then came another trolley carrying the bread ration, about 300 grams or two thin chunks, sometimes supplemented by a sliver of liver sausage or cheese. This was the sum of food and drink for the next twenty-four hours.

Burney soon realised that getting through ten hours of night on an empty stomach was an ordeal best avoided, therefore the challenge was to keep his bread untouched until the evening. He described in 'Letter from Buchenwald' the anguish of fighting hunger:

To be starving, to have a piece of bread to eat and nothing whatever else to do, and yet to wait six or seven hours before eating it is really a trial. I found it almost the hardest thing of my life. Some days I could feel the desire for food literally dragging the strength out of me, like the extraction of a tooth, only slower. If I felt strong on those days I went ahead and fought, walking up and down and forcing my mind onto other subjects. Sometimes I got through and got into bed feeling very pleased with myself. But sometimes it defeated me and after about half an hour my knees would give out and my mind seem to split, and I'd collapse onto the bed so completely worn out that I would break right down.

He discovered that after the slightest nibble of bread with his soup he would give in and greedily consume the lot whereas, if he turned his back on it, sometimes literally by hiding it, then when evening came, 'I had looked forward for so long and taken such pains to wait that at least two-thirds of my delight in eating it were consumed already in the anticipation.' However, abstinence brought its reward at night:

> The bread I had eaten made a yeasty bubbling in my stomach, as comforting as if a hot water-bottle were being turned over and over inside me. Anywhere else, this might have been called indigestion, but in Fresnes it signified the presence of matter in the digestive organs, and this was one of the beatitudes. It compelled stillness and, banishing the anxieties of the body for a while, quieted those of the mind.

Body and mind quieted, dreams of food began. The most frequent dream was of scrambled eggs: a line of bowls of scrambled eggs stretching from one end of a large table to the other.

After a few months of existence on a diet just about enough to keep him alive, Burney discovered a way of supplementing it. He broke into his oat-straw mattress and found that many of the oats had been left over after the threshing. He decided to eat them and spent hours collecting, husking and amassing them into a little pile, enough on a good day to give him two small extra mouthfuls. The price of that was bad diarrhoea but that had its reward too, for he succeeded in persuading his guard to provide torn pieces of newspaper which provided him, for the first time, with something to read.

Cold

The coming of autumn brought Burney another unwelcome companion and this was the cold: cold increased to a continuous shiver by his loss of weight. His arms were now 'mere sticks' and he could without difficulty pass his hand between his neck and his shirt collar. His only clothes for eighteen months were those he had hastily put on after his arrest, a cotton shirt and serge jacket and trousers. His socks were worn through by endless walking in loose shoes without laces and eventually they fell apart altogether. At night he covered himself with two threadbare blankets, one smaller than the other:

> I remembered being told that seventy five per cent of a man's body heat was lost through exhalation, and I tried to evolve a way of sleeping in a tent. But however carefully I pulled the blankets over my head and tucked them in, they came continually undone.

The following summer Burney was shivering even on the warmest days, and he anticipated that another winter would induce pneumonia. Also, his legs were beginning to swell from the feet upwards, the beginning of kwashiorkor caused by malnutrition that would last until the end of his war.

Contemplating how best to maximise heat from his two unequally sized blankets, he conceived the idea of wrapping part of the smaller one round his chest in the form of a crude waistcoat. Inspired by this improvisation, he looked round for tailoring tools. He noticed a small sliver of glass covered in dust below his skylight and then he managed to pick a piece of wire from what passed for bed springs: hence a sharp piece of glass as substitute knife and a wire as serviceable needle.

He realised he would have to sew a small garment in order to leave enough of the blanket to avoid detection, so the design he came up with was three strips of blanket to cover the chest and two supporting them over the shoulders, sewn together with thread from the same blanket. Thus, what remained of the blanket retained its rectangular shape. With a tailor's pride he added a collar, patch pockets, and even buttons.

Aware that so-called 'mutilation of stores' could be taken for sabotage, which carried a death sentence, he worked surreptitiously over the next few weeks behind his knees which were raised as cover while he sat on his bed facing the peephole. The Burney waistcoat was a minor triumph. Worn under his shirt, the rough wool next to his skin gave an extra illusion of warmth. It lasted until the last months of the war in Buchenwald, when he exchanged it with a Russian for a pair of boots.

Imposing a Regime

For the first weeks of incarceration in September 1942, Burney rehearsed his cover story for the interrogations he knew were coming. Otherwise, at this time, he was in a state of agitation, his mind racing with dread over his expected execution, guilt for failing his mother who had lost her other son a few months before, wild fantasy that he might be sent off to a prisoner of war camp, and anxiety that under torture he had betrayed his friends: 'All the while I paced the cell in ill-conceived frenzy, going through my pockets fifty times a day to see if I couldn't find just one cigarette. This was the elementary stage.'

As autumn drew on, Burney sensed that for the Gestapo he was out of sight and out of mind. If he were to survive, he would need a way of life, a regime of discipline. He began his morning with personal grooming, manicuring his nails with a sliver of wood peeled from the stool; then the daily wash using the erratic drip of water from the tap above the toilet. Once a week a guard came round with a blunt razor and dirty soap for a shave.

Then it was time for imposed stillness, sitting on his stool while he set himself mental exercises. What were all the counties in the United Kingdom? How many of the United States of America could he remember? What was the journey from one place to another, naming towns and people on the way? This programme lasted little more than an hour: 'Rarely had the shadow on the opposite wall begun to show when I reached the end of my repertoire and was reduced to the chief stock in trade of all those in solitary confinement: pacing up and down the cell.'

Burney found that the most calming course was straight up and down, taking five paces from end to end and pivoting round on the last step so as not to break the rhythm. Three hundred and sixty rounds took roughly one hour at a speed of one mile an hour. Sometimes he covered seven miles, he thought:

Hunger was always in the background. As soon as I had fallen into a steady rhythm of pacing, I would drift into daydreams, mixtures of memory and desire. But the journey's end was the chief delight, and my imagined steps were guiding me surely to supper, with pies and porridge and all the other things that fill you to stupor.

Instead, it was a bowl of watery soup and the bread he had to resist eating.

Burney's afternoons were for serious thinking. He realised early on that musings and daydreams were not enough to keep his mind active, and that if he was to retain a healthy mind and possibly survive further Gestapo grilling, he had to work at his mentality. He took a severe approach:

The essence of a healthy mind is to fight towards growth and maturity, and a healthy mind cannot include a degenerate will. I dug down into my wastepaper basket of memory and thought about what came out. Happiness, physics, metaphysics, economics and almost everything else. How much I got mostly depended on how much data I had stored away.

After sometime he became astonished that a result of his self-imposed education was the increasing power of memory. He could not only remember isolated facts but whole pages of books he had read years before: 'With a continuous effort my education came back, whether it was mathematics or Greek or chemistry or what have you, and it all fell into a pattern you might call philosophy.'

The Existence of God

Burney's endless mental preoccupation was with religion. He did not doubt the existence of God as creator and Prime Mover, but what had God to do with him? He had never taken 'His so-called words being the genuine article', nor had he believed in prayer, but now little by little the New Testament came back to him. In particular, he remembered the parable of the Prodigal Son, the story of the son who squandered his father's inheritance and returned home empty-handed to ask for forgiveness. Instead, the father welcomed him back and gave him a banquet. It is a story of redemption following repentance:

> Early on in my imprisonment I found myself in a daydream walking back from the old church in Herefordshire where we used to be taken every Sunday in the holidays. The fields had their August warmth and yellowness, the hopyards stood like orderly jungles waiting for the pickers, there were blackberries in the hedges and thirsty bullocks waiting in the shade. And across the stile and through the gate there was lunch.
>
> The vicar was an old and venerable man, with a fault in his speech. Now all I could remember were the opening words of his service, which never varied 'I will arise and go unto my Father, and will say unto him: Father, I have sinned before Heaven and in Thy sight and am no more worthy to be called Thy son.'

Now Burney saw himself as a Prodigal Son who had squandered his mother's love and the parable was an instruction to prayer. He says in 'Letter from Buchenwald' that he decided to ask God for forgiveness:

... for in my critical condition anything was worth trying
– anything which would give me the chance of dying with a
lesser burden on my heart: I could hear the lifts working for
the soup when the idea came to me to try and get forgiveness
from God, and I knew I had about twenty minutes before
it would get round to me (that is my estimation of twenty
minutes because I had no idea of time any more). So, I knelt
self-consciously at my bed and repeated first all the prayers I
knew and then made a sort of heated plea in my own words,
somewhat to the effect 'If it is by some chance you listen to us
and that what Jesus said was true, here's your chance to do
something about it'.

Then he dreamed of the banquet that would follow the
confession of the Prodigal Son. A few days later Burney heard
footsteps unexpectedly approach and stop outside his cell.
The guard unlocked the door and came in with a *feldweber*
(sergeant). The *feldweber* asked Burney why his hair was so
long and then ordered the guard to arrange a haircut. On the
way out he put his hand in his pocket, pulled out two pieces
of chocolate and put them on the table. 'Gut' he grunted and
walked out:

It is useless to try and describe the feeling I experienced when
I was alone again. I was indebted to the benevolence of God.
Here was the answer to my prayer, and a feeling beyond words
came over me, a mixture of undirected love, of relief and of
hope. I knelt hurriedly and said thank you in the most ritual
way I could think of; but I could not stay on my knees long.
The chocolate was too good, and I got up and took another
bite.

Here, thought Burney, was evidence of the Prime Mover
but the chocolate incident was not enough to turn him from
a vague sort of deist into a Christian, nor into a daily habit of
prayer. Then, at Christmas 1942, with German troops singing

carols in the yard outside, came another visitor. It was a Christian chaplain. At first Burney thought this might be a prelude to his execution, so when the chaplain offered him Holy Communion, he suspected it was the last rites. Flustered and caught unawares, he rebuffed the chaplain who gave him some Christian pamphlets and left: 'But I got a stimulus out of that Christmas which kept me thinking very hard about the whole Christian religion throughout the winter and right up to Easter.'

LONDON
5th March 1943

Darling Heart,
I love the weather, the heavenly blossom in the Park, the thicket carpet of crocuses, the early spring sun, the gliding swans. Above all, when, when, when will Christopher come back? When? He said in the spring, and that was a whole year ago and I thought that was an eternity that could not be lived through. I have lived through it and now I long with every fibre in my being, I long to see him again. If he doesn't come soon, spring will turn into summer and summer to winter and then yet another spring and that is too far away, and I know I simply can't wait until then.
Darling heart, you will never know how much I've missed you and how I have borne it all willingly feeling sure that I will see you in the spring. Now spring is here, and you are not and I tremble and have misgivings and moments of cold wet terror.

Later in 1943, after Burney had moved cells, another chaplain offered him a copy of the Bible in French, and this time he accepted. For the rest of his time in Fresnes he read most of the Bible through more than twice, except the books of Leviticus, Numbers and Deuteronomy. He enjoyed the Psalms and the Gospels because they were an 'assertion of the delight in being a creature of God who delighted in you being his creature'. He thought the Old Testament never became more than history and he preferred the

Greek histories of Thucydides and Herodotus. He could not understand how the God of Wrath could also be the God of Forgiveness. And who decided that the Book of Revelations should be annexed to the Christian texts? Why not Bunyan or even Blake?

So the Bible proved a mixed blessing but at least it filled his afternoons with reading. Then, so he writes in 'Letter from Buchenwald', around September 1943 he got hold of a book on St Thomas Aquinas and this had a seminal effect on him:

> I ceased to merely believe in God as a deliberate act of will and conscience. I actually knew now that He existed and that as a fact my own self was part of His intimate creation. It was like wearing a new suit. One didn't recognise oneself very quickly or easily and there was a feeling of something touching all the time. But I never let go again.

Many years later, wrote Julia, *when he was ill and had lost much of what he had held dear, he said, sadly, that his faith had once been like clothes, it had touched him all over.* But for now, in Fresnes and Buchenwald, Burney held fast to his belief that, to quote Voltaire, 'Dieu t'a fait pour l'aimer, et non pour le comprendre' ['God made you to love him and not to understand him']. He provided senses and a whole perceptible creation to that end. That was enough for Burney; further introspection and speculation about what kind of God or even what kind of religion was of little interest.

There was, however, a corollary to this: 'If, as I believed, the only absolute was God, and good by definition, there could be no such *thing* as evil: all it could be was an epithet meaning "less than good".' Burney no longer thought of good being opposed by evil:

> but of a spectrum which all originates from a single source and this accompanies a change of attitude. Pessimism becomes optimism, and the good of life is no longer overshadowed by

its imperfections. Henceforth, the tiniest window bringing light will always dominate the bleak and oppressive walls and dangerous passages beyond them. And we will fight for what we love instead of pursuing what we hate.

This belief must have provided hope and consolation in Buchenwald.

Burney was out of his depth in theological ponderings, as he admitted. Without the means of writing or studying or consultation he could not save himself from rambling: 'Words and ideas wandered slowly in untidy scrawls across my brain, blurred by the great fog of ignorance for which I had no lamp. Much of it was nonsense.' He confronted another metaphorical brick wall too. His belief in God 'was incoherent but unyielding', yet he found much of the Gospels, for instance, irrational: 'This seemingly insoluble antagonism between belief and reason threatened to explode in insanity.'

That must account for the preface to *Solitary Confinement*, dedicated to Julia. It is a difficult quotation from Shakespeare's *Richard II*, Act 5. Richard is a prisoner in Pomfret Castle:

For no thought is contented. The better sort,
As thoughts of things divine, are intermix'd
With scruples, and do set the word itself
Against the word:
As thus – *Come little ones*, and then again –
It is as hard to come, as for a camel
To thread the postern of a small needle's eye.

So far, so comprehensible. The quotation continues with language which for me is significant but its meaning highly speculative.

Thoughts tending to ambition, they do plot
Unlikely wonders; how these vain weak nails
May tear a passage through the flinty ribs

Of this hard world, my ragged prison walls:
And for they cannot, die in their own pride.

I take this to mean, in Burney's mind, that ambitious thoughts of free will and the meaning of life, for example, were limited by the poverty of his imprisoned mind and could not break free, like trying to tear a passage through rough prison walls with weak fingernails – and since there was no hope of escape, they died before they went any further. The famous literary critic, Frank Kermode, wrote in *The Sense of an Ending* that these verses from *Richard II* made 'exquisite sense' to him after reading Christopher Burney's *Solitary Confinement*.

Time Passes

Burney's days merged into weeks and weeks into months, with the only external variation brought by the weather. A few events disturbed the monotony. He changed cells. He suffered from dysentery and a medical orderly brought him balls of charcoal to eat. In spring 1943 a blackbird perched outside his window and 'sang loudly of hope and love and the freedom of the new earth'. He was taken out for exercise, with a gap between prisoners to prevent talking, but he picked up gossip that a general named Eisenhower was winning in the Mediterranean. Was Eisenhower a German, he wondered? On that occasion he found a snail and took it back to his cell for company.

One evening that summer, the cell door burst open, and 'a little red-headed sergeant scampered in and emptied the contents of a biscuit box on to my bed'. There were ninety-six whole biscuits and a dozen or so in fragments and they lasted Burney for a week, but brought back his dysentery. That summer, too, he heard Allied bombing raids overhead, and when he was caught hanging from his skylight to watch them, he was punished by the removal of his soup ration.

In the autumn, for a few weeks, he received food parcels

suspended on a cord from the cell above. They came from the prisoner next door, cell 260, who spoke to him through a small gap where the plumbing passed through the shared wall. He told him that the prisoner in the cell above could lower a food parcel. What Burney had to do was carefully remove a pane of glass from his window by scratching out the putty and prizing out the small nails holding in the pane, then remove a loose iron slat with a hook on the end from his bed frame. This was for grabbing the cord outside the window and pulling in the precious food. Miraculously, this worked for several attempts. Who was his benefactor? How did he get his food? How did he know about the iron slat with a hook on the end?

He was called 'Bernard', but his real name was Edmond Michelet. He was a captured Resistance leader but, as a French prisoner, he was allowed food parcels. Removing the bed hook was a well-known trick in Fresnes. The food parcels ended when Burney broke his pane of glass and then mistimed his grab for the cord so that the food parcel spilled on the ground. He was punished for that by several days without soup. That August, Michelet was removed to Dachau concentration camp, but he survived the war and became Minister of War and then Minister of Justice in French governments. He remained in touch with Burney.

Burney otherwise found contact with other prisoners unwelcome. He had been silent for so long that he was losing the confidence of speech. Moreover, he was so wrapped up in his own thoughts that he resented interference, whether from neighbouring prisoners tapping messages and questions along the pipes or from snatched conversations in the exercise yard. Burney told an American newspaper in 1946 that in all his eighteen months in Fresnes he was allowed ten-minute exercise sessions on three occasions and four showers. He was embedded in his life of solitude.

Another Christmas came.

16 December 1943

Darling Christopher,

I have returned to your letters [sent before you left]. *If when you wrote them, darling, they fell for the most part on rock, I can assure you they have reaped a full harvest since you left. I love them all and seem to understand so much about you that puzzled me. Do you remember the poem 'You touched me where resistance ends'? Clever you.*

I suppose the point of this letter lies in the fact that after two years, completely and utterly cut off from each other, we are bound to find changes in ourselves and each other. I love you as you were, and I know you know that I long for you with something stronger than intense excitement. We should know when we meet again whether it is to be everything or bleak futile nothing.

But maybe you are a step ahead of me. Two years is a lifetime really and you may have merrily danced away with another fairy! Chilly thought. But when I remember your last words to me I feel that cannot be so. I trust you into eternity. If you have changed then I shall have to change my skin. Because I am sure you have not, I can look on the possibility with complete calm – can even wish you well in your newfound happiness – honestly!!

Julia

The year 1944 arrived, and Christopher felt 'it was time to go', as he put it. His physical health had deteriorated so much that he no longer had the strength to do his morning exercises. His mental health was suffering because his brain no longer had the fuel to sustain his endless cogitation. Soon, he would have nothing left but cold and hunger. Yet he knew he would be reluctant to leave. In a most significant sentence, picked up by the poet Christopher Fry who wrote the introduction to *Solitary Confinement*, Burney wrote:

I knew that so many months of solitude, though I had allowed them to torment me at times, had been in a sense an exercise in liberty. For, by absolving me from the need either to consider practical problems of living or to maintain the many assumptions which cannot be abandoned in social life, I had been left free to drop the spectacles of the near-sighted and to scan the horizon of existence.

What he meant was that for weeks on end he had nothing else to do but force himself to seek out knowledge of himself and the big issues that mattered in his life, like the existence of a god and good and evil: these were the 'horizons of his existence'. One can only admire the self-discipline that allowed him to do this, a triumph of mind over matter. By relegating hunger, cold, fear and disgust to the back of his mind, he achieved a sort of 'serenity' that his peers would comment on in Buchenwald. He would need all this 'serenity', what Holocaust studies have called 'camp autism', to survive the next fifteen months of his ordeal.

Towards the end of January, a sergeant ordered him downstairs. He was placed in a cell with three young men who told him that a convoy of prisoners was about to be moved to Royallieu, near Compiègne, and then on to Germany. A string of buses for Royallieu arrived at nightfall and the Fresnes prisoners were crowded together in a shed for a night on the floor:

Silence and privacy were gone; an episode was ended. Solitude, with its mysteries and adventures, had passed over me like a wave and washed back into the spreading ocean of the past, while the next sea, cold and clamorous, already mounted.

CHAPTER 4

BUCHENWALD – DESCENT INTO HELL

In the Wagons

I came to Buchenwald in a convoy of two thousand
Frenchmen. We spent four days in [closed] wagons, 110 men
in a wagon, with no water and two small holes for air, which
were almost completely blocked by wire. There was no room
for everyone to sit down, however we crowded, and it was
immediately a question of every man for himself. In a few
hours there was not room for those who were standing to
put both feet on the ground. I stood up for the first night to
let another sit and had to remain standing for the rest of the
journey. When our thirst and bursting lungs began to oppress
us, they [the French prisoners] forgot all considerations for
each other. The fainting were allowed to faint by themselves.

SO WROTE CHRISTOPHER Burney in *Dungeon Democracy*. The
language is typically matter of fact, the detail about his feelings
virtually non-existent. However, for once there was a witness
to his behaviour who left a record, because in the same wagon
was one of the Newton brothers, Alfred. He and Henry, known
as 'the twins', were former SOE operatives codenamed *Artus*

and *Auguste* who had been captured in Lyons, tortured, and then sent to Fresnes. Now they would be Burney's companions throughout Buchenwald. In the twins' biography, *No Banners*, published in 1955, Alfred Newton gave a more graphic account of this nightmare train journey to the author Jack Thomas:

> A fight broke out at one end of the truck. A man recognised an informer who had sold him to the Germans. There were furious curses; then a muffled *Au secours!* There were groans and prayers for water. Men fainted, slid to the ground, and were trampled on. Many went mad and howled like dogs. A priest took a bottle of sacred wine from beneath his *soutane* to wet the lips of a dying wretch. Two bullies snatched the wine, drank it, urinated into the bottle and forced the priest to drink it. They shouted he was 'a capitalist lackey' and 'dirty fascist'. There was no room in the truck for any but 'organised workers and proletarians'.

Soon after this, one of the prisoners got out a hacksaw blade and began to saw through the planks. He was the Frenchman, G C Turck, codenamed *Christophe*, who, as we saw in Chapter Three, was suspected by SOE to have given the *Abwehr* the address of a safe house in Marseilles, but nonetheless he had ended up in Fresnes gaol. This hopeless escape was soon discovered and, as a punishment, the surrounding prisoners in the wagon, including Newton and Burney, were ordered to throw their shoes and outer clothes out of the train.

There was also another SOE agent in the truck, twenty-three-year-old Frenchman Maurice Pertschuk, codenamed *Eugene* but calling himself Martin Perkins as he was pretending to be an English student. Burney dedicated *Dungeon Democracy* to him and said in his debriefing after the war that Pertschuk was the only prisoner who 'kept his courage' during the journey.

They were all on the same train because Compiègne, north of Paris, was a transit camp from where 50,000 enemies of the Third Reich were deported to Germany by train, beginning in 1942. Compiègne was known as 'the antechamber to the death camps' because most of the Resistance prisoners ended in Auschwitz or Buchenwald. A big clearout from Fresnes and other French prisons began in January 1944.[1] *No Banners* continues:

> For three more days and four more nights they endured. Then, as wild animals sensing danger, they knew the nightmare journey was coming to an end. The train wheels slowed. There was a clanging of buffers, soon drowned by the clamour of voices and the barking of dogs. The planks were ripped away; the doors slid wide open. Outside, strong arc lights glared on ground covered by a foot of snow. A young S.S. man climbed into the truck, walking on the bodies of the dead and dying. Waving a long, black cane, he bawled 'Out, you vermin, *Schnell, ihr verfluchtes verbrechers*, Get a move on, you wretched criminals' ...
>
> If a man fell, a dog worried his throat or a shower of blows beat him to death. Bruised, bleeding and some barefoot, the survivors struggled on towards the darkness beyond the last arc-lamp.
>
> But the nightmare was not over. Long tongues of flame shot from a tall chimney, illuminating a pair of huge steel gates, mounted between giant pillboxes. Surmounting the gates was a German eagle holding a swastika in its claws. Below, in Gothic letters, was inscribed: *RECHT ODER UNRECHT MEIN VATERLAND* [My Fatherland Right or Wrong] and under that *BUCHENWALD KONZENTRAZIONS LAGER*.

On the gates themselves was written another slogan, *JEDEM DAS SEINE* [To Each His Own], a Roman maxim expressing the universal right to equality and justice, but was mockingly interpreted by the S.S. to prove their superiority over other races and their right to exclude them from society.

Buchenwald Concentration Camp[2]

Buchenwald, meaning 'beechwood', had been built with forced labour in 1937 on the northern hillside of Ettersberg, a little way north of the historic town of Weimar and not far from Leipzig. As Burney stumbled barefoot through the iron gateway in the near dark that early morning of 29 January 1944, he would have seen ahead the main square or *Appellplatz* where the twice daily roll calls took place. On the other side of Roll Call Square, he could just have made out the silhouettes of rows of long huts, perhaps sixty in all, facing down the hill. This was the Inmates' Camp, the Big Camp, and below, separated by barbed wire and on ground drenched in mud and effluent from above, was the dreadful Little Camp where Burney's fate would be decided in the ensuing weeks.

Off to the right of Roll Call Square was the crematorium, its tall chimney exuding the stench of death. Below that was a complex of buildings, the Disinfection Station, the Laundry and Bath, and the Effects Chamber where new arrivals handed over their belongings. This was where the pitiful procession from the train was now headed. A high voltage electric fence with no fewer than fifty-eight sentry posts surrounded the entire camp. All was ugly, ominous, and still, for the night had not yet lifted.[3]

Buchenwald was the largest of the concentration camps established by the Third Reich. The camps were for 'enemies of the Reich', political opponents of the Nazi regime and others who had no place under National Socialism, such as criminals, homosexuals, Jews, Roma gypsies and Jehovah's Witnesses. After the outbreak of war the physically and mentally disabled from across occupied Europe were also sent to Buchenwald and other camps to be used as 'guinea pigs' in medical research.

Concentration camps incarcerated 'enemies of the Reich' mostly without trial or length of sentence and in the harshest of conditions. They were not extermination camps like Auschwitz,

Treblinka or Chelmno, because extermination, mostly in gas ovens, was not their main purpose. Instead, after 1942, all concentration camps were placed under the S.S. Department of Economic Administration. Now the prime purpose of the camps became the housing of slave labour, and between 1942 and 1945 the number of the slave army grew from 90,000 to 700,000, imprisoned in twenty-three concentration camps and 160 sub-camps.

Inmates on outside work gangs were often worked to death, or near death through unremitting forced labour despite malnutrition and sickness. The S.S. had a name for this, *Vernichtung durch Arbeit*, meaning 'extermination through labour'. In Buchenwald there were many executions too, by a variety of methods, as Burney described to the BBC reporter Robert Reid who interviewed him at the entrance to Buchenwald when the camp was liberated: 'They hanged; they shot, they had patent traps where you stood on a trap door which let off bullets into your neck, they electrocuted, they injected with phenol, they injected with air, they injected with milk.'

The total death toll between 1937 and 1945 is estimated to have been up to 60,000.

The first Commander of Buchenwald was Karl Otto Koch, who supervised the construction of Buchenwald and then ruled it with unsurpassed brutality, actively aided by his wife Ilsa who became known as 'the beast of Buchenwald'. In 1941 he was transferred to Lublin where, with other S.S. thugs from Buchenwald, he set up the Majdanek concentration and extermination camp. Then even Himmler turned against him for his corruption and cruelty, and in April 1945 he was shot by the S.S. Ilsa Koch was sentenced to life imprisonment after the war and committed suicide in 1967 at the age of sixty.

Hermann Pister succeeded Koch as Commander of Buchenwald in 1942. He was less cruel and more efficient, running the camp as a smooth commercial operation.

Ultimately, he obeyed S.S. orders from Berlin, however vindictive, and he was condemned to death at the Dachau Military Tribunal in 1947. He died in prison the next year, aged sixty-three.

According to a survey in March 1944, soon after Burney arrived, Buchenwald contained 21,000 'labourers', as they were called officially, with a further 21,000 in the twenty-two Buchenwald sub-camps also under S.S. control. Many of the Buchenwald 'labourers' worked adjacent to the camp; 3,500 in the vast Gustloff Werke armament factory and another 500 in the DAW (*Deutsche Ausrüstungswerke GmbH*) which was in the camp itself. Perhaps half of the old lags who had been in Buchenwald since the early days had found soft jobs inside; in the laundry, the records office, or in shoe repairing and tailoring, and that is what kept them alive although their food ration was less. Life on the outside work gangs was brutal and few survived from sub-camps like Dora, where life expectancy was five or six weeks at most.

Fifty per cent of the prisoners were young men under thirty. Nearly fifty per cent were Russians and Poles, fifteen per cent French and twelve per cent Jews. Eight per cent were 'Reich Germans', the old Communists who had been in the camp from 1937. The numbers grew hugely towards the end of the war, so that in January 1945 there were 62,000 prisoners in Buchenwald. The only women were a handful of prostitutes sent from Ravensbruck concentration camp but, after September 1944, several sub-camps were set up for women under the Buchenwald S.S. where female slave labourers mostly worked in armaments and numbered more than 20,000.

The only Britishers in March 1944 were Burney, the Newton brothers, Martin Perkins (strictly speaking he was French) and an Anglo-American, Henry Crooks, who had been on the same train but quietly disappeared on arrival. Little is known about him. He was born in Calais, France, in 1905, had been arrested by the Gestapo for espionage in Lyons in June 1943 while working for the American consulate – was he part of Virginia Hall's messaging service? – interned in Fresnes and then put on the same convoy as the others. Shortly he would do Burney a significant favour and eventually he would survive Buchenwald.

It was now a grey and foggy dawn. The camp was coming to life. Emaciated figures shuffled about slowly and painfully on their way to morning *Appel*, some walking skeletons, others so bloated that they looked like puffballs. Some wore the blue and white striped uniform, others filthy civilian suits with large, coloured patches on the back. They spoke in a Babel of languages from Czech to Serbo-Croatian. 'It was a nightmare scene, from another planet', Burney told Robert Reid in his BBC interview on liberation. What happened to prisoners on arrival was described by Burney in a talk for the BBC written in the autumn of 1945 but not broadcast. Once again, he does not refer to himself, but his description of what he witnessed while working in the Disinfection Station, the *Desinfektionsstation*, in the winter of 1944/5 must stand for his own experience on arrival as far as the process was concerned.

> There was a low building, containing five rooms, which was the Disinfection Station of this camp. Outside this building, in a sort of wire pen, was a crowd of dirty unshaven skeletons dressed in striped ersatz cotton clothing, very few of them with shoes, some with their feet wrapped in bits of rags or paper, and although a few of them were standing, most of them were lying or crouching in the snow.

By this time conditions in the Disinfection Station were unimaginably appalling. Many thousands of Jews had been driven out of labour camps in Poland away from the Russian advance. That winter the population of Buchenwald and its sub-camps doubled to over 80,000 and for the first time the Jews became the largest inmate group in the camp. The convoy of prisoners Burney describes here had survived a forced march across Poland followed by ten days in open trucks in a perpetual blizzard, from which they emerged scarcely alive:

There were maybe a thousand of them and at the camp station there were a thousand more, dead and being scooped out of open trucks by gangs of prisoners. Watching them in their pen were two or three S.S. sergeants, looking bored, joking among themselves, and paying little attention to the proceedings. Closer around them stood a few men with ski caps, thick green overcoats and black jackboots. Every half-hour two or three of these men in green coats came out of the building and ushered in a further fifty of this mutilated wreckage. This was effected German fashion, with shouting and kicking and rubber truncheons.

I remember when I arrived at the camp I thought they were a brand of Nazis, but they were prisoners just as much as I was. They were the camp police and their job, which was delegated to them by the S.S., was to uphold that old German word, discipline.

The prisoners went into the building and were immediately hustled and shouted at until they stood stripped of everything they possessed. They were passed into the next room and were stopped by a man with a white coat whose job was to look for infections and lice. He and his assistant, both prisoners, also searched the naked bodies for hidden valuables, with hitting and kicking.

In the next room the first thing to be seen was a pile of corpses. They were piled up to fifteen at a time, and as soon as a pile was complete, it was carted up to the crematorium. Beside them would be fifty or sixty dying men, and a barber with electric clippers, going placidly around and clipping their hair off, in case they lived long enough to get through this disinfection. To cut the story short, of the thousand who arrived alive, three hundred would die before they could be re-clothed, and five hundred would die before the end of the day.

In that short scene that I have described, nearly all the

brutality came from prisoners, those men in green or white coats with the invariable black boots.

A year earlier Burney and the others had endured in the Disinfection Station the procedure of stripping and body inspection, total body shaving, disinfection in a communal bath of filthy water that stung the skin and then a shower, before being herded along an underground passage to the *Effektenkammer*, the clothing store. By this time the striped uniform supply had run out, so it had been replaced by cast-off clothes, some even ripped from museums in central Europe. Without any consideration of size, Alfred was given an ill-fitting green uniform that 'might have graced a Ruritanian cavalry officer'. To this was added a pair of socks and wooden clogs that had been made in the camp and were so uncomfortable that they caused inflammation of the feet.

The final act of initiation was registration. Considering the wanton destruction of bodies outside, the careful cataloguing of bodies inside the registration office was Germanic efficiency at its extreme. Burney was given the number 44461. He said he had been a 'farmer', an innocuous job description perhaps, and, on 15 February, his card was stamped 'Dikal', an ominous acronym for *darf in kein anderes lager*, meaning 'not to be transferred to another camp'; in effect, death. His height was 178 centimetres, he was 'slim', with 'grey' eyes, 'long' face, 'tilted' nose, 'small' mouth, 'complete' set of teeth and 'blond' hair; he was a 'pipe smoker'. Once again, the colour of Burney's hair is a mystery, as in all photographs his hair is dark. Anyway, it was a superfluous description because on registration his head had been shaved.

Burney, the Newtons and 'Martin Perkins' were then given a strip of cloth to sew on their jackets, printed with their number and a red triangle bearing the letter 'E' for 'Englander'. They were now 'Enemies of the Reich', with no name but the chilling label, *Nacht und Nebel*, meaning 'night and fog', a Nazi classification for political prisoners, meaning that they could disappear without trace.

Little Camp

Whether a prisoner lived or died depended on how he survived the Little Camp, in particular that initiation on arrival. This was the view of Eugen Kogon, a German Catholic inmate of Buchenwald from 1939, and an accomplice of Burney in the last weeks of the Camp. He wrote in *The Theory and Practice of Hell*:

> Every newcomer immediately had to traverse a course of profound personal degradation and humiliation. Naked, he was driven through the abyss that separated the two worlds 'outside' and 'inside'. It was the immediate effects of this terrifying act of compulsion that determined the ultimate destiny of a prisoner. There were two possibilities, and within three months it became apparent which would apply; either he would abandon hope and go into an irresistible mental decline, if he had not already perished in a physical sense, or he would begin to adapt himself to the concentration camp.

After an hour of searching, the Newtons and Perkins found Burney, as described in *No Banners* in the 'factional' style (fact overlaid with fiction) that was typical of biographies of the 1950s:

> His head was shaved, his face was puffed and flabby as a result of gaol privations, and he was wearing a too small outfit that made him look like the fat boy of the comic papers; yet he had an indefinable arrogance about him that commanded more than respect.
> They hailed him jokingly. 'Hey, Lord Muck! May we have the honour of introducing ourselves?'
> He stared at them haughtily. 'Are you British?'
> 'Yes.'

'Very well. As you see, I'm engaged at the moment. I'll see you in a little while.'

It was incredible but, as they were to discover, Christopher Burney was an incredible character.

To those who met him in Buchenwald, Burney was an upper-class Englishman with the stiff upper lip and sense of superiority of his class. His arrogance was also disdain, as he readily admitted in *Dungeon Democracy*. He recalled a threat from a *Kapo* (prisoner guard): 'You British walk about the camp as if you own it. Especially "der dicke" (my humble self), who looks at us all as if we were lumps of s—t (How right!).' There was something about Burney – insolent or principled, depending on your point of view – that commanded attention. On one occasion, as he recalled, he intervened to stop an S.S. man beating up a Hungarian Jew, an action that could easily have ended in his death. Burney's arrogance was part of his character, but it was also a protective armour. As Kogan wrote:

> The mind developed a protective crust, a kind of defensive armour that no longer transmitted every strong stimulus to the sensitive membranes. Pain, pity, grief, horror, revulsion, if admitted in their normal immediacy, would have burst the receptive capacities of the human heart.

Burney dulled his senses. His front of indifference or arrogance was a protective device to prevent severe depression, even hysteria. His withdrawal into an inner world was a practice he had learned in Fresnes, but it led to a kind of split personality, for while 'he surrendered his body to the terror, his inner being withdrew and held aloof' (Kogan). He would pay the price for this mental repression after the war.

Burney and the other Englishmen were marched off by an officious group of prisoners sporting black armbands that signified *Lagerschutz* (camp police) to the so-called Little

Camp on the lowest, northern edge of the barrack town. This would be their home for the next few weeks while in 'quarantine' and selection for 'labour allocation'. Initially they were 'quarantined' in a large blockhouse surrounded by barbed wire, but after two weeks they moved to the barracks. These were wooden, windowless, former stables where the inmates slept on shelves. By the summer of 1944 these stables each contained up to a thousand men. The overcrowding was such that some slept sitting on the floor or lying outside. It became so bad that, later in 1944, Block 61 was set aside for the giving of lethal injections to the dying in order to reduce numbers. The latrines were foul pits, either frozen or flooded, always full.

Rations were half those in the Big Camp. The Little Camp was the refuse camp, for the newly arrived, the infirm, disabled, weak, children and Jews. Many of the slave labourers here were recognised as 'Muselmann', a term common to the concentration camps with no clear derivation but meaning those who from starvation, exhaustion, and lack of will had given up hope and were rotting to death.

It was a deeply shocking initiation to Buchenwald, as described by Dutchman Leo Kok who had arrived on a similar transport to Burney a few days before:

As we were beaten out of the railroad cars with rifle butts at Buchenwald Station at the break of dawn on January 24, 1944, we were in a miserable condition after the terrible journey. There were three corpses in the car, and two who had lost their minds, in addition to the many who had lost consciousness... We finally entered the night, in wooden shoes, descending the high steps of the uniform depot into the dark, into the dirt, into the Little Camp, into Block 58, which was already full to capacity... Sixty men to a box, that is ten to each set of shelves, only possible if they arranged themselves like sardines in a tin. It was impossible to get undressed... Going out to relieve oneself was agony. The latrine was full because nearly everyone suffered from diarrhoea or dysentery. At night you had to grope for a free place with your hands, and then you ended up sitting down in another sick person's filth... When water was available we had to get to the washroom at five in the morning and most people avoided this because it was excruciatingly difficult to get through the mud in wooden shoes... We were yelled at everywhere and it took us days to figure out that the washroom attendants and the men on Camp Protection duty were inmates like us and not the SS.

(From the *Buchenwald Report*)

S.S. Rule by Proxy

From the beginning of Buchenwald, the S.S. believed first in delegation and second in divide-and-rule. By getting former criminals and anti-social elements like homosexuals to run the camp, known as the Greens and Blacks because of the colour of the triangles they wore, the S.S. gave them power over the Reds, that is the Communists, whom they hated. At every level of the camp hierarchy, from the *kapos* who ran the work Kommandos and the *blockältestes* (block chiefs) who, with their *stubendiensts* (attendants, literally room service), controlled the huts to the *Lagerälteste* (camp chief), who was ultimately responsible to the S.S. for the smooth running of the camp, Buchenwald was administered by the prisoners, initially by criminals.

This meant that the S.S. could live in barracks outside the camp, the officers enjoying family life in little bungalows with access to riding stables, all built by camp inmates. In case of trouble the S.S. Totenkopf Squadron kept two barracks of guards here too. 'Totenkopf,' literally 'skull', was the insignia of the Deaths Heads units of the S.S. that were formed to run the extermination and concentration camps.

The transition from Green to Red came in 1942 when Commandant Koch turned over the camp administration to German Communists. By this time power had corrupted the Greens, who in any case were not capable of efficient management, so when the Nazis wanted to expand an arms factory on the fringe of the camp, the Gustloff Werke, the Reds were ready. German Communists had been in the camp since Hitler rose to power. Tightly organised by ideology, unlike the Greens, they also contained proletariat who had worked in industry. It took little persuasion by the S.S., like being granted privileges to wash, grow their hair and wear uniform that wasn't the striped convict pyjamas, and they were ready to help the Fatherland.

In *Dungeon Democracy* Burney describes at length the 'Rule by Proxy' by which the S.S. delegated running the camp to the prisoners. He believed the Nazis alone were not to blame for the barbarity of Buchenwald, for the evil was contagious. It spread from the S.S. to the German Reds and then to other inmates running the camp to whom personal survival was all that mattered. Referring to the recent enemy, he wrote: 'My basic conclusion is that the vast majority of the non-Nazis of Europe, and more especially of Germany, are not material which, without careful selection and treatment, will produce a new civilised continent.' Bitter words, written in 1945, which were widely shared at the time. Burney saw little difference between the German Communists and Nazis; they both believed in domination and spoke fanatically about *unseres liebe Deutschland*, 'our beloved Germany'. He said in an interview in the 1970s: 'The German Communists were merely Nazis painted red. Lots of them thought of me as that bastard Burney.'

The Reds had enormous power. Just as the Greens before them, they controlled the allocation of food, so they could increase or reduce rations. They also ran a huge black market based on stolen prisoners' possessions, and, essentially, they controlled the Work Office, the *Arbeitskammer*, which decided who worked where. If the S.S. wanted a thousand men to be sent to the dreaded Dora, the sub-camp of Buchenwald where slaves lived and worked for their few weeks of life in underground tunnels building the V1 and V2 bomb sites, then the Work Office provided them. Each inmate had a card, an *Arbeitseinsatzkart*, and each Kommando was on a list in the *Arbeitskammer*.

The allotment of work meant literally who lived or died. Falling out of favour with a *Kapo* or denunciation as a 'capitalist' could mean being sent on transport to one of the sub-camps from which few returned. Initially, this is how the Reds got rid of resisting Greens, though a few criminal leaders were sent off to the hospital where the compliant S.S. doctor liquidated them with an injection. Now it was the turn of the many French and the few English, newly arrived from Compiègne, to have their fate decided. They were registered with the *Arbeitskammer*.

From early on in Little Camp, Burney was a marked man. As an upper-class Englishman he was automatically a capitalist, and somebody on his convoy, whom he does not name, denounced him as one of the biggest holders of arms shares in England. Within the first three weeks he was placed three times on the transport list for Dora, alongside the Newton brothers and Perkins, and it was only the intervention of a Dutchman, Pieter Cool, who worked as a medical orderly in the Institute of Hygiene, Block 50, that somehow got their names removed from the list overnight. An advantage of being a conspicuous Englishman and Christian was that group bonding with like-minded Europeans came to the rescue.

Burney had been saved from probable death, but the alternative was still dreadful. He was sent to the *scheisse-kommando*. The sewers of the camp emptied into a concrete pool. Chemicals were added to the excrement to make fertiliser, and this was carried by the prisoners to the fields below Little Camp, referred to as the garden. The Reds reserved this Kommando for those they wished to degrade. To add to the humiliation, the S.S. or Red overseers would whip the hod carriers so that they slipped and were covered with human excrement; sometimes they were pushed into the pool.

When Burney gave a BBC talk in 1954 on 'D-Day in Buchenwald', he remembered first the *scheisse-kommando*:

> The picture that always comes to mind is a winter picture of a column of men, dressed in ersatz cloth, with no coats and open wooden clogs, carrying hods of manure down through dirty snow to what was unhappily called the garden. I remember waiting my turn, watching in the distance this long slow line of men and boxes. Every now and then there was a wavering in the line as some S.S. man decided it was time he kicked someone.

When he was not carrying excrement, Burney was digging ditches in the freezing snow to take power lines to the Gustloff Werke or hewing stones from the limestone quarry for building construction. He found this particularly dangerous: 'If a guard took a dislike to a prisoner he would call him over, throw his cap over the perimeter fence and order him to fetch it. As soon as the man was outside the fence he was shot.'

After a fourteen-hour day that began at four in the morning, on half rations, he was then marched back to camp for the evening *Appel*; that meant standing in the snow an hour or more. Finally, after bread and thin cold soup, he would lie fully dressed and caked with mud or excrement on a wooden shelf squeezed next to the other English prisoners. It could not last. Both Alfred Newton and Martin Perkins contracted pneumonia and were carried off, near death, to the hospital.

On his *Arbeitseinsatzkarte*, Burney's experiences shovelling human excrement and then working in the quarry to hew out paving stones are described in what may best be described as euphemism: for labour detachment Number 14 is *Entwässerung* or 'de-watering' and Number 12 is *LagerKommando* or 'street cleaning'. Or perhaps these refer to other Kommandos? The archivists at Buchenwald today say that the *Arbeitseinsatzkarte* record keeping was unreliable. Nor is there any reference that by late April Burney had joined the *Lagerdolmetscher* ('Camp Interpreter') *Kommando*, which he assuredly did.

The 'Incredible' Burney

It was now, according to Alfred Newton, that Burney began to earn his reputation as 'incredible'. He asked to speak to the International Camp Committee, a powerful but illegal body representing the Communists from many countries but dominated by the Germans. It had been formed initially to maintain the power of the Reds but now it worked to reconcile national differences between Communists and take their various interests into account. On the Committee, ideology was more important than nationality. Later, when German defeat seemed likely, it prepared for the liberation of the camp.

Burney's pitch was an intentional ego trip. He gave himself the rank of Captain and insinuated that he was more than a 'farmer' which was how he was registered. He claimed he was a 'landowner' who was well-known in Government circles and he was sure that the British Government knew about Buchenwald. When the Anglo-American armies liberated the camp, not the Russians as the Communists hoped, they would want to know what happened to these English officers. The Committee, like the Nazi overlords, would be accountable.

This threat was an 'incredible' gamble, and according to Newton it made Burney 'the most hated man in Buchenwald'. Here was a member of the British Establishment, if not a capitalist, threatening a committee of Communists; but there must have been a sense of quiet authority and composure about him that was convincing; and it was in character. The Committee was impressed. It helped that he spoke, in his own estimation, 'good' German and he was 'reasonably fluent' in Russian and Spanish as well as 'perfect' in French. Perhaps his promotion to a camp interpreter stemmed from this meeting.

Burney and Henry Newton were moved to Big Camp, *Grosse*

Lager, where they were joined by the others after they got out of hospital. The Newton brothers were shoved into Block 14 where Henry Newton was made *stubbendienst*, the orderly who dished out soup and bread, which had its advantages. Burney was assigned to Block 38, a stone-built two-storey block containing mainly 'political' prisoners like himself and Czechs, most of whom had been incarcerated from the early days. He was given one smelly blanket.

Community life, including meals, took place in the blocks. The food ration in 1944 was supposed to consist of 300 grams of bread per day, 400 grams of potatoes, 250 grams of vegetables and up to 30 grams of meat (mostly horse), as decreed for slave labourers by the S.S. Department of Economic Administration. Those not on outside work camps received eighty per cent of the ration. This may sound reasonable but in practice the amount of food was much reduced so that, according to a survey in March 1944, eighty per cent of Buchenwald inmates in Big Camp were 'undernourished'. From then on until the end of the war, that is the duration of Burney's time, the food allocation was reduced to near starvation level. This gave rise to the Buchenwald slang word *Tonnenadler*, meaning 'rubbish bin eagle', applied to an inmate who through starvation and lack of restraint plundered rubbish crates and dumps. On the other hand, such was the history of Buchenwald that some inmates still received food parcels, and there was a black market among those who had somehow obtained money.

In Little Camp the food supply was reduced to a thin soup and a piece of bread. This had to be collected from Roll Call Square where long queues formed daily, inmates carrying or dragging the dead with them to claim their food ration too, after which the corpses were left on the ground.

Burney's 'indoor work' in Buchenwald was still in a house of hell. It was back to the *Effektenkammer* and the Disinfection Station, the *Desinfektionsstation*. He was acting as interpreter already, but he was not spared the routine of body searching, shaving and the piling up of bodies; all the while working among the bewildered, the exhausted, and the scarcely alive. Although conditions here were not at their worst until the following winter, already in the first quarter of 1944, 15,000 more Jews were inducted into Buchenwald.

After the war, when Julia watched a newsreel report about the liberation of Buchenwald, she could scarcely believe it:

> *I could not believe Christopher had worked in that part of the camp; I thought there must have been a more salubrious annexe for gentlemen and officers. When I asked him about this, he replied shortly that he worked among these doomed creatures, and often had the job of collecting and piling bodies in stacks of fifteen. He added that they were slimy and smelly, and he never wanted to talk of them again.*

About April 1944, Henry Crooks introduced Burney to a Czech international hockey player who spoke good English. He invited them round to Block 12 where, he said, he had friends who could help. It was a special block with central heating:

> It was occupied in a mysterious way by some of the interpreters and a few other Czechs. We came in through a screened door to a bright, warm room with a smell of frying onions and we saw a group of neatly dressed gentlemen with long hair, creased trousers, shiny shoes and, believe it or not, one whole beard. Two or three were painting, another cooking, at one table an earnest discussion was being held over what smelled like coffee; and the rest were reading. We shook hands, were given coffee and cigarettes, and till the curfew whistle blew we discussed in English Anglo-Czech relations, literature, and music.
>
> I remember saying to Harry as we walked back to our block through the wind, 'I can hardly believe it. It's not Buchenwald.

If I could spend the rest of my life as they live, I wouldn't ask more.' It was true at the time.

It was the Czechs who ran the Interpreter Kommando or *Lagerdolmetscher* – 'one of the two best Kommandos in the camp', Burney wrote – and soon he was an official member based in the Czech Block 20. The backbone of the block were senior Czech citizens who had been interned since the Nazi occupation of their country in 1938, and ever since they had kept their privilege of receiving food parcels. These were shared out communally and, said Burney, the Czech community of Communists and non-Communists lived more or less amicably together; peace and fraternity were the aim. Burney owed a particular debt of hospitality to Dr Holek, former Editor of *Národný Listy* (The Times of Prague), and an influential figure in the camp. It was due to him, Burney wrote in *Dungeon Democracy*, that the German Communist opposition to his soft job was squashed.

Burney's life in Block 38 was less harmonious. One day its Russian members 'bounced' to death one of their number for being an informer. Burney had a number of Russian acquaintances, and these included two Russian POW army colonels who sat on the clandestine International Camp Committee. He had friends in the right places. From this time Burney's life became more bearable.

CHAPTER 5

BUCHENWALD – LIVING HELL

16 June 1944

I think it's your birthday today – or tomorrow – so I thought I would write and send you my fondest love and wishes.

Useless to say how much I miss you or how much I long to see you again.

Love, Julia

Dungeon Democracy

NOW THAT BURNEY was in the Interpreter Kommando he could wander around Buchenwald and get to understand the meaning of 'concentration camp'. He determined, if he survived, to write *Dungeon Democracy*, in part a description of the behaviour of the different nations in the camp and in part an account of how power was operated from the S.S. downwards. To this he would add the chapter 'Curtain', his dramatic diary of the last weeks of the camp in which he played a prominent part. He obtained contraband paper to take notes, although this was a minor offence leading to *funf und zwanzig am arsch*, 'twenty-five strokes on the backside', with the handle of a pickaxe.

Burney believed that if he looked under the surface of horror and determined what caused it, he could contribute to retribution and prevention. He saw himself in Buchenwald as a witness to history and for this he needed detachment. He wrote in the Introduction to *Dungeon Democracy*:

> I fear passion in books because passion clouds the mind so that the eyes see only the horrible surface of events and cannot judge their real place in human history. The true perspective remains hidden behind the red fog of impenetrable emotional reaction.
>
> I have watched men die in filth and squalor and the stench of their own rotting flesh. Most were so far down the pit of inhumanity that they were unable to know or feel more than tortured dying animals, but some had still kept enough of their own souls and their own values to appreciate the pathos of their agony.
>
> What I saw filled me with loathing and pity. But vengeance is the right of God alone and we must content ourselves with judgement and execution. The evidence for conviction abounds but we need a clear sight to achieve the ultimate good of all evil experience and the ultimate end of every judiciary body, which is to avoid the recurrence of the evil.

He goes on to say, 'I have tried as far as possible to leave personal things alone,' so his book is not a personal account; far from it. He leaves out entirely episodes in which he played a prominent part. Sometimes he refers to himself in the third person and sometimes he gives others assumed names: Eugen Kogon, for example, is Emil Kalman. It took me some time to realise that Burney used the actual names of the Nazis but gave fictional names to some, but not all, prisoners to protect their identity. Suspicion of authority must have become ingrained.

By the late summer of 1944 thoughts were turning to the end of the war. The Russian offensive had pushed through Belarus to the Polish border, where Russian troops would soon discover the eastern Nazi extermination camps of Treblinka and Sobibor. In the west the Allies were consolidating their

D-Day landings in Normandy. Optimists in Buchenwald began plans for the camp liberation and took a more pro-active stance towards survival.

In his unobtrusive way Burney moved through the camp observing and making contacts; the French were in Blocks 26, 10 and 31, the Czechs in Blocks 20 and 38, the Poles in Block 37 and the numerous Russians were everywhere. The Jews who had got out of Little Camp had their own blocks too. There was little community spirit in these blocks, never mind co-operation with blocks of other nations, for as Burney said later in his BBC interview with Robert Reid:

> If you wanted to be disgusted with humanity, all you had do was come and live here. People were stealing, they were killing each other for a slice of bread, they were always quarrelling, there was always a lot of political intrigue. One group hated another, and the other group hated the next and so on.

Nevertheless, as a sign of more optimistic times, in 1944 each nation began to form its own co-ordinating committee; the Polish Cooperation Committee, the Comité des Intérêts Francais, the Dutch Committee, the Italian Solidarity Committee, and so on. Then there was the International Camp Committee which hoped resolutely that the time was drawing closer when the Soviet Union would liberate the camps and Communism would triumph.

Non-political opposition, as Burney called it, more appropriately non-Communist opposition, was centred in the camp administration itself, in the Hygiene Institute of Block 50. This innocuous sounding unit had been established by the Waffen S.S. to develop new treatments for injuries and diseases afflicting German troops, such as typhus. 'Guinea pigs' for this research were housed in the feared Block 46, where horrific experiments took place. The doctor in charge of both these blocks was S.S. *Sturmbannführer* Ding-Schuler.

Working as his First Secretary in Block 50 was the Austrian Catholic journalist and later professor, Eugen Kogon. 'He stood head and shoulders above all,' wrote Burney, 'he was the principal saviour of the 23,000 prisoners who were there to greet the tanks of the American Third Army'. Ding-Schuler was close to Heinrich Himmler, the *Reichsführer* of the S.S., but Kogon was close to Ding and would visit him at home in Weimar where he was known as 'Onkel Eugen'. He had persuaded Ding that the Third Reich was doomed, and Ding-Schuler needed to save his own skin. Then there was Heinz Baumeister, a one-time Social Democrat politician from Dortmund and now the Second Secretary in Block 50, who was prepared to use his many contacts outside the camp; Burney calls him 'Heinrich Bilder'. With Kogon and Baumeister was Professor Alfred Balachowsky, once in the Resistance but spared because he was from the Pasteur Institute in Paris and an expert in producing an anti-typhus vaccine.

Two Dutchmen were medical orderlies in Block 50; Jan Robert, a former Olympic masseur and child psychologist, and Pieter Cool (called Peter Kool in *Dungeon Democracy*), an ex-naval officer whom the Newtons nicknamed 'Battleship' because of his size. He had already saved the Englishmen from probable death on three occasions. They acted as liaison between the group and the International Camp Committee, and they all took the initiative in saving prisoners from death when they could.

Finally, there was Franz Eichhorn whom Burney calls 'Fritz Edelmann', chief barber to the S.S., a former motor dealer in Dusseldorf. He had gained the confidence of the Camp Commandant, the indecisive but order-obeying Hermann Pister, who was loose-tongued during the intimacy of the shave. This information Edelmann would pass on.

After the dreaded evening *Appel*, which could require standing for hours until the whole Big Camp had been counted, including the stiff cold corpses of those who had died or been murdered during the day and were dragged to Roll Call Square, the three Englishmen with Perkins would meet up in the *Effektenkammer*. Here Maurice Pertschuk, alias Martin Perkins, had the task of handing out clothing to new arrivals, while Alfred worked nearby as a clerk in the registration office. The *Effektenkammer* had the only clean latrines in the camp, so here they would hold their daily 'cabinet meeting' (after *cabinet*, the French for WC) 'chaired' by Burney, whom they had appointed 'Senior British Officer'.

It was at this time, the summer of 1944, that Julia Burrell consulted a clairvoyant:

> *'Pick a card,' she said. Then she said, 'There is a brown-haired man, he loves you very much and he will come back to you in an aeroplane. He is very, very ill.'*
>
> *'Is he wounded?' My heart was in my mouth for I knew she was talking about Christopher.*
>
> *'No, he is not wounded, but he is very, very ill. He is not wearing a uniform. He is wearing strange clothes.'*
>
> *'What kind of clothes?'*
>
> *'Strange.' After a pause, 'He wouldn't willingly hurt a hair on your head.'*
>
> *'When will he come?'*
>
> *'He will come. He loves you and there is much beauty and happiness around you.' Then, sounding worried she said, 'There is something sharp and I do not understand for it is there, the sharpness, in the happiness...'*

Burney to the Rescue

In the *Effektenkammer*, on 18 August 1944, Burney told the others of his fears for thirty-seven members of the Allied Secret Services who had been despatched by the Gestapo to Buchenwald on the last transit train from Compiègne. He had already met them, he said, as related in *No Banners*:

I've tipped off the new chaps about what goes on here. I've
also had a word with Comrade C – – [one of the International
Camp Committee]. He's damned pessimistic about their
future, and quite sure this new crowd had been brought here
for immediate execution. The point is what, if anything, can be
done about it?

Burney was earning a reputation as diplomat and fixer, but
the fate of the Resistance agents, mostly French and British,
was beyond his help. On orders of the Reich Department of
Security, they had been sent to Buchenwald for execution and
were housed in the quarantine Block 17, unwittingly awaiting
their fate.

Two days later, on 20 August, another trainload of Allied
prisoners of the Reich arrived from Paris, the last before the
city's liberation. It included 168 airmen, mostly from the US
Air Force and Royal Air Force, who had been shot down over
France while bombing strategic installations before and after
D-Day. Rescued by the Resistance they had been captured
by the Gestapo and were crucially found to be wearing
civilian clothes and were without their 'dog tags' (military
identification). They were branded *Luftgangsters* or 'terror
fliers' and sent to Buchenwald DIKAL, *darf in kein anderes
lager*, 'not to be moved to another camp'.

Stanley Booker, aged ninety-eight in 2021, is the one airman
still alive and his story stands for the others.[1] He had been a
navigator in a Halifax bomber shot down just before D-Day.
Parachuted to land, he evaded capture for five days before
being picked up by the Resistance with the intention of passing
him along a usual escape route. Like over forty per cent of the
other airmen, he was betrayed by the Gestapo double agent,
Jacques Désoubrie. He was found to have Resistance papers
on him, so tortured in the Gestapo headquarters at 11 Rue
des Saussaies in Paris and sent off to solitary confinement in
Fresnes. Here he pondered the injustice of fate for six weeks
before his fourth floor at Fresnes was evacuated on 14 August

and the whole batch of prisoners sent on the nightmare train journey to Buchenwald.

It was in the Disinfection Station that the future leader of the airmen, Squadron Leader Phil Lamason, a New Zealander, first came across Burney.[2] He rarely talked about Buchenwald after the war, but he gave a long interview to his local newspaper when he was eighty years of age in 1999:

> They'd taken us into this room and there were about a dozen guys shaving all the hair off our bodies... There was one bloke who came up to me, he was working as one of the shavers in there, and he said to me, 'My name's Burney, and I'm an Englishman.' I asked him what the hell he was doing in here? Speaking very quietly he told me he'd been operating behind German lines and he'd been caught 'and now I'm in here and they have almost forgotten me'. He asked me who I was, and I told him the story of what had happened...

Stripped, shorn, scalded by disinfectant, dressed in convict stripes, Stanley Booker, Phil Lamason and the other airmen emerged into Little Camp. They had no idea what a concentration camp was or why they were there. The initial reaction was shock and horror, as expressed by the American airman, Joe Moser:

> I was filled with a sense of dread. I felt it deep within my gut... at the faces staring at us... empty, vacant, bony, skeletal faces. No empathy or pity. Just empty, dead stares – I wondered if I would be reduced to such a state. If this was a POW camp, it was far, far worse than anything I imagined when trying to prepare myself to be a prisoner.[3]

Black armband *Lagerschutz* steered Booker and the rest of the airmen towards a corner of Little Camp strewn with rocks, near the barbed wire. This Rock Pile, as they called it, would be their quarters. Phil Lamason, the tough looking New Zealand

Squadron Leader with a boxer's broken nose, took charge. They were prisoners of war, he said, not political or criminal prisoners; they must conduct themselves like a military body; they were in a fix, but he would get them out of it. Large tureens of soup arrived, 'little more than grass or nettles soaked in hot water with vile tasting black bread,' one airman remembered. Without bowls the airmen could only drink by dipping their hands into the tureens. They threw scraps of bread towards a group of pathetic 'musselmanner' who fought and scavenged like starving dogs until Lamason put a stop to this degradation. It was then that Christopher Burney turned up, as Booker recalled:

> Suddenly a shadowy figure came across wearing the striped uniform. He asked in English where our commanding officer was and then he went over and had a private conversation with Lamason. He went away and came back with two other prisoners about an hour later. They carried about a dozen bowls and a bucket of potatoes.
>
> Then I didn't see him again for a while. We didn't know his name, but I later found out it was Burney. He kept himself to himself and didn't mix with us.

On 24 August, a daylight raid of US Flying Fortresses flattened the Gustloff Werke armaments factory outside the camp, killing at least 400 prisoners and injuring 2,000 others. The airmen agreed to help fight the resultant fires in the camp. They picked up leaflets showering down from the sky which showed photographs of Germans in uniform, with the caption in Gothic German print, 'These men are German prisoners of war in England. They are treated according to the rules of the Geneva Convention.' Was this some kind of hint? Was their existence known after all? But in the short term the raid made their treatment worse. Spat at and called *Verdammt terrorfliegers*, they were summoned to Commandant Pister's office where he vented his hostility. Probably unknown to them, a large amount of arms was smuggled back into the camp after the raid; and this became the base of the International Camp Committee's secret supply.

Over the next few days Lamason met Squadron Leader 'Tommy' Yeo-Thomas, formerly an agent for the RF section of SOE known as *Shelley*, and now the leader of the thirty-seven Resistance agents awaiting death in Hut 17. The meeting went badly. To avoid certain execution in Paris, Yeo-Thomas had adopted the identity of Squadron Leader Ken Dodkin with whom, back in England, he had trained in SOE techniques of avoiding detection; but Lamason had flown with the real Dodkin and saw immediately that he was not the man in front of him. Lamason sought out Burney who told him the truth, in utmost confidence.

Lamason recognised Burney as a man in whom he could confide. They were kindred spirits, pro-active about survival and good at knowing the right people, but also discreet. The same could not be said of Yeo-Thomas. They found him indiscreet and impulsive, despite his huge bravery and inspiring leadership. In his 1999 interview, Lamason was keen to put the record straight:

Burgess [author of *Destination Buchenwald*] gives Yeo-Thomas credit for helping get us out of Buchenwald, but in actual fact he had nothing to do with it. He was given a great write-up after the War, probably I think because he was so highly decorated... I sort of quite liked the guy but he had a great big ego so I treated him with kid gloves. Half of Yeo-Thomas's own blokes didn't want a bar of him [could not tolerate him]. People have written books on Yeo-Thomas, saying how he had his men very well disciplined... that's all bullshit, he didn't have them disciplined at all... He was very much a loner...[4]

There were two issues over which Lamason and Yeo-Thomas disagreed. The first was a hair-brained scheme of Yeo-Thomas's for agents and airmen to break out of the camp assisted by Russian POWs using arms they had secreted away, and take over the nearby Norha airfield from where they would fly back to Allied lines. Lamason thought this was a non-starter, though he tried to be tactful. The second was Yeo-Thomas's invitation to Lamason that their two groups should integrate as far as possible. Lamason firmly declined. It was vital for him to insist on the Prisoner of War status of his airmen which should guarantee them the protection of the Geneva Convention, even though Buchenwald did not accept this. Any dilution with resistance agents would make his task more difficult.

After eight days and nights on the Rock Pile, the airmen were installed on the shelves of nearby Block 58. There was a large group of Roma children with them in the Block, but they were soon dragged out by the S.S. and forced, crying and screaming, into a large, windowless, black pantechnicon. The back of the van was closed and it drove away. An ominous silence hung over the camp. It was rumoured that this pantechnicon was a mobile gas chamber, similar to those used elsewhere in the Third Reich.

One Saturday morning Booker met Burney:

Once a week we were checked for lice and if our clothes were crawling with them, we were showered and sent off to the *Effektenkammer*. Christopher Burney, who seemed to have an office nearby, came and spoke to me in English. Then he came back with a wonderful jacket with a fur collar. 'You'll be glad of this,' he said, 'winter is on its way'. We came to see him as Mr Fixit. He was our only contact with the German authorities, so if we wanted something we got it through Squadron Leader Lamason, and he asked Burney.

Lamason continued to protest to Commandant Pister that the airmen were POWs and would not work as slave labour. He would not 'step back' (hence the title of his biography: *I Would Not Step Back*) even if faced by an S.S. firing squad.

Without work the airmen hung around Block 58, daydreaming about life after Buchenwald. They formed the **KLB** Club, *Konzentrationlager Buchenwald Club*, and discussed post-war meetings where activities and exchanges would take place. It was a way of counteracting their fear that they were irretrievably lost. As Stanley Booker said, 'We all knew the war was going well, but we could not contemplate that anyone could possibly know where we were, and we might disappear without trace.'

Murder – and Escape

On 9 September, the camp tannoy system blared out the names of sixteen of Yeo-Thomas's men, ordering them to report to the Main Gate. They marched off, singing, 'It's a long way to Tipperary'. Booker, who had been alerted by the tannoy announcement, dashed to the wire and watched them go: 'There was the awful spectacle of them all gathered outside. I saw them led across the courtyard and into a building. They walked in, marching through the doorway. And we didn't see them again.'

The next day those sixteen men were beaten up, marched to the mortuary block below the crematorium known as the *leichenkeller* (corpse cellar) and there executed. They were tied back-to-back in pairs, nooses of piano wire were strung around their necks, and they were hoisted on to steel hooks just below the ceiling: strangled to death, thrashing on the end of hooks. The bodies were heaved down, piled on the electric lift and sent upstairs to the coke-fired crematorium.

Probably shortly after this ghastly tragedy, Lamason was tipped off by a German Communist that a friend in the camp administration (was this Franz Eichhorn, the barber?) had heard Pister say he had received orders from Berlin that the airmen were to be exterminated. This hearsay may well have been true, though it would have been a mass execution with enormous international ramifications unless the 168 deaths could have been disguised, however unlikely, as natural causes. The indecisive Pister considered the options and Lamason kept the rumour to himself. Now there was an even more urgent need to get the airmen out, so Lamason consulted Burney who said he would try and help.

After discussions with the International Camp Committee and Eugen Kogon's network in Hut 50, they considered that the best, if slim, hope was to smuggle a letter out of the camp stating that a large group of RAF, USAF and other Allied aircrew were being held illegally in Buchenwald Concentration Camp. This would be given to a trusted prisoner on an outside work group at the Nohra Luftwaffe airfield nearby, with instructions to get it up the chain of command to Berlin.

Very possibly, Burney had the idea for this letter as he would use the same ploy to save lives during the last weeks of the camp; he may well have drafted it too. Lamason said in his interview that Balachowsky got the letter out, but elsewhere Baumeister has been named. In fact, in January 1946, Balachowsky gave this deposition during the trial of Hermann Goering, Commander in Chief of the Luftwaffe, at the International War Crimes Tribunal in Nuremberg:

> In Block 50 we had a visit from Luftwaffe cadets. These cadets, members of the regular German armed forces, passed through the camp and were able to see practically everything that went on there. They came at the invitation of *Sturmbannführer* Schuler. We received several visits.[5]

Perhaps this was Balachowsky's contact? Now it was a question of waiting, more in hope than expectation.

Shortly after this, around 15 September, Yeo-Thomas disappeared and that was the last Lamason saw of him. The story of his extraordinarily courageous escape, together with Harry Peulevé and Stephane Hessel, has been told many times. Christopher Burney had nothing to do with it, although he was one of the very few who was privy to the secret.

In summary, Yeo-Thomas was contacted by Eugen Kogon and Professor Balachowsky from Hut 50. With the connivance of *Sturmbannführer* Ding-Schuler, who saw an Allied victory coming, they proposed a scheme for saving three agents. One of them had to be Yeo-Thomas who, thought Ding-Schuler, might plead his case for clemency after the war. All three had to be fluent French speakers because, after being injected with a high fever wrongly diagnosed as 'typhus', they would be hidden upstairs in Hut 46 until three genuine typhus sufferers, all Frenchmen, died of the disease. Then their identities would be exchanged.

On 19 September, Peulevé and Hessel, with high fevers, joined 'Dodkin' in Hut 46. They remained hidden on the first floor, while a few days later three Frenchmen with genuine typhus arrived in the ward on the floor below. They waited for them to die.

During this intermission in a drama of life and death, a distinguished former Luftwaffe fighter pilot named Hannes Trautlof arrived at Buchenwald, ostensibly to inspect the bomb damage at the Gustloff Werke. The truth was he had heard the rumour of a large group of Allied airmen incarcerated in the camp and he had decided to investigate. He was spotted by one of the airmen, Bernard Scharf, who spoke fluent German. Over the barbed wire Scharf begged for rescue. Trautlof had the ear of Hermann Goering, who was outraged when he heard the news and demanded instant release of the airmen. Had Trautlof been alerted by the Buchenwald letter after it had been delivered at Norha? Had the letter reached Goering directly in Berlin as was afterwards rumoured? Whatever the truth, Trautlof's report initiated the release of the airmen.

On 4 October a further fifteen SOE agents were summoned for execution and one of them was Peulevé. Ding-Schuler convinced Pister that Peulevé was in the hospital dying of typhus, but for good measure one of his team would execute him with a lethal injection. This was a lie, of course. The fourteen agents were executed on 5 October, this time facing a firing squad. The three survivors in Hut 46 continued to wait for the Frenchmen to die.

On 14 October an official arrived at the camp S.S. offices from Dulag Luft in Wiesbaden, where Allied airmen were interrogated and transferred to POW camps after capture. He addressed the assembled airmen in the camp cinema:

> Recently it came to the attention of the Luftwaffe that you were being held in this place, so the S.S. tell me, by mistake (howls of derison from the audience). You will be released from this place and transferred to a prisoner of war camp, this time under Luftwaffe control (hubbub of excitement).[6]

And so it was, on 19 October, that Stanley Booker and 151 other airmen (fourteen remained for a short while in hospital and two died in Buchenwald) found themselves once again in cattle trucks, but this time with stoves, fresh straw, and an open door, bound for Stalag Luft III prison camp in Sagan. Chunks of bread and sausage were handed out and all, including guards, joined in the singing of 'Lili Marlene'.

Did Booker know that his release had begun with Burney, among others, and a letter? The answer is 'no' because Lamason and Burney had kept it secret. Stanley Booker:

> At the time we didn't know there was a letter. It was only many years after the war that we learnt about it, and then we thought that Yeo-Thomas had got it out when he escaped. Now I know that it was Christopher Burney with a small group of friends who organised it and got it out.

To the airmen, rightly, their release was due to the Luftwaffe. Both Lamason and Burney carried their secrets into peacetime. It was only in the 1980s at a reunion dinner of the KLB Club that Lamason revealed they had all been under sentence of execution. Burney does not even mention the episode of the airmen in *Dungeon Democracy*.

Booker adds a short epilogue to this story:

> In 1982 I went back to Buchenwald, the first airman to do so. I wanted to get our records back from the Gestapo archive to prove to the RAF that we had been in a concentration camp for two months, because they would not put it on our service record.
>
> I formed a close relationship with Herr Rothman who worked in the museum and had actually been a *kapo* in Hut 17 in 1944. He gave me the impression that he had found Yeo-Thomas rather a braggart who was making false claims. There was 'another Englishman', he said, with a close circle of contacts including a Dutchman [Jan Robert] who had got the letter out of the camp. He said us airmen had a lot to thank him for, and he obviously meant Burney.

On 20 October, the day after the release of the airmen, the three Frenchmen Marcel Seigneur, Maurice Chouquet and Michel Boitel were registered dead and cremated in the names of the three SOE agents. Peulevé and Hessel walked out of Buchenwald a few days later bearing their new French identities on their way to a relatively lenient sub-camp at Schönebeck, one hundred miles away.

Shortly afterwards the remaining Resistance agents were summoned for execution and the names announced included Dodkin and Hessel, an administrative mix-up for they were already officially dead. It was not until 9 November that Dodkin moved out of hiding in Hut 46 and was taken to Gleina sub-camp. Eventually all three survived the war and Julia's memoir records that Peulevé and Hessel were reunited with Burney in her London flat, where they 'talked in hushed voices' about their experiences.

One more Resistance agent out of the thirty-seven remained alive in Buchenwald. He was Squadron Leader Maurice

Southgate (*Hector*) who had been in the camp hospital during the cull and somehow survived. Henry Newton found him a cushy job in the tailoring Kommando but from now on the four English agents with Maurice Pertschuk must have dreaded the camp tannoy summoning them to their own execution.

CHAPTER 6

BUCHENWALD – THE LAST WEEKS

The Worst Winter

THE WINTER OF 1944/45 was one of the coldest in European history. Working in the Disinfection Station, Burney saw piles of frozen corpses arriving off the open wagons. One day he stood at *Appel* for over two hours in a howling blizzard; only the intervention of a French West Indian prisoner who gave him his coat, he says, saved him from pneumonia.

Burney's life was at its lowest ebb. The war was dragging on and after nearly a year in Buchenwald he did not expect to survive. Using his contraband paper, he wrote to Julia over several days at the turn of the year. In an extended metaphor, the walk up the grassy valley behind Oakfield house in Hay on Wye, past the waterfall above Llanigon and rising to the sunlit Hay Bluff, has now become his *via dolorosa*:

> My darling Judy [*sic*],
> When we walked round the hills at Nether Auchendrane I told you about the valley behind my house which seemed to symbolise in some way our future. Perhaps that future is now past, and if the beginning of the valley looked full of promise, as in my blindness it did, it took some strange turns after it passed out of sight round the shoulder of the hill.

At first it was strewn with stones and rocks on which I cut my feet, but it soon led onto a high plateau, barren and swept by the bitterest of all winds, which tore off what protection I had and cut through me, froze, and whipped me constantly.

In the sky I could see the reflection of a view more beautiful than any I had hitherto imagined, but it was no more than a reflection and of the plateau I could see no end. I felt only the wind and my nakedness before it, the death of despair gnawing at my heart and of insanity at my brain...

Though my blood has run cold here, and I know that passionate longing in such an exile is not possible, yet I know too that I still love you and sometimes through the cold and hunger I feel the lack of you more than anything else and more deeply than ever I felt it during the feverish separations of the old days.

In early January1945, Christopher's mother received a letter from Major I K Mackenzie of the War Office:

Dear Mrs Young,

I very much regret to inform you that we have lost touch with your son, Lieut. C A G Burney, and he must be considered a prisoner.

As you may know, he had volunteered to work in connection with the Resistance Movement in France, and therefore there are certain circumstances in connection with his arrest which make it essential, in the interests of his own safety, that you make no enquiries about his whereabouts except through me. In other words, he may be held prisoner as a French civilian, and any enquiries about him in his own name may draw attention to him and jeopardise his safety.

Once again, may I say how sorry I am to give you this bad news, and to say that there is every reason to hope that your son will eventually be recovered.

Yours sincerely

Burney's Role in the Last Weeks of the Camp

Burney wrote afterwards that, even among the old-timers in Buchenwald, the last few weeks were the most dangerous in its existence. Would orders come from the S.S. in Berlin to evacuate the camp west and southwards, leaving many dead on those death marches? Would the S.S., led by the S.S. Totenkopf squadrons and reinforced from Weimar, try to exterminate the camp using flame-throwers? Would Pister order the execution of camp inmates considered the most subversive, including Burney? Would inmates exploit the prevailing anarchy and carry out revenge murders against each other? Finally, would Allied planes and artillery attack Buchenwald? All these threats were realised to some degree.

Burney's account in *Dungeon Democracy* of the collapse of Buchenwald Concentration Camp begins on 25 March:

> Emil [Eugen Kogon] informed me that Ding had just returned from Ohrdruf, where Kommando S3 was employed digging tunnels for the accommodation of the train of Hitler's headquarters and other important Nazi offices. [Ohrdruf is sixty kilometres due west of Weimar and was in the line of the advance of the American army.] A conference was held of all senior officers at Ohrdruf to decide what to do with the prisoners if the Americans showed up in force. Suggestions were made, first to gas them in the tunnel, second to blow them up. Both were squashed on technical grounds. Himmler was telegraphed for instructions. He replied that criminals and prominent political prisoners should be executed and the rest marched eastwards to Buchenwald.

Dispassionate as ever, Burney is describing the fate of concentration camp prisoners on the defeat of the Third Reich. Would Buchenwald be next? Since the beginning of the year the dissolution of the camps had dominated life in Buchenwald. Trainloads of dying survivors from camps in the east were daily arriving in Little Camp, half dead from hunger, thirst and cold. 2,000 emaciated men were crammed into each stables, the dead being thrown out at night to make way for the living. The population of Little Camp grew from 6,000 to 17,000 in the first three months of the year, even though 14,000 prisoners died during this time in Buchenwald and its sub-camps. The crematorium ran out of fuel: bodies piled up outside and only rats flourished. Food rations were reduced to a minimum. Life was a desperate struggle for survival.

From early April the boom of guns could be heard as American troops attacked the German defences at Eisenach and Kassel, one hour away. 'These were days of extreme nervous tension' writes Eugen Kogon in his account of the last days as printed in *The Buchenwald Report*, which is a very similar account to Burney's own in his last chapter of *Dungeon Democracy*, titled 'Curtains'.

Now that it was clear that the Americans would liberate the camp there was new tension between Communists and 'capitalists'. Burney reports the resolution of German Reds at the end of March: 'It is in the highest degree regrettable that the Anglo-American capitalists should liberate us. We will do all in our power, even under them, to retain the position we have always held.' Burney observes with distaste the change of allegiances. He tells of a Frenchman:

> When he arrived, he claimed to have been Secretary of the
> Communist Youth of France or some such thing and was
> therefore treated with honour and respect. But at the end,
> when the Americans were on their way to us, he forgot the
> saviour creed and came crawling to me for favour and special
> treatment.

Burney was recognised as one of the leaders of the 'non-politicals'. As part of the network based on Block 50, he knew what was on Pister's mind, and as the English interpreter he would obviously play an important part when the Americans arrived. This increased his unpopularity among the German

Communists. Alfred Newton described to Jack Thomas in *No Banners* how he was arrested by two of the camp police and dragged to *Lagerschutz* headquarters. *Der Anglo-Amerikaner* was beaten up, but heard the leader of the German Communists say:

> 'You confounded blunderer! You've brought in the wrong man. This chap is the one with the brother. I want the Scotsman, of course. [Burney was proud of his eighteenth-century Scots ancestry.] The one who walks about the camp as if he owns the place. The one who speaks Russian.'
>
> It was Burney they wanted, Alfred reflected. He was the only one of the five who spoke Russian, and he had used his talents to good effect in establishing friendly relations with the Red Army officers among the prisoners.
>
> [Nevertheless, Alfred was forced to stand to attention all night in the hut latrine.]
>
> After the morning *Appel*, Alfred had a chance to speak to Henry and Christopher Burney. They knew what had happened and Burney had made a strong protest to his mysterious 'friends' who assured him there would be no repetition.

To Alfred Newton this was the 'incredible Burney' again.

The Killing of Maurice Pertschuk

On 26 March, Commandant Pister asked the German Reds to assemble in the camp cinema. He told them he had no wish to evacuate the camp, though he would obey orders, and he wished to hand it over in good order. It was up to them to maintain discipline.

Any optimism the Englishmen felt was obliterated three days later when Martin Perkins was summoned to the Main Gate. At the time, Burney said in his debriefing after the war, they both assumed that 'Perkins' had been mistaken for

'Dodkin', alias Yeo-Thomas, who they knew the Germans were trying to locate (as we know he had 'disappeared' the previous November having changed his identity for a dead Frenchman) and a simple face-to-face identification would sort out the confusion.

But Perkins did not return. Later that day Burney discovered that he had been beaten up, shoved in a van that made the shuttle service between the Gate and the Crematorium and then hanged from a hook in the mortuary. Burney's reaction in *Dungeon Democracy* was laconic: 'This darkened the picture, for he was my best friend. It also made the future look grim for the rest of us.' However, in his dedication in the book, he allowed himself some emotion: 'To the memory of Maurice Pertschuk, hanged in Buchenwald Crematorium on 29 March 1945, who fought more gallantly than any of us and died more sadly.' He was just twenty-three and the camp would be liberated within days. In his debriefing, Burney said that Perkins was hanged by the S.S. through 'mere vindictiveness' to compensate for the disappearance of Dodkin.

According to Alfred Newton in *No Banners*, Burney feared the worst whatever he said after the war:

Christopher Burney walked with his friend to the *appel* square. Then Martin went on, alone towards the Gate. Watching the slim, boyish figure striding away, head erect and shoulders squared, Burney's cold, realistic mind failed him. His throat choked and the tears ran down his cheeks unashamedly.

The real reason for the execution of Maurice Pertschuk is harder to pin down. The official reason given in the Buchenwald museum is that, from his arrival, Pertschuk passed himself off as Martin Perkins, an English student with no political activities (he is described as 'student' on his Registration card) and it was only in March 1945 that the Gestapo discovered his real name and SOE resistance work, punishable by execution. Eugen Kogon added to this explanation. He wrote that the

Gestapo Zentrale ordered the execution of Pertschuk 'in the spring of 1945' and the S.S. officer in Buchenwald charged with carrying out the order took with him the file cards of both Martin Perkins and Kenneth Dodkin (Yeo-Thomas), who had officially 'died' already. Kogan and others thought that the execution order was only for Dodkin, so they made no effort to save Pertschuk. Only later did they learn that the execution order was for both.

Hiding Underground

The Easter Weekend of 30 March to 2 April passed in 'typical German fashion' writes Burney, with free workdays. The contrast between bureaucratic efficiency and scarcely imaginable cruelty lasted until the end. The non-politicals of Block 50 put it to good use. Eugen Kogon, Jan Robert and Burney decided that their armed revolt would take the form of preventing a larger, reckless insurrection led by the Communists which they feared would result in a bloody suppression by the S.S., who by now numbered 3,000 heavily armed men. A rising would be premature. Burney writes that his group had three pistols and a few hand grenades with which they hoped they could hold the main secret arms dump, the location of which they had discovered, and use it to 'arm reliable men if order had to be kept'. Luckily, this very flaky initiative was not necessary.

Kogon states in *The Theory and Practice of Hell* that Captain Burney emerged as the leader of the non-Communist group which, independently of the Communist Party, was preparing its own plans for the imminent liberation of the camp. It turned out that these differed little from Communist plans except, writes Kogon, that the Communists held the power in the camp and were intent on keeping in that way. Only Communists would hold functions once the camp was liberated and, in the meantime, total secrecy was observed, as was the Communist practice. Burney, on the other hand, worked on the principle of the best man for the job, so he assigned one third of the proposed new functions to Communists. Understandably, they reported back to the Party. In the end this was of no consequence because as soon as the camp was liberated the Communists, represented by the International Camp Committee, took over until the Americans arrived, as we shall see; but twenty years later it became an issue. In 1966, *SOE in France* was published and M D R Foot gave his version of events:

It says much for Burney's stoicism and serenity that he was able to get a resistance movement of a kind started up: but he made an intelligible, disastrous mistake in setting about this laudable but hopeless task by selecting his men on his own assessment without regard to their political views. Consequently, his group was penetrated by the Communists who kept their own Party informed and kept Burney away from the communist arms supply. Burney and his surviving companions – Southgate and the two Newtons – were lucky not to be liquidated before the Americans arrived a few hours later.

That last sentence offended Burney. *The Sunday Times* reviewed the new book on 1 May 1966, and interviewed the Newton brothers, Southgate, and Burney. He retorted:

That part is a load of rubbish – I don't know where that story came from, and it was certainly not checked with me. Far from liquidating me, they hid all the four remaining British officers for some days when the S.S. was trying to execute us. The Communists saved our lives.[1]
    (In this article Burney is quoted tendentiously on two other matters which are discussed in Chapter Notes.)

More urgent in these last days of S.S. control was the finding of a hiding place, should the last four Englishmen be summoned for execution. The need was desperate because on Tuesday, 3 April, the *blockaltester* of Hut 14 whispered to Alfred, *Acht geben heute abend. Die kommen fur dich und dein bruder. Und die andere zwei auch* – 'Beware, tonight. They're coming for you and your brother. And the other two as well.' Once again, Kogon came to the rescue. He got the four into a 'two-foot crawl space' under the floor of Block 56 in Little Camp, which had been reserved for Party members should a similar emergency arise. The *stubendiensts* in this block were Russians, and for ever after Burney thanked them for saving his life.

Lying under the floorboards with a Jew who had found the same hidey-hole, motionless, without light, in the dirt, and with the tramp of wooden shoes on the floor immediately overhead, they would not have heard the camp loudspeakers ordering them to the Main Gate, even if the call came. Burney wrote 'the night I spent there will always remain one of the most comic-opera nights of my life.' Actually, the Englishmen were there for forty-eight hours.

Violent End of S.S. Rule

On 4 April the death marches in and out of Buchenwald alerted the whole camp that the end was near. Arriving at Buchenwald were survivors of the death march from Orhdruf who had been herded to complete exhaustion for seventy-five kilometres by the S.S., being shot at along the way by Hitler Youth and German women. One hundred bloody corpses lay along the last short stretch from Weimar to the camp.

Ordered to assemble in the *Appelplatz* for another death march out of the camp were the remaining Jews – 'Jews step forward' – but this time the S.S. could not execute the order, even helped by the *Lagerschutz*. The Jews broke rank, tore off their identity badges and ran towards Little Camp or slipped unnoticed into Aryan blocks. From then on, the routine of twice daily *Appel*, a ritual of S.S. authority, could not be enforced.

The lists and numbers of which inmates were in what blocks was in chaos, and that made it easier for Burney and others to submerge into anonymity when necessary.

Burney emerged from hiding, though he took the precaution of removing his prison number and changing his red triangle with the letter 'E' for 'F' for French. After consultation with his friends in Block 50, he and the Belgian minister Paul Soudan, the French Under-Secretary of State André Marie, and Pieter Cool, the Dutch naval officer, wrote a letter to Commandant Pister. Kogan describes them as 'leading personalities among the foreigners in the camp'. Burney adds that he was discouraged from signing because 'my position was too delicate', but in the end he added his name because 'my signature, or rather the designation underneath it, would undoubtedly carry more weight than all the others put together'. Was he referring to his undoubted status when the Americans would arrive in a few days?

The letter asked Pister to stick by his declaration of 26 March not to evacuate the camp, and promised him a good word at the time of retribution after the war. The reliable S.S. barber Franz Eichhorn delivered it to Pister who was in bed at the time. Eichhorn reported back that Pister could not decipher the signatures but that he seemed 'highly elated'. He saw it as a document that might provide him and his family with safety. As his excuse for not evacuating the camp he announced, 'In an emergency a period of time can elapse between an order and its execution'. Time had been gained.

The S.S. prepared for revenge. Ding-Schuler returned from his home in Weimar and informed Kogon that the Gestapo had ordered the immediate execution of forty-six prisoners whom they suspected were leaders of the resistance. That evening the full list was handed to the roll call officer for announcement the next morning. The named persons should 'come to the Gate', a recognised euphemism by now for 'proceed to the crematorium'. The names included Communists as well as the non-politicals of Block 50, like Kogon himself and Jan Robert, but not Burney. It was, Burney said, 'purely a matter of personal vengeance', a list drawn up without much knowledge by an ex-prisoner who had volunteered for the S.S. to save his skin. The camp leadership was put on alarm and the forty-six went into hiding. Burney and the other Englishmen gave up their cellar to some of them and disappeared into the camp. Burney's parting words:

> Keep on the move. Never sleep twice in the same block. And if it comes to the worst, snatch the guns out of their hands and make bloody good use of them when you can. (*No Banners*)

April 6th was the day of decisive showdown. Only one of the forty-six appeared 'at the Gate' and the S.S. could not hold a roll call, their daily instrument of control. From then on, the S.S. entered the camp only at night and heavily armed. Nevertheless, Burney and the non-political leadership argued that an uprising would be premature; it would end after a few hours in a bloodbath with the S.S. the winners.

That day Himmler gave the order for Buchenwald to be evacuated and the camp resistance decided to prevent this as far as possible. News came through that Allied paratroopers had landed nearby, disguised as civilians. Kogon, Burney and the others decided to write another letter to Pister, pretending that it came from 'James McLeod, Major, War Office, London'.

> Commander
> Transports are leaving Buchenwald. They are death transports – like the one from Ohrdruf! The terrible tragedy of Ohrdruf must not be repeated. We have seen it with our own eyes.
> Woe to the commanders in Buchenwald if this is repeated.
> The name of the camp has come to be abhorred by the entire civilised world.
> Much has been improved under your rule. We know that.

You may be in difficulties today from which you see no other escape than to send thousands on their way. Stop! Stop immediately – *Schluss damit, sofortiger schluss!*

Our tank commanders are on their way this minute to settle accounts. You have one more chance!

Burney says that he could not write the letter as his handwriting would be recognised, so Jan Robert took over and Eugen Kogon, showing impressive cool and courage, smuggled it out of the camp himself by hiding in a crate of vaccines on its way to Ding-Schuler's house in Weimar. Sewn into his tunic was a recommendation written by Burney to the American who would find him. 'Thank God, eventually all went well,' says Burney. The letter from 'Major James McLeod' sent from Weimar was delivered to Pister and he continued to waver.

Another call for help left the camp; this time via an illegal transmitter made overnight by three Polish electricians:

An die Alliierten! To the Allies
An die Armee des Generals Patton To the Army of General Patton
SOS!
We bitten um Hilfe. Man will uns evakuiren. Die S.S. will uns vernichten
We ask for help. They want to evacuate us. The S.S. want to destroy us.

It seemed that this could be true. Without orders from Pister and in scenes of chaos and cruelty, squads of S.S. with machine guns forced a partial evacuation of the camp. When the order came to empty Little Camp, they were assisted by the German *Lagerschutz* and Block Chiefs with their *Stubendiensts*, behaving, in Burney's words, 'with a horrible display of brutality, beating and kicking and swearing at wretches who were too weak to walk or even stand up. The beast was beginning to reappear among the prisoners.'

Despite resistance, over the next five days more than 20,000 prisoners were evacuated, mostly on foot, with very little food. Probably one in three died either through exhaustion or S.S. murder on death marches towards the concentration camps of south Germany. Some prisoners went willingly. Eight hundred Russian POWs marched out, followed by military contingents from the Poles and Czechs. They overcame their S.S. escorts and joined the American Third Army.

Twenty thousand prisoners remained in Buchenwald. By now, 10 and 11 April, tension within the camp was scarcely bearable. It was rumoured that an S.S. contingent, armed with flame throwers, was on its way from Weimar to liquidate the camp. American fighter planes were seen and heard shooting up military targets in the vicinity of Ettersberg. One flew low over the camp and threw down two loaves of bread and a can of gasoline, which some inmates took as proof that the wireless *SOS* had been received. American artillery was pounding Erfurt and the road to Weimar was closed. One prisoner wrote afterwards:

> During the night of Tuesday to Wednesday, most comrades slept fully clothed because everyone reckoned with the possibility that it might come to a final showdown with the S.S. that night. It could be in the form of mass murder, a bombing by German planes, or a mass evacuation transport. Then we heard that Erfurt had fallen, and the S.S. were preparing to flee. In this last night the final victims of these mass murderers fell. Sixteen men were hanged in the crematorium, and twenty-four were brutally slain in the washrooms of the cell blocks.
>
> (Stefan Heymann, in *Buchenwald Report*)

Burney wrote: 'We had nothing to do but wait, listening to rumours and trying not to think about liquidation. We had waited so long that the idea of liberation was now no more than a habit.'

Liberation of the Camp

Next morning, 11 April, Pister told the *Lagerälteste 1* (Camp Chief) Hans Eiden, a German Communist, he was leaving and Eiden should take over, handing the camp to the Americans when they arrived. Burney was told this by Fritz Eichhorn as they watched German artillery and infantry fall back on the plain below. At about 2pm twelve American tanks entered the Ettersberg forest north of the camp and after fierce resistance an S.S. reserve company gave way. At 2.15pm four more American tanks moved by on the outskirts of the camp from the east. It became clear that American tanks had broken through on all sides. The S.S. left their posts in the camp and disappeared. Burney wrote:

> Two hours later, when the coast was well clear, daring prisoners hoisted the white flag from the mast on the Main Tower, and Jan Robert and I, who were watching from a room of Block 50, saw them taking the hidden weapons from the 'secret' dump. They were very childish, forming bands of different nationalities and marching about looking as if they had defeated the entire *Wehrmacht*. The S.S. magazine was raided too and there was much trigger happiness, men shooting each other, shooting themselves and shooting into thin air.
>
> At five, the first American tank came into the camp, and I went up to touch it and make sure that it was true. But in that atmosphere, it was hard to appreciate what had happened.[2]

Units of the US Sixth Armoured Division entered Buchenwald and were the first Americans to see a functioning concentration camp. Perhaps officer William Kolbe was one of those to whom the Newton brothers gave a guided tour:

My first impression was one of disbelief in view of the emaciated people in striped uniforms, their sunken eyes; you could feel the horror they had experienced. And then I saw the red brick ovens in which there were still human skeletons, and hooks outside for the bodies. As I looked round some more, I saw the shelves on which the prisoners had had to sleep; the most horrible scene, however, was that of the flat quarry carts with hundreds of corpses piled up on them and covered with lime... a completely unbelievable scene which I shall never forget.

Burney offered to help the American officer who found himself responsible for thousands of jubilant but starving survivors wandering around the camp, some of them armed and bringing in captured S.S. guards whom they threatened to kill. It was still a battlefield.

In fact, since the middle of the afternoon the International Camp Committee (Communist) under Hans Eiden had begun its administration of the camp with commissions set up to organise security, rations, medicine, clothing and information. This effectively ran Buchenwald until the Americans took over on 13 April, bringing up huge supplies of medicine and food with the personnel to supervise them. The 120th US Army Evacuation Hospital moved 4,700 sick inmates from the camp barracks to the former S.S. barracks nearby; at least a quarter of them died over the next few days.

Burney noticed that two German Communists, excluded from the ruling executive because they were too friendly with the 'capitalists', were the only two who knew about catering: 'I had to interfere and put the two of them up to the American commander as being the only people fit to do the work.'

It was Burney who passed on the American order that carrying weapons risked being shot as 'franc-tireurs' ('free shooters', outside the law). This went down badly with the Communists, but Burney agreed that armed guards should be posted that night because there were insufficient American troops. The next morning, Burney writes, 'to do them credit three or four thousand men were disarmed without incident'. On Burney's advice, the remaining Russian POWs were allowed by the American commander to keep their rifles. The senior Russian officer had asked Burney to pass on the message: 'We wish that all orders for Russians should come direct to us and not through the camp leaders. We have suffered long enough from these Germans (the Communists) and wish the indignity to end.' 'It did,' Burney explained, 'they did not like each other but nobody liked the Germans.'

'We had reached the end,' Burney wrote. That night the four Englishmen slept in a villa evacuated by one of the S.S. officers. Burney shared a room with the platoon commander of the Eleventh Rangers of Sixth Armoured Division, and Burney wondered if the American could sense the emotions that kept him awake:

> I was not drunk with freedom – freedom of movement, freedom from want – for I had in some way trained myself to stay spiritually free, and when that is achieved the other 'freedoms' become less noticeable. But I was stunned and blinded by my sudden entry into the daylight of friendliness. I became light-headed and talkative as the protective tension I had acquired slowly relaxed.
>
> It might be easy to wax sentimental over that first night. I shall not do that. But I know that of all the virtues, simple friendliness is the greatest, and I am grateful that my re-baptism into the world was pronounced in the language which, though some may sneer, expresses it best of them all.

On 14 April Burney was standing at the Buchenwald gate when he was interviewed by Robert Reid of the BBC programme *War Report*:

> PRESENTER: To justify – or at least to palliate – the existence of these places, German civilians frequently asserted that

only 'criminals' were sent to them. The assertion scarcely accounts for the presence of a British officer in Buchenwald. He was Captain C A G Burney of Hay, Hereford, and he described his experience of fifteen months in the camp in conversation with a BBC correspondent, Robert Reid:

REID: Who ran the place?

BURNEY: The place was run by the S.S.

REID: What were they like?

BURNEY: Well, the best example you can get of what the treatment was like is the arrival here. Our arrival took place in the middle of the night, with a temperature of about fifteen below zero. We'd had our shoes and some of us had had our clothes taken away from us on the train to prevent us from escaping, and when the doors were opened in the station, we were pulled straight out of the wagon by an S.S. man, given a hit over the head – I was pushed into a dog that bit my arm; another S.S. hit me again, kicked me in the backside, and then off I went.

REID: Now, were there many atrocities in the camp?

BURNEY: Yes. The means of execution were varied, and applied with great frequency... They hanged, they shot, they had patent traps where you stood on a trap door which let off bullets into your neck, they electrocuted, they injected with phenol, they injected with air, they injected with milk.

REID: Did you see any burials or any bodies?

BURNEY: I must have seen thousands of bodies since I've been here. Most of the bodies were cremated, but towards the end they ran out of coal, and they had too many bodies.

REID: Was there any real community spirit inside the camp?

BURNEY: I can't say there was, frankly. If you wanted to be disgusted with humanity all you had do was come and live here. People were stealing, they were killing each other for a slice of bread... One group hated another, and the other group hated the next and so on.

REID: And how would you sum up your experience here?

BURNEY: Well, I couldn't say it over the microphone. It's been shocking, but on the other hand, it's so stunning it's almost unreal. I think probably when one has been back among civilised people for a while one just forgets it.

REID: You think you've really been out of civilisation, do you?

BURNEY: Oh yes, absolutely out of this world. Everything which happened over here was without relation to anything that has happened before, and therefore one had a special year of life which was just somewhere else, in another world. It might have been on Mars.

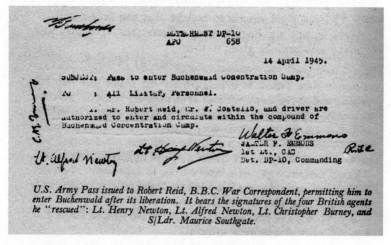

U.S. Army Pass issued to Robert Reid, B.B.C. War Correspondent, permitting him to enter Buchenwald after its liberation. It bears the signatures of the four British agents he "rescued": Lt. Henry Newton, Lt. Alfred Newton, Lt. Christopher Burney, and S/Ldr. Maurice Southgate.

Robert Reid's press card replicated from *No Banners*.

According to Alfred Newton, Reid could not get over the inscription over the Gate: *Recht oder unrecht, Mein Vaterland.* "'My Fatherland, right or wrong", he repeated, "nay, I'm not likely to forget that one."' Then the four surviving Englishmen signed Reid's US Army Pass before piling into his jeep with an armful of K-rations (boxed meal rations used in combat) and were driven to General Patton's US Army Headquarters in Gotha, sixty kilometres away.

At some time, Burney must have been to the *Effektenkammer*, because for his re-entry into the world he had swopped his stripes for grey flannel trousers and an army battledress top. A Russian had given him a pair of Buchenwald-made boots in exchange for his Fresnes-made waistcoat; the boots had an array of matchsticks under each toe cap to swell and absorb water – a talking point when he got home. He may have removed his concentration camp stripes, but the effects of his suffering were clear for weeks after he returned home. Julia said *his face was as bloated and as white as a dandelion puff*.

At US HQ, Burney was asked to prove his identity. He said he lived in Herefordshire. It so happened that the interrogator knew Hereford. 'What's the best pub in town?' he asked. 'The Green Dragon', Burney responded. Next day the four surviving Englishmen were in the air, bound for Hendon, England, in a US Army Transport aircraft.

CHAPTER 7

HOMECOMING

Coming Home

CÉSAR, ARTUS, AUGUST and *Hector* were driven to the Berners Hotel in London where they were met by Maurice Buckmaster of SOE, his chest displaying medal ribbons. 'Good show, Christopher,' he said. 'I see it has been for some,' Burney replied with uncharacteristic bitterness.

He was refused a whisky as it was after hours, so he took a taxi to the Connaught Hotel: from the horror of Buchenwald to the poshness of a top London hotel, Burney took it in his stride. Here the god of Herefordshire was smiling on him for, just as The Green Dragon in Hereford had proved his identity to the American interrogator, so on reception he met Emmy, a Czech refugee who had stayed at Oakfield before the war. She gave him a room and a bottle of whisky.

The next morning, he went to SOE headquarters in Baker Street to collect what he could of three years back pay. He found that his suitcase of clothes, typewriter and talismanic cigarette case, left there for security reasons before he disappeared into France, had all been lost in the winding down of F Section. He was fixed up with a medical appointment and a date for the first of two debriefings, and then it was off to St James' Park underground station for his reunion with Julia – the dream come true.

Julia had been at her desk in the Secret Intelligence Service (MI6) headquarters at Westminster when the phone rang.

There was a pause, and then Christopher's voice said 'Julia'. I suppose I said 'Yes'.

'Can you have lunch with me today?' I must have said 'Yes'.

'Where shall we meet?' Without thinking, I gave my usual reply to a lunchtime invitation: 'St James's Tube station at 1 o'clock.'

'I'll be there.'

I put the telephone down and then the awful truth dawned that in my haste and excitement, I had committed myself to a three-hour wait before I could see him again after such a long time.

When at last we did meet, we stood in front of each other and exchanged a perfunctory kiss. I did not notice he was wearing a strange assortment of clothes; an army battledress top, thin grey flannel trousers over which were pulled home-made wellington boots. His head had been shaved, but long enough ago to have grown a moleskin skullcap of short hair. His face was as bloated and as white as a dandelion puff. I noticed none of this; I only knew I was in his element and that I was in Heaven.

'Where have you been?' I asked, breaking a long silence. 'It will take time to tell.' Pause. 'Are you married?' 'No.'

They went to have lunch in her flat nearby in Marsham Court.

In the little kitchen I began to peel potatoes. My hands were trembling so badly that I was taking half the potato with the skin.

'Look out,' Christopher shouted, 'you're wasting food.' For someone whose diet had been rotten manglewurzels, a potato was a precious luxury. We were both in emotional shock.

Julia had planned to take a new boyfriend of convenience back to Nether Auchendrane on the night train. Now it was 'owning-up time', as she put it. He was discarded and she made the journey to tell her parents she intended to marry Christopher. Her father had not softened with the years: 'If you marry him, you'll be a long time dead,' he said, showing a remarkable lack of tact. 'You will always be welcome here but he won't,' he continued by letter after she left for London. This did not deter Julia one bit; she had not waited three years for nothing.

Meanwhile, Christopher spent the night at the Berkeley Hotel where the two ladies at the next table, who perhaps had heard him on the radio, discreetly paid for his dinner. News of the unimaginably dreadful concentration camps produced a British generosity to survivors. Christopher was given a free lease on another flat in Marsham Court, his stepfather's tailor stitched him two suits and Lobb, the St James shoemaker, made him a pair of shoes in return for displaying his camp-made Russian boots in the window with a suitable plaque. When Julia stayed up in Nether Auchendrane, Christopher went down to Hay where Dorothy found him an assortment of clothes, including a hat. The visible signs of Buchenwald became less obvious.

Vera Atkins wrote Dorothy a letter: 'I know Christopher is spending the weekend with you and I'm sure you will agree after seeing him that he is in a very wonderful state, both mentally and physically. All our officers who return from Germany are given an X-ray examination and an interview with a psychiatrist.'

Perhaps it was the elation of being re-united with Julia, as well as his extraordinary detachment; whatever, Burney was in control of his emotions and capable of remembering one of the dreadful episodes in Buchenwald. This was in response to a letter from the Canadian Ambassador to France who was investigating the execution of the three Canadian SOE agents,

John Macalister, Guy Sabourin and Frank Pickersgill, on 9 September the previous year. The task of replying was too much for Alfred Newton, but Burney could remember all too well. He wrote a sincere and comforting letter:

> I saw them constantly right up to their execution and they behaved wonderfully well. I also heard from a prisoner who worked in the crematorium that they died as bravely as I should have hoped to do had my turn come. I cannot say more. Sympathy from someone unknown would cut little ice with the families, though they most certainly have mine.[1]

SOE was able to reassure Burney about a nagging worry. He had feared in Fresnes that under his brutal interrogation he might have passed out and revealed the identity of his contact in Caen, Madame Terrien, as well as Jacques Foure in Paris. He had not, but Madame Terrien and her two children had been killed in an Allied bombing raid at the time of the Normandy landings in 1944.

Burney's debriefing on 13 June reads as a taciturn, unhelpful session; not surprising as by this time he believed that SOE had dropped him into France knowing that AUTOGIRO had been effectively penetrated: therefore, his chances of survival were very limited. He may well have thought that if he had been saved for another mission then his three years of suffering might have been avoided.

There were rewards. Burney was upgraded to the rank of Captain with the South Wales Borderers and Major General Gubbins recommended him for the Military Cross. The citation reads:

> Burney was severely interrogated and beaten up by the Gestapo. He stood up to these hardships with the greatest courage and endurance, and did not give away any vital information. He was kept in solitary confinement in Fresnes prison until the 24 January 1944, when he was transferred

to Buchenwald Concentration Camp, where he spent fifteen months undergoing severe hardships. Throughout this period, he showed qualities of endurance and unselfishness of a high order, and played a large part in keeping up the morale of his fellow prisoners. For his courage in undertaking a hazardous clandestine mission in occupied France, and for his fortitude and self-sacrifice during his two and a half years in captivity, it is recommended that he be awarded the Military Cross.

On the citation this award was crossed out and the Military MBE substituted, presumably on the grounds that the MC may only be awarded for 'gallantry in active operations against the enemy' that is, in battle. The Newton brothers were similarly decorated. A few years later he was offered a Croix de Guerre by the French Government, but he did not bother to collect it. He was obviously dismissive of medals. (For more on the award of the Burney MC, see Notes for Chapter Six.)

Burney was given six weeks paid leave and for the next six months he had two priorities. The first was to marry Julia and the second was to write and get published his exposure of the German concentration camp system, in particular Buchenwald.

Meanwhile, he had an important (undated) letter to write to Dorothy:

I had to write because I couldn't say this speaking, but I've known since 1942 that there was no reasonable chance of Rog coming back. When I was in prison I used to think so much about it and about you and I wished that if I could come out I would make it better for you. Now I am out, and you know how bad I am at saying things, but more than anything in the world I want you to have a little happiness.

Please don't grieve too much for Rog. I don't know why he died and I lived, but we rarely understand things like that. I promise you there was nothing slow or horrid about it, so don't imagine things that weren't. I know I can never be two for you, but I'll try all I can to be as good a one as I can.

He added the thought-provoking comment of someone who faced death daily over the three years of incarceration: 'Dying's only painful really if you're guilty of something bad and he wasn't.' Does this state of mind account in part for Burney's serenity in Fresnes and Buchenwald?

Wedding

After six weeks' sick leave Christopher was issued with battledress and *posted to a dull desk job somewhere in the suburbs*, in Julia's words. Their determination to get married, despite her parents' opposition, was unabated. Christopher wrote a formal letter to Julia's father, Gordon, asking for 'his daughter's hand in marriage', as they did in those days, and the couple followed this up with a weekend visit. It was not a success. Waiting on Ayr station for the train back to London, Christopher moaned, 'I'd rather go back to Buchenwald than ever have another weekend like this one'. Julia related one conversation at the dinner table:

> *Julia's mother: 'I can't believe you could have been through so much and be so normal.'*
> *Christopher: 'What do you expect? That I should eat with my fingers?'*
> *Julia's father: 'What did you eat in Buchenwald?'*
> *Christopher: 'Mangelwurzels.'*
> *Julia's father: 'That doesn't sound too awful.'*
> *Christopher: 'It is if they are rotten.'*

Gordon Burrell's disapproval on the surface was about money, as Christopher related to his mother in a letter:

Trouble in the henhouse. We got nothing but a terrific lecture

from the father about money. It really was vulgar beyond words. He asked me why I did not go into business instead of the Foreign Office [Christopher had applied, as also to the BBC and *The Times*] because I could make a fortune, and so I more or less said that I'd no shopkeeper's blood in my veins, thank God!
Poor Julia was so ashamed of him. It was pathetic.

It seems that, under this display, Father Burrell's continuing disapproval of Christopher's 'commando' past was up against Christopher's army snobbery of 'stockbrokers and bookmakers' as he put it later in the letter. The lovers decided to post their engagement in *The Times* and get married in London, if necessary without the Burrell permission.

Their reception at Oakfield in Hay was far more welcoming. Dorothy met them at Hereford station in the Armstrong Siddeley, *that looked like a large black box on wheels*, Julia thought, and drove them along *twisted, deserted roads through beautiful scenery* until they reached Hay:

> *Then, just as a rabbit pops down a hidden hole, so the car turned abruptly into a narrow drive with huge, unkempt hedges on either side. Suddenly a rose-coloured brick house came into sight, with a white climbing rose hanging loosely to the front. We turned sharply into a yard and came to a stop with the nose of the car almost touching a wall covered with pink rambler roses. Christopher's house seemed to be a mixture of Beatrix Potter and* The Secret Garden, *with 'Ma' fitting comfortably into both stories.*

During the war the main part of the house had been taken over by the Red Cross, so they gathered with Christopher's older sister Joan in the kitchen. It was just as you would expect from an old-fashioned country house kitchen, with a temperamental Aga cooker, a rack above on a pulley for drying clothes, a stone sink with jam jars alongside containing washing up mops, and a long pine table round which at least ten people could sit. It was warm and comfortable, like 'Ma' herself, as Julia called her from then on. That evening the drawing-room fire was lit and the family photographs fetched from a cupboard.

Next day Christopher took Julia for a long walk up that symbolic valley he had described to her twice: the first time soon after they met with the promise of happiness to come; the second during that grim winter in Buchenwald, when it was the *via dolorosa* of pain. *Now*, wrote Julia, *I felt, as he did, that it held the promise for all of us that was secret and good and eternal.*

Soon after this she recalled the occasion when Christopher drew out of his wallet a long gold tiepin with a cluster of diamonds at its head that had belonged to his grandfather:

> *'Ma thought it could be made into an engagement ring. What do you think?' I noticed it ended in a murderous point. I suddenly remembered Mrs MacDougal's puzzlement when she was telling my fortune. She said she saw, in the midst of all the happiness I would one day enjoy, something unexpectedly sharp. I saw now clearly what she could not understand. The beautiful diamonds that would be my engagement ring were presently part of a rapier-like pin! My memory jogged, I remembered her saying that Christopher would return in an aeroplane, not wearing a uniform but a strange assortment of clothes. She said he was not wounded but he was very ill. It took the tiepin to remind me of all the clairvoyant had told me that evening in the kitchen when she had read my cards.*

Christopher and Julia were married at Candlemas, Saturday, 2 February 1946, at the local church near Nether Auchendrane. The Burrell parents, realising that the marriage would take place whether they consented or not, had thrown themselves into organising it like *over-excited party planners*. It was a great success. Ma softened the hearts of the Burrells, although Julia said that in the wedding photograph her father *looked as though he would burst into tears*. The couple were both in tears when the vicar said 'The Cross is made by crossing out the "I". Remember this in your marriage.' Stern advice.

On the eve of the wedding Christopher wrote to Julia:

> Next time I see you will be in the Church, and I wanted to be sure that I love you perhaps more humbly than you think, and that when we do see each other again it will be the greatest moment of my life. You know I believe in God, and I believe too that of all the trusts that He had given me your happiness is the first. So please show me where your happiness lies so that I may not fail.
>
> All my love, always.

Publication of *Dungeon Democracy*

Christopher Burney wrote *Dungeon Democracy* in only three months, mid-May to mid-July 1945, working in his Marsham Street apartment. It is a short book of 40,000 words, written without his notes which he had hidden in the camp but lost in the pillage of the last days. Macmillan wanted to publish *Dungeon Democracy* but did not have enough paper so he had to wait until the end of the year before Heinemann published it on both sides of the Atlantic. He wrote in too much of a hurry, he later admitted, and he was suffering under the surface from emotional trauma. How could a writer in a matter of weeks pass from Buchenwald Concentration Camp to peace of mind in London? Julia wrote to Dorothy in August that *Christopher has a pathetic little chalk white face with eyes as black and shiny as wet coal*. His weight was down to eight stone from the eleven and a half before the war.

What drove him to write late into the night was his urge to relate how he had witnessed in Buchenwald the degradation of humanity. This had a corollary. Unless Europe could return to civilised values then 'it will mean back to Buchenwald for me and a maiden trip for most of you'.

To comprehend *Dungeon Democracy,* it is necessary to put it in the context of Europe just after a world war that had destroyed civilisation. Europe was still a savage continent. In fact the war had not ended, it had broken up into a variety of other wars: civil wars (Greece and Yugoslavia), ethnic cleansing (Poland and Ukraine), political violence between communists and capitalists (France and Italy), national resistance against the spread of Russian totalitarianism (the Baltic states). Violence was endemic in continental Europe; vengeance and hate were everywhere. Law and order and morality had broken down, exemplified by looting, the proliferation of rape like never before, and the casual murder of refugees. Europe was on the move with countless refugees crossing the continent seeking food and shelter. Burney's cri de cœur about the end of civilisation presaging the return of concentration camps does not seem exaggerated.

The liberation of the concentration camps at Buchenwald and Belsen in April 1945 provided the most potent images of the depravity of war. First there was the dispatch from Buchenwald by the American radio reporter Ed Murrow on 15 April. He described the crematorium:

> There were two rows of corpses stacked up like cordwood. They were thin and very white. Some of the bodies were terribly bruised, though there seemed little flesh to bruise... All except two were naked. I tried to count them as best I could and arrived at the conclusion that all that was mortal of more than 500 men and boys lay there in two neat piles...
>
> I pray you to believe what I have said. I have reported what I saw and heard, but only part of it. For most of it, I have no words. Dead men are plentiful in war, but the living dead... and the country round about was pleasing to the eye... American trucks were rolling towards the rear filled with prisoners. Soon they would be eating American rations, as

much for a meal as the men in Buchenwald received in four days.

This was followed by Richard Dimbleby's *War Report* from Belsen, which was held up by the BBC because it was so disturbing. *War Report* also carried Robert Reid's interview with Christopher Burney on 19 April (although it had taken place several days before). Then came newsreel films showing shocking, scarcely believable, pictures of stick-like children playing next to human corpses and bulldozers shovelling piles of corpses into mass graves. Images like these condemned Nazi Germany for ever.

Moreover, the whole German nation seemed to be implicated. In the words of Colonel Spottiswoode, the military governor of Belsen, to an audience of local Germans forced to help clear up the camp: 'The existence of camps such as this is such a disgrace to the German people that their name must be erased from the list of civilised nations. You must expect to atone in toil and sweat for what your children have committed and for what you have failed to prevent.'

As the historian Keith Low wrote in *The Savage Continent*:

The discovery of the concentration camps shaped the moral attitude of the British public to the war. Now everything was justified, the mass bombing of German cities, the insistence on unconditional surrender, the violent revenge of the Russian army. In 1945 there was no sympathy for the German people, no agreement that they were victims too.[2]

In this state of public opinion, Christopher Burney's descriptions of Buchenwald in his radio talks and in his book were restrained. He did not hide his disgust of German behaviour, far from it, but he cast the net of blame wider. His 'basic conclusion' was that the Nazis alone were not responsible for Buchenwald, for 'the vast majority of the non-Nazis of Europe, and more especially of Germany, are not material which, without careful selection and treatment, will produce a new civilised continent.'

His condemnation would have been shared by a teenage Jewish girl hiding in her Amsterdam attic in 1944. In innocent words she accounted for the cruelty of the age:

> I don't believe that the big men, the politicians and the
> capitalists alone, are guilty of the war. Oh no, the little man
> is just as keen, otherwise the people of the world would
> have risen up long ago. There is an urge and rage in people
> to destroy, to kill, to murder and until all mankind, without
> exception, undergoes a great change, wars will be waged,
> everything that has been built up, cultivated and grown, will
> be destroyed and disfigured, after which mankind will have to
> begin all over again.

Anne Frank died in Auschwitz the following year.

The most exciting chapter of *Dungeon Democracy* is Burney's day-by-day account of the liberation of Buchenwald, 'Curtain', an account which is confirmed by Eugen Kogon's *The Theory and Practice of Hell*. The most controversial is his 'Conclusion' which follows and the most important in understanding the concentration camp system is the 'Rule by Proxy' that begins the book. In between is his semi-anthropological description of the other nations that shared the camp with the Germans, mainly in 1944 the Russians, Poles, Czechs, French and Jews. Some of Burney's views are shocking to read today, but they came from a restrained observer and were not challenged by any of the book's reviewers. The world at war was a world away from today.

Burney liked the Russians:

> They were clannish and independent; they had their own
> moral code and gave nothing for any other; and they behaved
> as members of a proud nation among a crowd of humbugs and
> degenerates. They hated the Germans, despised the French,

In MEM_
ORIUM | G.A.BURNEY. | JULY, 1916

A Burney knight in armour bearing the flag of St George in Kenchester church.

The Burney plot, Kenchester churchyard.

Thandiana Hill Station, 1925. From left, Joan wrote: '"Chucha", Mr Martin (tutor), Daddy, Gen Hardie, Roger, me and Ma.'

Oakfield House, Hay on Wye, 1902.

Burney family reunited in Herefordshire in the late 1920s.

Christopher in his SOE issue 'Damon Runyon' suit, Oakfield 1942.

'Christophe Brunet' identity card.

Plaque outside Gestapo HQ, 84 Avenue Foch, Paris.

Cell graffiti from the Second World War, Gestapo HQ.

Fresnes Prison today.

Solitary confinement cell, identical to that occupied by Christopher for 526 days and nights.

The drawings of Auguste Favier who survived Buchenwald but died of TB shortly after.

Transport; three days and nights in a closed wagon with almost no water.

© Auguste Favier family

Arrival: Disinfection Station for stripping and body inspection, total shaving, and disinfection in a communal bath.

© Auguste Favier family

Little Camp: windowless stables housed 1,000 new arrivals on shelves.
© Auguste Favier family

Little Camp: daily clearing of the dead from the stables as 'Muselmänner' look on.
© Auguste Favier family

Maurice Pertschuk.

Phil Lamason, 1942.

August (Henry Newton), *Artus* (Alfred Newton), and *Hector* (Maurice Southgate centre) back home after their release.

The wedding of Christopher and Julia, February 1946.

Happy days!

Cromlins the Quarrel by Barry McGlashan is owned by Christopher's daughter Juliette. It reminds both of us of the allegorical story 'Descent from Ararat'.

Christopher, aged 52, in Paris in 1969.

Roger would bring Cambridge friends home to Oakfield; Peter Godden hiking with Roger in the Black Mountains, 1939.

Roger shared confidences with his older sister 'Jo'.

Roger was formally inducted into the Royal Naval Volunteer Reserve as a rating in July 1940.

'For…mi…dable!' Roger's first impression of *Surcouf* in drydock at Portsmouth, New Hampshire, October 1941.

Surcouf sailing into diplomatic deep waters, Christmas 1941.

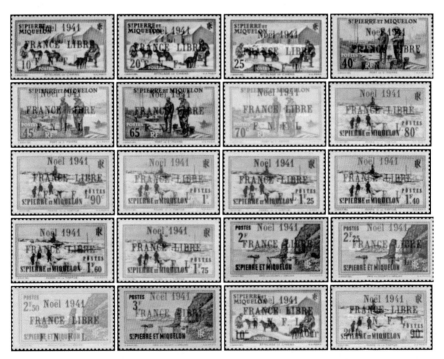

'These stamps are worth a fortune,' Roger wrote when he posted them home. The already rare St Pierre & Miquelon stamps were overprinted with: 'Noel 1941 FRANCE LIBRE FNFL'.

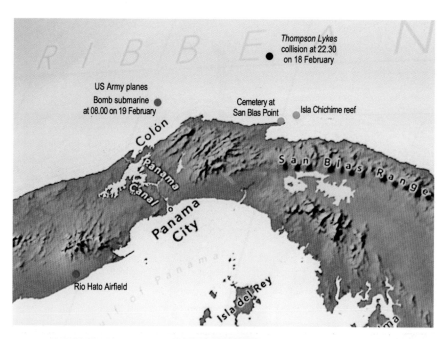

US Army planes
Bomb submarine
at 08.00 on 19 February

Thompson Lykes
collision at 22.30
on 18 February

Cemetery at
San Blas Point

Isla Chichime reef

Colón

Panama
Canal

Panama
City

San Blas Range

Rio Hato Airfield

Isla del Rey

Map of Caribbean coastline showing approximate locations of the *Thompson Lykes* collision and the bombing of *Surcouf*. The bombers flew North from Rio Hato Airfield to location 'R13', an intersection of US Army Air Corps radio stations used as a navigational aid.

WHO SANK SURCOUF?

THE TRUTH ABOUT THE DISAPPEARANCE OF THE PRIDE OF THE FRENCH NAVY

JAMES RUSBRIDGER

Who Sank Surcouf?
by James Rusbridger.

Surcouf Memorial in the port of Cherbourg, unveiled by de Gaulle in 1951.

scorned their minor Slav brethren and in return were fawned upon and secretly loathed by all and sundry, except the Poles, who just frankly hated them.

In particular, he admired the Russian POWs who had their own blocks and maintained military hierarchy and discipline. They knew they were winning the war and were full of youthful self-confidence. Although they liked the few British as fellow combatants against the Nazis and treated them with kindness, they were ignorant about British life. Their knowledge seemed to be based on communist propaganda and the novels of Charles Dickens, as Burney discovered in a revealing conversation with 'Bolshoi' Sasha, a young artillery lieutenant from Voronezh with whom he spent much of his free time:

> Burney: 'What's your view of the British?'
> Sacha: 'A few people who have a lot of money and smoke pipes with gold rings round them, and millions and millions of people who live in black houses and can't afford to smoke.'
> Burney: 'It's really all the fault of propaganda. Why, when everyone says they are trying to avoid war, do governments allow propaganda against each other to such an extent?'
> Sacha: 'I suppose that if a government feels or knows it is not the best but still wants to stay in power, it has to tell its people that other kinds are worse or it would be thrown out.'

While he was writing *Dungeon Democracy* Burney went round to the Russian Embassy several times to try and find out what had happened to Sacha, loyal Communist and patriot. He was told nothing and supposed, later, that like most Russians in Buchenwald he had been repatriated and then sent off to the Gulag by Stalin because he had been politically contaminated by the West – extreme proof of Sacha's perception. Later in 1945 Burney was invited by the Anglo-Russian Friendship

Society to visit Russia on a goodwill tour led by the fellow-traveller socialist M.P. John Platt-Mills. He declined. He liked Russians a lot more than Communists and the 'Iron Curtain' was coming down.

Burney despised the French, though he said he was grieved to say it. As refined and civilised Europeans, they found survival in Buchenwald more difficult than the rough peasants from the East and the Germans targeted them too, precisely because of the supposed superiority of French civilisation. The Work Office, the *Arbeitskammer*, transported as many Frenchmen as it could to the dreaded sub-camps as soon as they emerged from quarantine in the Little Camp. Faced with this prejudice, Burney explained, the French appeared to have given in:

> It was more than anything a sign of the moral wear and tear suffered by the defeat and humiliation of occupation that few Frenchmen in Buchenwald found the inner strength to stand up against the seemingly overwhelming forces of brutality and corruption which seemed to gather specially against them as the upholders of a 'degenerate civilisation'.
>
> ... They were slovenly, greedy, lazy and succumbed both physically and morally more readily than any other people... and they were painfully aware of the depths to which they had fallen. There was no flicker of real spirit.
>
> ... (As for resistance) *'Ce n'est pas le moment. Il vaut mieux rentrer sain et sauf chez soi.'* Safe and sound, yes, but deprived of the last shreds of honour.

Extreme views from someone who later found in France a refuge from his personal troubles, but one shared yet again, though more tactfully expressed, by Eugen Kogon – 'one of the few good Germans', thought Burney.

Burney's particular target was the Comité des Intérets Français which he stated in *Dungeon Democracy* was nothing more than a front organisation for representing French

Communists on the International Camp Committee, often against the interests of fellow Frenchmen. He cited the example of an elderly member of the Michelin tyre family who had been sent to Buchenwald by the Gestapo for ordering the destruction of rubber to prevent it from falling into German hands. To the Comité he was a manufacturer and therefore a capitalist who deserved to be sent off by the *Arbeitstkammer* to one of the sub-camps for slave labour. He died in Ohrdruf after three weeks.

Immediately after the war there was a period of reckoning in France when Communists and Gaullists settled old scores. 'Patriotic committees' of workers were set up inside factories to arrest bosses as 'class enemies' if they found any evidence of collaboration. Burney spoke up as an anti-Communist witness to what he had seen in Buchenwald and later his evidence in *Dungeon Democracy* was noted in France.

The Jews, wrote Burney, 'provided by far the most glaring example of Nazi brutality. To the S.S. the Jews were only fit to die,' either by being worked to death or simply murdered. Surprisingly, he adds that about 500 German Jews who had been interned in Buchenwald since before the war 'knew the score' and, by keeping as low a profile as possible, survived; but for the Polish and Hungarian Jews, many of them survivors of other concentration camps who had arrived in the winter of 1944, death was almost inevitable. 'It is impossible for any civilised person who has not himself seen it to imagine that such a lack of charity towards suffering could exist,' Burney added but, in an observation that would get him into trouble in America after the war, he went on:

One thing must be admitted: they behaved badly themselves. They were annoying in the extreme in their obsequiousness, even to the S.S., and even among themselves they behaved more like animals than men, fighting and robbing even the dead and dying of their clothing. Sensible men would have realised that treatment such as they had endured must inevitably have affected their better natures and would at least have tried to bring them back to humanity by behaving humanly themselves. But anti-Semitism is endemic in all Central and Eastern Europe.

There was one radio talk Burney wrote that autumn that the BBC tactfully decided not to broadcast. 'Your case is more forcefully put in book form,' wrote Eileen Molony in Talks Department. Burney took her advice and inserted it in *Dungeon Democracy*. This was his answer to the question on everyone's mind: how could Germans have done this?

The German is not essentially bad, but he is made bad by the conditions of German history. He is an hereditary subject to despotism; therefore he is a potential despot. The only rule he has known is that of the secret police, the jackboot and the bark, and every German not only fears that rule and obeys it but employs it when it is his turn.

Having been subject to 'warrior kings' since the accursed Frederick the Great, the Germans will always have new Dachaus and Buchenwalds (in different shape), a Gestapo under a new name and sergeant majors disguised as judges. They just don't know any better.

Unsurprisingly, with these views, Burney did not recommend a return to German self-rule after the war. The Allies needed first to educate a new political class that believed in justice and not 'destiny'; that put morality over ideology, whether it was the ideology of Nazism, or Red fascism, as he referred to German communism. The morality of justice, Burney said, was based on natural law which was derived from Greek and Roman civilisation and found its ethical base in Christianity. This was the British belief: 'Life in England, despite superficial inequalities and isolated injustices, has rested for centuries on this foundation of absolute justice.' Therein, Burney wrote in his BBC talk on Buchenwald, lay the fundamental difference between British morality and German ideology.

He went on to write that the British were individualists with conscience while the Germans always obeyed orders:

> Take as an example our own prisoners, who were put to work by the Japs on the jungle railway in Siam. They had a terrible time, but they developed not brutality towards each other but rather an increased will to help each other. Every one of them had, either in greater or smaller degree, a conscience of his own and a will of his own.
>
> Whereas in Germany, what began as a purely military despotism has now become a sort of tyranny so that, even in peacetime Germany, there is the ingrained rule to give or obey orders. You go into a town hall to ask for something and you will be greeted by a bark, and you will be expected to stand to attention.
>
> More broadly, German political theory has to assume the nation as having the form of the Army. One man like Frederick or Hitler who is greater than God, an armed executive, and a docile mass, and that is the ultimate shape which is taken by every political variation which comes out of Germany.

Burney's 'Conclusion' to *Dungeon Democracy* attempts to answer the broader question of why mankind in general in Buchenwald was reduced to inhumanity – 'You may judge for yourselves the amorality, the cowed seeking of refuge in a herd, the longing for revenge, the leadership of animal emotions.' Other than saying that the ideology of totalitarianism, both fascist and communist, had replaced Christian-based morality he has no answer. Instead he ends by concluding that mankind is precariously balanced:

> Now we are at a crisis. In the next years the balance will fall. On the one side lies this idea of right, of reasoned self-discipline and a search for justice: on the other, evolution to a

world of herds, led plunging and fighting for material gain by
a few godless megalomaniac bulls.

Dungeon Democracy was not a best seller either side of the
Atlantic, although Julia wrote that the small print order and
the lack of a reprint was only because of the shortage of paper.
The reviews, she said, were 'glowing' which reflected her wifely
admiration, but that was not far from the truth: '*The Dungeon
Democracy* is an attempt to analyse the illness of our time. The
result is one of the most remarkable books of the year' (*The
New York Times*, Sept 1946). 'His views are often arresting and
entirely fair' (*The Times Literary Supplement*, October 1946).
Christopher was invited by the Book of the Month Club of
New York to speak on the radio in a programme called *Author
Meets Critic* and Rebecca West, whom *Time* magazine titled
'indisputably the world's number one woman writer', said
Dungeon Democracy was 'the most important book for 25
years', though she did not want her comment to be used as a
review.

Yet, who remembers *Dungeon Democracy* now?

What of retribution? Justice, in its judicial sense, was
obtained as early as 1947 in the Buchenwald Trial held as
a military tribunal organised by the US Army in Dachau.
Twenty-two S.S. were sentenced to death by hanging, five
to life imprisonment and four to long prison terms. The
death sentences were reviewed the following year and
several commuted to long terms of imprisonment. Camp
Commandandant Hermann Pister died in prison of a heart
attack in September 1948 having been sentenced to death, and
Ding-Schuler, Head of the Hygiene Institute in Blocks 46 and
50, committed suicide in prison in August 1945, so neither
benefited from any possible leniency resulting from the efforts
of Christopher Burney and others to save lives during those
last days.

Burney wanted to give evidence but, according to Julia, he

was *turned down on the grounds that he would be biased*. It is hard to see how someone who has been in hell for fifteen months could be unbiased, but Burney had declared his hand. He had identified as murderers four S.S. guards in a submission to the Buchenwald Trial. Two of them were:

SS Oberscharführer WINKLER. Aged 50, 5ft 10ins. Slim build; grey hair; grey face; pale eyes; wears gold ring, looks like a snake. Must be regarded as a murderer.

SS Obersturmführer KAMPE. 5ft 11ins; slim, dark brown eyes. Known to have tortured British officers before their execution.[3]

Elsewhere, ex-prisoners of war were invited to file their own charges of war crimes in an affidavit. Burney filed fifteen charges against Nazis, including Pister, relating to offences of murder, brutality and death by injection in Rue de Saussies, Fresnes, and Buchenwald. This was his vengeance.

BBC

In August 1945 Burney was asked by Vera Atkins to give a short talk on the BBC French Service about his experiences of the Resistance and of Buchenwald, as part of a series introduced by Colonel Buckmaster. This he did, avoiding his heavy criticism of the French that would shortly appear in *Dungeon Democracy*. It brought him to the attention of Christopher Salmon, the Assistant Director of BBC talks, who asked him to prepare a fifteen-minute talk called *Solitary Confinement* for the Home Service. Working through several drafts and more meetings, Salmon obviously taught Burney that the best 'talk' is one that is shaped as a story, beginning at the beginning and ending at the end. This can't have been easy because the producer of the French Service talk had reported to Salmon, 'I had to pluck the whole out of a great deal of natural reserve'.[4]

Eventually Burney recorded *Solitary Confinement* on 3

November, and then followed two months of BBC wrangling about when to broadcast such a difficult subject. Eventually, the wrong decision was made; the broadcast was buried on Tuesday, 8 January 1946, at 10.45pm, a time when most listeners were in bed. Later in the week the talk was discussed by the BBC Review Board where this feeble decision deservedly drew 'flak'. The minutes of the meeting reported: 'Why had such a fine talk been buried in a graveyard slot? It was difficult listening, but it was uniquely personal and deserved to be more widely heard, even by the whole family.' So *Solitary Confinement* was given the prestige placing for a repeat of 7.30pm on Sunday, 3 March, BBC Home Service, and this time Christopher read it 'live' in the studio. He repeated the talk once more, on the Third Programme that October.

The Sunday evening broadcast, especially, attracted dozens of letters, all preserved in Burney's broadcasting file. Like the Mass Observation reports popular then, the letters say a lot about the mood of Britain just after the war, at least the mood of BBC Home Service listeners who, like Radio 4 listeners today, seem predominantly middle-class, middle-aged and living in the south.

Most of the correspondents are female, many of them deeply affected by the broadcast: 'What woman could listen to your experiences and not shed a tear for you, poor boy.' 'The tears I shed for you are utterly futile but I should feel unhappy for the rest of my life if I did not discover if all is well with you now.' Some express gratitude: 'You did this for us! What absolute fiends the Germans were, and I expect always will be.' 'Please be quite sure that you have saved England from a far more terrible fate than we can conceive; we have every reason to be proud of you.' Others want to share their grief: 'My two brothers were killed in the war, many of my friends are dead too, so it is good to be reminded that there are people left who have proved they can face anything as you have; sometimes it seems that all the best people are dead.' All are full of admiration: 'I salute your gallant spirit! Such a tremendous spiritual victory is a challenge to high endeavour.' 'I'm impressed by your sanity, which you only kept through sheer guts; what enormous resource of character you must have.' And a surprising number want to show their thanks by offering gifts; a free holiday in Scotland, ration coupons, even a pair of field glasses belonging to a husband killed in battle.

Christopher Burney would broadcast several more times over the years – *Moral Courage* (1952), *Ten Years After D-Day* (1954), *The Spirit in Jeopardy* (a discussion in 1956) and *Silence* (a TV interview in 1963) – but none made anything like the impact of *Solitary Confinement*, both the BBC talks and the book of the same name that followed later.

Married Life

Readers of Christopher's books and listeners to his broadcasts asked what happened to him after the war? He replied that 'nothing had happened', to which Julia added sadly, *I always thought it strange not to mention getting married.* Obviously, the events of the Burney war years were defining experiences of tragic intensity, compared to which marriage, family life and earning a living had their day-to-day monotony. To the reader of this book, his post-war life can be of little interest and therefore little justification for the invasion of privacy to relate it, except in bare outline.[5]

Between 1946 and 1950, for the first five of the seventeen years of married life referred to by Julia, Christopher and Julia lived in New York where Christopher worked as personal assistant to the Dutch Assistant Secretary-General of the United Nations, Adrian Pelt; then for several months in 1950–1, they followed him to the UN Trust Territory of Libya, living in Tripoli where Pelt was the Commissioner charged with writing the official report on independence. Their daughter Juliette was born in 1947 and son Peter two years later. Julia wrote in her memoir, *Our luck lasted seventeen years, and was crowned by the arrival of our children, Juliette and Peter.*

The Burneys flew off to New York in March 1946 in good spirits. As Julia put it, *the cinema organ played at full throttle as we flew, hand in hand, into the sunset of a promised land, unmarked by war, where hearts were warm and food unrationed.* They were disappointed. Christopher found the job frustrating, and no doubt would have preferred to work for *The Times* or the BBC or the Foreign Office, all of which considered employing him. At one stage he thought of applying to Oxford University to study for a degree.

In the circumstances, Christopher must have been delighted to meet up again with his fellow survivor from Buchenwald, Stephen Hessel, as both were working for the UN. Judging from Julia's and Christopher's letters to Dorothy and sister Joan, these were happy years domestically. Christopher was an adoring father and loving husband; Julia was admiring and always supportive. But the physical and psychological illnesses caused by Christopher's war lurked under the surface.

CHAPTER 8

THE ENDURING EVIL

IT IS TRAGIC to realise that the marriage between Christopher and Julia ended effectively after seventeen years because, Christopher said, he found Julia impossible to live with. Drinking heavily, losing his faith, profoundly depressed, he left the family, first to Guatemala and then to France. Julia, too, had a nervous breakdown and the two teenage children were left torn between the two. Julia had no doubt of the cause:

> Our magical reprieve came to an end as eventually the result of Nazi barbarity caught us, many years later, in its wicked net, giving our story it's sad end.

This is easy to read but tragic to imagine when one considers the miracle of their reunion after the war and the intensity of their love. Who can tell why marriages end except the couple themselves? However, undoubtedly what we now call post-traumatic stress became a most significant, and increasing, disorder in Christopher's life, hastening his premature death.

The legacy of Buchenwald affected these years: just as dark clouds over the Black Mountains above Hay unpredictably inundate those below. Salutary to think that the Buchenwald survivors who gathered in Christopher's apartment in Marsham Court soon after the war, talking in hushed voices about their experiences, 'Tommy' Yeo-Thomas, Harry Peleuvé,

Pieter Cool and Alfred Newton, all had their lives blighted by PTSD and died prematurely in what should have been their middle years.

What were the symptoms of Christopher Burney's illness and what effect did it have on his life?[1]

Enter Post-Traumatic Stress

From the start, Christopher was failed by the British medical profession, by the War Office and by SOE. 'Well, you seem to have had a good war,' opined the Harley Street dietician who mistook starvation oedema for fat. When Christopher developed both a duodenal ulcer and a hiatus hernia as a result of his wartime diet his doctor, a sympathetic Hungarian called Zolly Lietner, sent SOE and the War Office a medical report recommending discharge from the army on medical grounds. Neither offered any help. Christopher was amused by the army psychiatrist who enquired about his sexual dreams in solitary confinement and was perplexed by the answer that he only dreamed about rows and rows of scrambled eggs. Christopher and Julia resorted to 'Johnny', Lord Tweedsmuir, a family friend, who threatened to raise the matter in the House of Lords and this time – as so often in those days – name dropping worked and the army offered a discharge on psychiatric grounds with a pension of £100 per year.

In New York the following summer the army required another medical report and the Jewish doctor who examined Christopher, wrote Julia, having taken offence at what he considered anti-Semitic remarks in *Dungeon Democracy*, recommended that the pension was discontinued. The War Office took his advice. That left Christopher with a one-off payment of £225 over two years, awarded in 1947 under the German War Reparations scheme for forty per cent disability defined as 'nervous depression, liver damage and visceral disorders, all resulting from malnutrition and excessive nervous strain beginning in 1943'. He also received a generous pension from the French Government, given to former members of the Resistance which allowed him later when living in France to put a yellow badge on his car with the initials 'GIG' for *Grande Invalide de Guerre*.

At this time it seems that Christopher's ill health was more physical than psychological but his mental health was precarious. Julia wrote to Dorothy from New York:

> *It's a strange thing how anything sudden affects him. I was ragging with him the other evening and gave him one or two fairly hard smacks with the back of my hairbrush on his bareness and the next day he was really quite off colour, and when he went in bathing the other day, he wasn't at all well when he came out. One gets to learn these things. I suppose it's just a case of time.*

What does Julia's euphemism 'off colour' mean? Irritable? Fearful? Depressed? For someone who had suffered such violence it took little to disturb Christopher's peace of mind. Above all, he hated talking about the war and fobbed off social conversations with his usual laconic *hauteur*, as Julia recalled:

> Questioner: *'How did you endure such horrors?'*
> Christopher: *'I worked up to them gradually; it was not as if I went from this room to Buchenwald in a split-second. I'm sure madness would have been the result if that had happened.'*

Silence was the official remedy for post-traumatic stress. Survivors of Japanese prison camps were told that if they ignored their nightmares they would go away. Christopher did broadcast and write about his experiences, but he avoided the intensely personal – 'Letter from Buchenwald' and *Solitary Confinement* being the exceptions. There was nothing to be said. Fellow survivor Harry Peuleuvé felt the same, so did Stephen Hessel. A post-war friend of

Yeo-Thomas recalled introducing him to another Buchenwald survivor:

> I had conceived in my ignorance that their shared experience would develop into comradeship, that they would dive happily into reminiscence, but there was nothing whatsoever for them to say. In that instant I knew the depth of the terrible experiences they shared. They were not as other men, and I was far removed from them.

The inability to communicate trauma is expressed vividly in *The Body Keeps The Score: Mind, Brain and Body in the Transformation of Trauma* by Professor Bessel van der Kolk:

> All trauma is preverbal... Traumatised children 'lose their tongues' and refuse to speak. Photographs of combat soldiers show hollow-eyed men staring mutely into a void. Even years later traumatised people have enormous difficulty telling other people what has happened to them. Their bodies re-experience terror, rage, and helplessness, but these feelings are almost impossible to articulate. Trauma by nature drives us to the edge of comprehension, cutting us off from language based on common experience.
>
> This doesn't mean that people can't talk about a tragedy that has befallen them. Sooner or later survivors come up with what many call a 'cover story' that offers some explanation for their symptoms and behaviour for public consumption. These stories, however, rarely capture the inner truth of the experience. Even the experienced CBC reporter, Ed Murrow, struggled to convey the atrocities he saw when the Nazi concentration camp Buchenwald was liberated in 1945: 'I pray you believe what I have said. I reported what I saw and heard, but only part of it. For most of it I have no words.'

Burney's work in Libya completed, Julia and the children returned to London and Christopher worked briefly in Geneva at the UN headquarters before he resigned, disillusioned with international peacekeeping, and re-joined the family. For a short while he worked on the staff of the Institute of International Affairs in Chatham House. In 1954 they moved out of London to The Orchard, Much Hadham, in Hertfordshire, from where Christopher commuted during the week.

How was Christopher to earn a living? Once again connections came in useful. While still at Chatham House, he was recruited by Siegmund Warburg as a manager for the British and French Bank, founded in 1947. It described itself as 'the Franco-British flagship for commercial, financial and diplomatic relations between France and Great Britain. In many respects it acts as a vehicle for the commercial growth of the Empires of Britain and France in their African colonies.' Christopher wrote to his sister Joan in 1952, 'The Warburgs gave us a very sumptuous dinner and I think we got on all right. It's not going to be very interesting for a couple of years, but I think it's worthwhile if he is on my side. Meanwhile I'm becoming very good at adding.' He and Julia soon went off to Nigeria for three months.

For the next ten years Christopher found himself in the unlikely role of banker, commuting into the City during the week and helping Julia with the young family at weekends. Juliette remembers him as a loving father, taking her to parties with the other daddies and showing affection, though restrained by the formalities of the age. Yet for someone with his adventurous past, it must have been mundane, to say the least, and when this decade of his life was over, and he was living in France, he wrote to Joan about 'the wasteland of the City. Here, there's not a stockbroker in sight.'

What should have been an event of excitement was the publication of *Solitary Confinement* in 1952, with its Foreword by the celebrated poet and playwright Christopher Fry. But the publishers were new and poor: Clerke & Cockeran telephoned him the very day of publication to warn him not to cash their cheque for £50 as they had gone bankrupt. The small print run scarcely made an impact, and *Solitary Confinement* was soon unobtainable: like Burney in Fresnes it disappeared without trace.

Publication of *Solitary Confinement*

However, in 1961, Macmillan republished *Solitary Confinement* in one volume with *Dungeon Democracy*, and this time it became a *cause célèbre*. The *Times Literary Supplement* wrote its first leader on 13 April 1961, with the title OUT OF PRINT:

> It is cheering when a book of real quality seems to break through a barrier of indifference and bad luck. Ten years ago, Mr Christopher Burney wrote a short work called 'Solitary Confinement' which is one of the classics both of the last war and of that long process of imprisonment, brutality, and sudden death in which the war itself was only one extra acute and well publicised stage. The publisher quickly went out of business, the book out of print. The public soon forgot it in favour of the simpler, but more immediate and trivial jottings of Anne Frank.
>
> Yesterday it was re-issued in a new edition by another publisher and here it is once more with its singular balance of contemplativeness and self-ridicule, of the philosophical, the religious and the urgently physical, of spiritual gropings, and the sharp, vivid glimpses of the outside world; all clearly and detachedly described. It seems possible that the hibernation has done it no harm. The book's depth and range of reference are more evident than before; that richness which is there to be dug into not only by ordinary readers but by philosophers, psychologists and priests who want to see their ideas tested by an intelligent and sensitive individual in an extreme state.

Rebecca West was on hand to make another extravagant claim – she had described *Dungeon Democracy* as 'the most important book for twenty-five years'. She wrote in the *Sunday*

Telegraph: 'Readers who are genuinely inquisitive about their own souls, and other people's, and (these being as they are) about the prospects for our species, should read *Solitary Confinement'*. The reviews on both sides of the Atlantic were many and fulsome and must have proved to Christopher, still in 'the wasteland of the City', that he was a writer of distinction.

The originator of this publisher's *coup* was Alan Maclean, Christopher's editor at Macmillan. He became a close friend of the Burneys during the 1950s and stayed with them at Much Hadham during the weekends, partly to escape the pestering of the press because he was the brother of the spy Donald Maclean who had defected to Russia in 1951. His publicity blurb for *Solitary Confinement* called it 'a classic work which will illuminate the minds of its readers for years to come'. In May 1961 Maclean received a letter from Prime Minister Harold Macmillan, later to become chairman of the family publishers: 'I have now read both Mr Burney's books. He is clearly a man of considerable talent and I hope he will prove a successful writer. He sounds a most charming personality, whom I would one day like to meet.'

Worsening Post-Traumatic Stress

Julia wrote that for the early period after the war, such was Christopher's self-control that he seemed not to think about Buchenwald: *memory did not even manage to sneak through his strength of will into his dreams.* But in 1952 came the first relapse. One Sunday morning in London, Christopher brought her a weekly treat of breakfast in bed and then went back to the living room with coffee and the Sunday papers:

> *Ten minutes later he came to me and said, 'Get a doctor quick, I'm ill'. I wondered what he had eaten that had perhaps poisoned him and told him to lie down. 'If I lie down, I shall die,' he replied. When the doctor arrived, he was lying down and could move no part of his body. The doctor said he had suffered either*

a heart attack or a stroke, gave him an injection, and said he would call in the next day.

I immediately rang Zolly who came at once. He said he doubted it was a stroke or heart attack and when I told him Christopher had been reading the papers, he said something he read had probably touched off a memory in his subconscious. He gave him another injection which would put him to sleep for twenty-four hours, after which he would give him a proper examination in his surgery.

He found nothing wrong physically and thought a psychiatric probe would be unnecessarily cruel in the light of all he had gone through. I often wondered, in the light of what happened later, whether this was the right decision.

Christopher had suffered a panic attack when in response to a sudden shock, the heart rate suddenly increases, breathing becomes shallow and a feeling of faintness intensifies. The body's response to this, psychiatrists say, is 'fight' or 'flight':

When traumatised people are presented with images, sounds or thoughts related to their particular experience, the amygdala [the emotional part of the brain] reacts with alarm... even years after the event. Activation of this fear centre triggers the cascade of stress hormones and nerve impulses that drive up blood pressure, heart rate, and oxygen intake preparing the body for fight or flight. (*The Body Keeps The Score: Mind, Brain and Body in the Transformation of Trauma*)

Sometimes the panic attack turns into catatonic collapse when the so-called dorsal vagal nerve shuts down the body and you cannot speak or move for a short time. This is presumably what happened to Christopher, *terrifying* to Julia and her young family.

A second incident of 'nervous disorder', as it was called then, occurred two years later when Christopher was asked by the BBC to broadcast a talk on the tenth anniversary of D-

After further discourse, similar in introspection and complexity to the mental exercises in Fresnes gaol but expressed in very accessible dialogue, 'Ego' and 'Alter Ego' descend the mountain in a spirit of optimism. It is clear to me that *Descent from Ararat* is a key to understanding the state of Christopher Burney's post-traumatic stress fifteen years after the war, first his loss of memory and thoughts of suicide and then his attempts to convince himself that life was worth living. It deserves more attention.

Those who have suffered from 'transient memory loss' will know that this is completely disorientating. The 'injured man' wrote: 'Of myself, my name, my past I could recall nothing... I had escaped from my memory.' This is another symptom of post-traumatic stress. After years of suppression the mind temporarily wipes out the memory of the experience except for its surfacing in nightmare.

Ego: 'I'm afraid I've lost my memory...'

Alter Ego: 'You've just stopped remembering about yourself. Probably it had become too unpleasant. Brains are very efficient and on the whole co-operative. So don't be in a hurry to start remembering again. I rather envy you... In a way, your brain behaves like your ears. When the noise becomes too bad, then you go mad by degrees. The safety-valves go wrong and the whole system blows up.'

Ego: 'You haven't told me why you think I was going to commit suicide.'

Alter Ego: 'When a person's awareness of his own being is put in doubt... he can no longer account for himself. He gets privately lost... Your hold on your own being had been weakened and you were not far short of saying "Oh well, that's done for".'

Ego: 'I've still no idea who I am.'

Alter Ego: 'Good heavens, what do you want to know that for? The only important thing is to be sure who you are.

Don't even try to see yourself *as* anything, just *be*. Whatever happened to you went wrong and when your memory comes back, I hope it will be like a flat map and not real country, something you can recognise and not feel. The most important thing is your own being. I do believe, "Thou shalt love thy neighbour as thyself", but I think that means you should start by loving yourself – valuing is perhaps better.'

Ego and *Alter Ego* find an overhang to shelter under and, 'as first light had just managed to prevail over the storm-laden eastern sky and I could make out that rain was still falling', they massage each other's feet to keep warm. They discuss the philosophy of life, as one does in the early hours.

> *Alter Ego*: 'Learn to be content that you are; that is the first truth. Remind yourself that the intangibles that you perceive when you are most conscious of being are the first realities. God, wonder, beauty, love… Shun the abstract bogeys like the plague, Good, Evil, Perfection, Sin and all the rest. They're the only excuse I know for believing in devils.'
>
> *Ego*: 'But surely, conversation would be difficult without them?'
>
> *Alter Ego*: 'Good and Evil are my pet aversions. You remember the story of the Garden of Eden? People always seem to think it was the tree of good and evil when actually it was the tree *of the knowledge* of good and evil.'
>
> *Ego*: 'What makes you think that my demons are not real?'
>
> *Alter Ego*: 'Because they only exist in your brain. They are the way you have learnt to look at things, the associations you have built up and had built up for you. We are supposed to believe that an absolute power of evil exists, which has led to the Devil and Hell and all that paraphernalia. Demons aren't true, but all the bad intelligence you have been given leads you to think they are. People call this brain-washing nowadays.'

Alter Ego concludes with heartfelt advice:

'If you remember that the most important thing about you is
that you are, that it is your own being that sees beauty and the
reflection of God, you'll be able to live life instead of arguing
with it... Sit quietly and stop arguing, as you sit under a
summer sky. Then you can consent to anything without any
violence to your reason.'

As they walk down the mountain, *Ego* feels 'a warmth like
love and a wondering expectancy like opening a well-packed
parcel':

'Life was astir. Some wild duck flew past to the west, a pair
of swans flew past making with their wings the first sounds I
had heard apart from our own voices. A pair of hooded crows
alighted wickedly on the hill opposite. A rainbow curved over
the summit we had left.'
    Alter Ego: 'Do you remember the rainbow was a sign from
God to Noah promising him there would not be another
flood? Always look at rainbows. Don't analyse them into
raindrops and light. Just look and realise how beautiful they
are, especially the ones made by little clouds passing over the
moon just before dawn.'

They descend the mountain and see a search party coming
towards them.

    Alter Ego: 'There's no need for me to stay any longer. I've a long
way to go in the opposite direction.'
    Ego: 'It seems odd after all these hours that you should
suddenly fade away, here and now, in the middle of nowhere.
After all, you're the only thing I remember about myself.'
    Alter Ego: 'I don't think that will last long, and I cannot be
any more use to you now. You've got to get down again, plant
your vineyard and drink your wine.'

But *Descent from Ararat* did not exorcise Burney's demons. Its publication in 1962 to respectful if uncomprehending reviews coincided with a number of events that broke up his marriage and hastened his decline. Like the stranger on the mountain, *Alter Ego* with his positive reassurance seemed to disappear.

War Requiem

At Christmas 1962, Christopher and Julia received a card from Benjamin Britten and Peter Pears and with it an invitation to attend a performance of their *War Requiem* on 9 January. *War Requiem* had its premiere the previous May at the consecration of Coventry Cathedral, and presumably their invitation came because Britten had dedicated it to Christopher's brother Roger, among others. He had been their friend until his death on 19 February 1942, on the submarine *Surcouf*.

After the performance Christopher wrote from Much Hadham to 'Mr Britten':

> It's really an impertinence to send you anything in return for the service of the *Requiem,* which I am sure is the greatest work of art done for many years. But herewith is all I have to offer beyond my esteem. My mother would like you to know how grateful she is for all your kindness to Roger.

But listening to the *War Requiem* was a traumatic experience for Christopher. Two years later Julia revealed this in another thank you letter for a Christmas card to 'Mr Britten':

> *I am writing because Christopher has what the doctor calls 'a severe nervous depression'. It overtook him just before he met you after the Requiem and we have had fearful times since. He is not up to much and he certainly can't write letters. It seems to be an affliction so terrible it defies description. He can't even read.*
> *His mother died this autumn. She was 76 and only lived for*

a few days after a stroke. She was pleased when you sent her a copy of the Requiem. *I never knew Roger, but she loved him best and as the years past there were fewer and fewer people left who could share this memory with her. So it was particularly joyful for her when you remembered.*[2]

The *War Requiem* may have reposed the soul of the late Roger Burney but, not surprisingly, it severely agitated the mind of Christopher. His daughter, Juliette, supposed it was due to 'survivor's guilt', a phrase identified in the 1960s as common to Holocaust survivors among others, self-blame for surviving when others did not. As Christopher listened to the *War Requiem*, did he blame himself, as he had done in Fresnes prison, for the grief he had caused his mother for allowing himself to be captured within months of the death of Roger? Did he imagine that he was walking unwittingly with his friend Maurice Pertschuk towards Pertschuk's execution below the Buchenwald crematorium?

That period of the early 1960s was the beginning of the end of Christopher's marriage and the worsening of his post-traumatic stress, for shortly afterwards he abandoned wife and teenage children and left for Guatemala. He was to spend most of the remainder of his life living on his own abroad.

Christopher dated his 'nervous breakdown' from 1963 in his re-application to the War Reparations Scheme to increase his disability pension from forty to sixty per cent. He listed his symptoms as 'nervous depression, chronic colitis and hepatitis causing constant pains in abdomen, very nervous. Had a breakdown in 1963 as nerves were cracking. Unable to work.' His claim was accepted and a one-off grant of £1,640 was decided by the Ministry of Pensions.

It would be wrong to think that PTSD had taken over Christopher's life. Outside his immediate family, the friends and relatives I have spoken with thought he was getting through life like everybody else, though hard drinking and depressed at times. That same year, 1963, he made a speech at the wedding of Joan's daughter, Lucy. The groom, James Mackenzie, remembers the speech as witty and composed, though on the few occasions they met he found his uncle-in-law 'taciturn', with the disconcerting habit of waiting to be spoken to before replying. James found him 'formidable'.

Later in 1963, Christopher was invited by Julia's wartime boss, Mark Oliver, to stay at his ranch, the Finca Los Andes at Guatalon in Guatemala. Apparently, Christopher's doctor, the wise Zolly Leitner, recommended the visit so presumably there were health reasons for leaving home. The *Daily Telegraph* commissioned a few articles and Christopher, always keen to write serious journalism, accepted the job though he never wrote the articles. On the eve of his departure, he learned that Harry Peulevé had died of a heart attack in Seville, aged only forty-seven. Yeo-Thomas, in Paris, 'wept bitterly' when he heard the news. Similarly haunted by his wartime experiences and disillusioned with post-war life, he would die the following year, aged sixty-three. The timing of Peulevé's death was coincidental, of course, though in retrospect it was ominous.

Christopher told Juliette, then aged sixteen, that he had to get away: 'It's not my fault, forgive me.' Relations with Julia were strained. She wrote in her memoir that she was suffering from depression too, and whereas Christopher kept a tight lid on his emotions she became tearful and demanding; this he found hard to bear. About this time, Alan Maclean at Macmillan re-published *Solitary Confinement* and *Dungeon Democracy* in one volume. He wrote in the Preface: 'I don't think he [Christopher] ever found again the serenity of spirit, composure of thought and the simple faith which he fashioned and earned in Fresnes. But he never forgot it, and nor should we.' Peter Burney pointed this out to me as his explanation of his father's increasing isolation. To reinforce that thought, here is what Christopher wrote in his own Preface that followed:

Solitude is liberty indeed, bounded only by the obsessive appetite and the animal lust to roam. But liberty is a rare and refined spirit, so strong that Providence in its wisdom has arranged that there shall be little of it, making men live in a society to which solitude is repugnant.

Alone in France

Between 1963 and 1968 Christopher Burney lived alone at a variety of addresses in Paris. One, he told his daughter, was a hostel for Algerian immigrants and another, he told his sister Joan, was on the site of a former famous brothel at Number 4 Rue du Générale Aube. He stayed at a more salubrious address too, 9 Boulevard Malesherbes, Paris 8eme. He was employed by the British Embassy to edit a small French-language 'propaganda sheet', as he described it, disseminating good news about Britain. For someone who until recently, according to his wife, was too distressed to read much or write, this must have marked a lessening of his PTSD and he told Joan he was enjoying his first work for three years. He soon took a more subversive view, explaining to her how he was trying to turn the 'propaganda sheet' into a French *Private Eye* and mocking himself for trying to write a special edition on 'English Gardens', about which he knew nothing.

Initially, Burney spent time visiting and nursing Yeo-Thomas, who was bedridden with a serious kidney complaint and general bodily breakdown. Yeo-Thomas was melancholic and bitter about the state of the world. 'I am a terribly disappointed man,' he told the *Daily Express* in 1963: 'sometimes I wish I had died after my escape from Buchenwald'. According to Peter Burney, his father's depression did not have a political dimension, although he was critical of the United Nations ever since he had worked there and thought little of Gubbins, Buckmaster, and the way SOE had been run. He had, said Peter, 'moved on'. Yeo-Thomas died on 26 February 1964 and his funeral was held in the pouring rain at the British Embassy church. Presumably Christopher was there.

Incidentally, Peter remembers going fishing with his father in France and meeting up with a friend of Christopher's who had been involved with SOE. This was just after M D R Foot's *SOE in France* was published in 1966. Neither thought much of it and took for granted that the leadership of SOE had been 'let off lightly' because the book was part of a Government Official History Series. Christopher did not mention his outrage at Foot's description of his role in the last days of Buchenwald.

Another wartime contact who Christopher revisited was the dentist Jacque Foure, now with an American wife and twenty years on from those wartime years. Mostly his social life was with journalists and SOE survivors headed by Sam White, the Paris correspondent of the *Evening Standard*. They held long and bibulous lunches at fashionable restaurants like le Crillon and Hirondelle. Once Christopher invited Juliette along and she noticed he left without paying so she went back to attend to the bill. 'Don't worry,' said the waiter who had fought with the Resistance himself, 'we just add the cost of his meal to another bill. No-one seems to mind.' The elderly waiters were protective of Christopher, Peter remembers. They realised he had suffered during the war and told Peter what a hero he had been.

Christopher was drinking far too much: gin at lunch, whisky at supper. He chain-smoked Gauloise cigarettes. No doubt because of his underlying depression, alcohol brought to the surface a nasty temper that embarrassed his family. His physical health was bad. In his occasional letters to Joan during this period he told her about his ill-health that seemed to affect much of his body: 'gut problems', respiratory problems like pneumonia and bronchitis, 'heart problems and everything else that resides in the rib cage'.[3] In 1972 he was back in London at King Edward VII's Hospital for Officers for two weeks with a 'heart virus'. Juliette visited him but he did not want Julia to know: 'On past performance it would take a bottle even to get us coherent.' This caused Juliette a lot of grief.

In 1967 he celebrated his fiftieth birthday with an all-night binge in Paris that resulted in a car crash in which he fell through the windscreen and spent more days in hospital with 'stitches and scars'. Writing in her memoir Julia remembered that Mrs MacDougal, the fortune teller of Nether Auchendrane, had foretold a car crash involving Christopher but not Julia and that, at that time, 'both of them would be very, very ill'.

In 1964 Dorothy died. Christopher and Joan corresponded about the will, and he added news about his life:

> As you know, I've made rather a mess of most of my life. There are theories and theories about why and I'm hanged if I know the answer. If I weren't worried about the others, I'd be quite content. I earn a modest living doing a useful job and I have no great needs. The doctors have put me on three months forced leave in the country and I've been lent a cottage provided I maintain its garden. It's surrounded by trees, so I sweep leaves and plant bulbs and saw wood to keep myself warm in the evening.

This cottage was in the small Normandy village of Fains; La Carottiere, La Noe du Bois par Fains 27. Christopher would spend the next eight years of his life there because in August 1967 he wrote to Joan to tell her he had been 'fired from his job [in Paris] for reasons of economy'.

Although he did not disappear from view, even his family did not know where he was living. He was discovered in Fains in 1973 by the journalist David Pryce-Jones – himself from the Hereford area. He wrote a lengthy piece about his visit for *The Daily Telegraph Magazine*, calling it 'A Ghost on the Files', because Christopher describes himself as 'a resident of nowhere'. The profile paints a rare physical description of Burney:

> Mr Burney stands waiting at the large gate. He has a very French pair of glasses with smoked lenses, and a Gauloise in hand... He looks lean and tanned. In spite of being 56, in spite of hair streaked grey, in his flannel trousers and corduroy jacket he has the air of an older unruly student – which in a general intellectual way is what he is.
>
> We go for a late meal in the small town nearby. Mr Burney does no cooking, though he buys food in the local market, questioning each day, he says, what value the food has been to him. He is known roundabout as *l'ecossais (Scotsman)* as though insisting on being accurate about the ultimate origin of the Burney family. For company he has *Bonhomme*, a hound from Brittany brought in a crisis of loneliness.
>
> So he lives alone with no more possessions than he could cram into his little grey Simca and be off. His treasured possessions are a barometer and a corkscrew his father took to the 1914 war.
>
> He finds London rather scruffy now when he stays at the Travellers Club. He still has his shoes made in St James's. He wears a signet ring on his little finger. Such English style is an armour in itself, for it has the full force of manners and habits firm enough to have saved him when put to the supreme test.

Interesting that Pryce-Jones picked up on Burney 'the upper-class Englishman', as Alfred Newton had described him when they first met in Buchenwald. This had been his reputation in the camp, for better or worse. As Eugen Kogon wrote in *The Theory and Practice of Hell*, the carapace of class may have contributed to his survival: 'The rational and political opponents of the Nazi regime were those among the prisoners who had some claim to superiority, by reason of their individuality or their allegiance to a given group, social stratum or class.'

The subject came up again that evening when Pryce-Jones questioned 'Mr Burney' about his survival like 'a ghost on the files', both of them aware that he was the interrogator and Christopher the prisoner in his solitary confinement. 'There's a theory widely held by all sorts of people that I'm round the bend,' says Christopher about his abandonment of family and security.

> 'The words people generally use about me,' he says with some apology, 'are "tough" and "arrogant".' Arrogance, with its ingrained reaction to "funny little chaps" is perhaps the one and only attitude which enables a man to contend with loneliness and starvation. Plenty of former inmates have stated that those who best survived concentration camps were sure of their own righteousness, like Jehovah's Witnesses, or at least of their identity, like aristocrats or born leaders, those who were able to keep their self-respect – including Mr Burney, "an unsuccessfully rebellious upper-class Englishman" as he says of himself.

The questioning inevitably turns Price-Jones to question himself:

> We can only guess what would happen to the rest of us if we were to suffer the fate of so many less fortunate races in this century. All the same, we have a pointer here, and more than that, an individual witness, for the history of Europe at its worst caught up among so many millions of victims a certain kind of Englishman at his best.

Concentration Camp Syndrome[4]

While Christopher was living in Normandy a seminal report was published by the Department of Adult Psychiatry at the Medical Academy in Kraków into the effects of the concentration camp experience twenty-five years after the war. Over one hundred survivors had been interviewed over much of that time and the first conclusion was that PTSD seemed to be progressive; 'KZ-syndrome was shown to occur in fifty-eight per cent of former prisoners five years after leaving the camp, and in seventy-seven per cent after thirty years, which confirms the syndrome's chronic and progressive nature.' Why should this be so? Why the awful experiences seemed to leak out over time the report does not explain, but it certainly applied to Burney. Similarly, the physical effects of internment in the concentration camps, or *Konzentrationslager*, were endured by Burney too. Survivors reported lung, gut, heart failure, and nervous breakdown, leading to alcoholism, depression and anxiety.

At the gateway to Buchenwald all those years ago, Burney said he regarded the last fifteen months as 'life on another planet' and 'when one has been back among civilised people for a while one just forgets it'. The opposite was true. Survivors could not forget and suffered from depression and unhappiness, as the report stated:

> They were all overwhelmed by the misery of human existence, they wanted to know how it was possible that so much evil accumulated in the limited territory of the concentration camp and how it was at all possible that they managed to survive. Every former camp prisoner could admit the same as Maria Zarbiska did: 'I witnessed such horrible things, such deep human misery, such great savagery, the elimination of all possible human elements and simple instinctive reactions of tender hearts and I can certainly claim I saw everything that a human being can see and experience both in hell and in heaven.'

The report reiterates what Eugene Kogon had observed and written up in *The Theory and Practice of Hell*:

> The initiation into the camp hell was a shock that was stronger than any other trauma of human life. All authors dealing with

the concentration camps emphasise the initial reaction to imprisonment which was generally experienced, and which led to death in many prisoners. A prisoner had to adjust to camp life within the first several weeks or months, otherwise he had to die.

How to adjust to camp life? The report concluded from its many interviews that it was essential for prisoners to withdraw into an internal world and become as indifferent as possible to life around them. It coined the phrase 'camp autism'. Burney must have found this easier than most because of his upper-class 'auteur' and his experiences in Fresnes gaol over eighteen months. Here his self-discipline had taken him beyond indifference. He had, as he wrote after his release from Buchenwald, 'trained myself to stay spiritually free'. It is hard to imagine the self-discipline that must have entailed.

Prisoners had to have the will to survive: 'the will to survive was so essential to the ability to survive.' Without it, according to Professor Stanislaw Pigon, who had survived Sachsenhausen Concentration Camp and contributed to the Kraków Report, the drift into surrender could be total:

> You could see it in a prisoner's eyes. Those eyes, heralds of death in the camp, were a special problem. I saw them so many times. We learnt their meaning by experience. As a farmer can forecast the weather looking at a cloud that covers the sun, we were also able to see the quietly approaching death in the eyes of some prisoners. We already knew someone would be dead in three days' time.

This surrender into the expectation of death defined the term *Muselmann* that was used throughout the concentration and extermination camps. It's origin is not clear but might refer to the belief that Muslims were fatalistic – 'Life is in the hands of Allah' – and no human will can prevent that: or else that the prostrate figure of the inmate too weak to stand was similar to the Muslim at prayer. The result was apathy, very different from 'camp autism'. Death came quickly when giving up on life was added to starvation and exhaustion.

The report also stated that 'camp autism' needed to be complemented by finding 'an angel in the camp hell', meaning that prisoners who survived said they had formed intense friendships with one or two companions in distress with whom they found a common humanity. Probably with Burney the special friend was Maurice Pertschuk, to whom he dedicated *Dungeon Democracy*. As always there was the intense and loving memory of Julia to whom he wrote 'Letter from Buchenwald' that terrible winter of 1944/45. Then, of course, there was Burney's belief in God.

The belief that humanity still existed among inhumanity and would triumph in the end was central to survival. The report again quotes Professor Stanislav Pigon. He wrote that every prisoner who struggled to survive needed a firm belief in humanity, a 'higher castle' of conviction that was impregnable:

We found ourselves in a situation where we had to find such a 'higher' castle in ourselves, a base that could never be destroyed, cling to it with all our might and never loosen our grasp on it, not even for a moment. These are not empty words. I found such a base in myself, and perhaps that is why I managed to survive. It does not matter now what the base was; it matters that I found it and that it was my refuge where I could hide from the onrush of hatred. Such an ability was not a matter of age but a matter of how great one's fundamental strength was.

Burney shared this deep belief in humanity. In the *Smithsonian* magazine in 1993, the best-selling American author Robert Wernick wrote:

My friend Christopher Burney, an English secret agent who spent many months in Buchenwald, once told me that the theory behind the Nazi concentration camps was that with a proper dosage of brutality, cold, hunger and fatigue, all human beings could be reduced to the level of animals. But he discovered that the theory was wrong, for even in most atrocious circumstances a kind of natural aristocracy would assert itself. There were remarkable people who in the face of everything would refuse to surrender their humanity, men like the French West Indian who once took off his coat to save Burney from pneumonia during a two-hour roll call in a howling blizzard, men who would risk their lives to bring a friend a spoonful of jam.

Last Years

Christopher Burney returned to London in 1976, living mostly in Rothsay Court, Harleyford Road, SE11. He was partially re-united with Julia, and the whole family would spend Christmas with Juliette at her marital home in Aberdeen. Julia offered a divorce, but Christopher rejected it: there was no other woman in his life, but he had to live alone. He had been stuck in an emotional impasse for years, as he had written to Juliette some time before:

> I'm sorry I'm such a messy father. I know it doesn't make you happy, but I can't see any way out. I wish to God things were different but they're not. Basically, anything I write to you is senseless. Birthday presents aren't important, but happiness is. I would much rather you were happy but I'm damned if I know what I can do about it.

His social life centred around the Travellers Club and it was here that he died on 18 December 1980, just before he was due in Aberdeen for a family Christmas. He suffered a heart attack after a good lunch as he sat in his favourite library chair. As Alan Maclean wrote, with understatement,

'Few of his wartime colleagues would have forecast such a peaceful exit'.

His friends from the Travellers Club organised a memorial service held in the Queen's Chapel of the Savoy on 12 February 1981. William Buchan, later the Third Baron Tweedsmuir, gave the First Reading, a quote from *Solitary Confinement*:

> On reading the Bible... I was worried too by the old notions of 'evil' and 'sin'... If, as I believed, the only absolute was God, and good by definition, there could be no such thing as evil, all it could be was an epithet meaning less than good...
>
> Perhaps that is all it has ever meant... And with what result? Fear, inhibition, moral despair and, above all, such preoccupation with the negative that men had no energy left with which to look positively after what was good. The Devil is only a dark glass.

But Christopher's devil was real. The tragedy of his later years, Julia wrote, was that *his depression deprived him of love, for me and for God, and his misery was profound.*

James Mackenzie, married to Christopher's niece, attended the memorial service and the wake in the Travellers Club. He met Yeo-Thomas's partner, Barbara, and M D R Foot and shared a table with 'old desperadoes', by which he meant former SOE agents from Britain and France. He listened with awe to their reminiscences. One of them turned to him and said, 'those were terrible years – but we wouldn't have missed them for anything'. Would Christopher Burney, could any survivor of Buchenwald Concentration Camp, have had any possible empathy with them?

NOTES

Chapter 1: The Making of a Rebel

1   I am grateful to his daughter Juliette and his son Peter for lending me the family papers. Above all they lent me a copy of Julia's memoir, then Christopher's scrapbooks containing reviews and correspondence about his books, then the all-important account of his debriefing by SOE. Other papers included a leather pouch containing Dorothy's (his mother) correspondence with him and his schools about his education; and later her account of his teenage wanderings.

As I wrote earlier, I could not have written this book without quoting extensively from Julia's memoir. She makes her entry in this chapter, commenting retrospectively on this period in his life.

Clearly, I could not have written about Christopher Burney without quoting extensively from his writings; his three books and his radio broadcasts. Juliette and Peter Burney own the copyright of his published material, and it goes without saying that I am grateful for their permission to quote as I wished. This applies to Julia's memoir too.

2   *Out of Bounds*
I am grateful to the librarian at Wellington College, Caroline Jones, who trawled the college archives for evidence of Christopher and provided details of his time there, such as the proceedings of the Debating Society. Importantly, she guided me to the school shop from where I bought a copy of *Out of*

Bounds, The Education of Giles Romilly and Esmond Romilly, this copy published by Umbria Press in 2015. It ends with an 'Afterword' by Patrick Mileham who was educated at Wellington thirty years later. He places their autobiography in the genre of school reminiscences of this period and finds it 'immediate and utterly believable... I can vouch for the truth and integrity of Giles's and Esmond's experiences'. 'Afterword' has much of value to say about Wellington College at this time in the context of a turbulent period in British politics, some of which I have quoted.

3   Fighting the Germans

For information about the Narvik campaign of 1940 I visited the museum of the South Wales Borderers in Brecon. Apart from details about the SWB in the campaign, I found there *The Doomed Invasion* by Jack Adams, published by Pen & Sword in 1989 and used it for my brief account. I also noted in the *SWB* magazine of 1981 a tribute to Captain Christopher Arthur Geoffrey Burney 'who was commissioned into the South Wales Borderers as a Supplementary Reserve Officer in 1936 and joined the 2nd Battalion at the outbreak of war. After the Norway campaign he was among the first to volunteer for the French Section of SOE and carried out his highly dangerous mission with cool courage until he was captured by the Germans.'

Later I came across an account of the Narvik campaign from the French army's point of view. It's 1st Light Infantry Division included the Demi-Brigade of the French Foreign Legion which was composed of many Jewish refugees who were banned from fighting for the French army itself. Anxious to prove their loyalty to France and fight the Nazis who had made life impossible for them in Germany and Poland, they joined the Foreign Legion. Their battle for the retaking of Narvik was brutal, and just when victory was achieved it was snatched away by the need to return and defend France – a doomed venture as we know. I found this account in *House of Glass* by Hadley Freeman, published by Harper Collins in 2020.

4   Finding Love

For the wooing of Julia Burrell by Christopher at Nether

Auchendrane, 1940–2, I have quoted from her charming memoir – where else? It shows an intensely romantic side to his personality that no-one who knew him in the grim years to come could ever guess at.

Chapter 2: The Short Life of a Secret Agent

1   The official history, *SOE in France*, was written by a former British Army Intelligence Officer, M R D Foot. It was first published in 1966 and with a revised edition in 2004. In between there were revisions and excisions. My account of the SOE background to Christopher Burney's time as a secret agent in 1942 comes mainly from M R D Foot's revised edition, *SOE in France: An Account of the British Special Operations Executive in France 1940–1944*, published by Whitehall History Publishing in 2004.

As M R D Foot writes, he was handicapped by a clash between scholarship and security and, as usual, security won. Although he was given full access to all the surviving files, Foot was not allowed to refer to them specifically and he had to hand over his notes showing exactly where he had obtained his material. There were other restrictions too. He did not interview Christopher Burney and, had he done so, he might have corrected the misapprehension that Burney was 'tall with blond hair', for he was neither.

Freed from these restraints and benefiting from less guarded memories with the passing of the years, Sarah Helm's book on SOE, *A Life in Secrets; the Story of Vera Atkins and the Lost Agents of SOE*, published in 2005 by Little Brown, is considerably more critical of SOE than is the official history.

2   The Fascination of SOE
In the media, I am sure, it is because of the women agents of SOE. In 2020, seventy-five years after the end of the war, out came a new book, *A Woman of No Importance*, about Virginia Hall, an American SOE agent known as 'the limping lady' because of her wooden foot, who led two successive secret lives in France. (Her wooden foot, which she called Cuthbert, did not prevent her

walking fifty miles in two days over the Pyrenees in 1942 to evade capture.) A public campaign was marshalled in 2018 to have the head of another SOE heroine, Noor Inayat Khan GC, printed on the new £50 note. She lost out, honourably, to the Enigma code-breaker Alan Turing, but now a film has been made about her. In 2012 Clare Mulley wrote *The Spy Who Loved: Secrets and Lives of Christine Granville, Britain's First Special Agent of World War II*. Christine Granville, née Krystyna Skarbek, codename *Pauline*, became a sort of posthumous media magnet. She was the 'bravest of the brave', beautiful and promiscuous, murdered in 1952 by one of her jilted lovers.

There have been many fictional accounts of SOE heroines on screen and in books. The most notable in my view is *The Girl Who Fell from the Sky* (2008) by Simon Mawer, but perhaps the best known is *Charlotte Gray* by Sebastian Faulks (1998) because it was made into a film. There is a museum dedicated to the SOE heroine Violette Szabo GC in Wormelow, for she was a Herefordshire girl. Our fascination continues but is it not a little morbid, even prurient? For out of the thirty-nine female agents who worked secretly in France, twelve were murdered and three others survived concentration camps.

There are two twenty-first century biographies that indirectly relate to Christopher Burney. The first is *A Life in Secrets* (2005) by Sarah Helm, about the organiser of SOE, Vera Atkins. Through this secretive and enigmatic woman, we enter the soul of the organisation. After the war Vera Atkins was Burney's frequent contact with what was left of SOE. The other biography, *Spirit of Resistance* (2008), is about Burney's friend and fellow Buchenwald survivor Harry Peulevé, who asked Burney to become godfather to one of his children.

3   After the war a large number of SOE files were destroyed, either to reduce storage space or by a fire in the Baker Street offices in 1946. This applied particularly to files on the early years of SOE, files on the training of agents and files on the particular circuits in France. This must account for the absence of Christopher Burney's personal file and, probably, for an absence of a file on the AUTOGIRO circuit with which he was involved. However,

the all-important two debriefing papers on Burney, written after his return in 1945, remain – see below.

4   *Aunty's War* by Edward Stourton (Penguin Books, 2018) is the story of the BBC during the Second World War. His account of 'personal messages' radio to occupied France is well worth reading.

5   The biography of Virginia Hall, *A Woman Of No Importance* by Sonia Purnell, was published by Virago Press in 2019.

6   Charles Grover-Williams, alias *Sebastien*, set up the CHESTNUT circuit in Paris and operated it successfully until his capture in 1943. He was executed at Sachsenhausen concentration camp in the spring of 1945.

7   The Christopher Burney Debriefing Reports

There are two. The first was obtained officially from the 'SOE Adviser to the Foreign and Commonwealth Office' in 2002. It is dated 26 April 1945 and titled, simply, 'Interrogation of Lt. Christopher Arthur Geoffrey BURNEY'. Part 1 covers 'Source's Mission' ('source' being Burney of course), 'Take-Off Until Arrest' and 'Arrest and Interrogation'. Part 2 is titled 'Security' and goes over the same ground again, in particular the 'Responsibility for Source's Arrest'. Apparently, this was based on a previous interview with Burney before 26 April and that was based on a paper that Burney had submitted. Part 3 is concerned with 'Source's opinions on People Met in Buchenwald, in particular Martin Perkins, Eugen Kogon and "Turk" [G C Turck] with a list of "Germans who may be of interest as being favourable to the Allies".' The whole report runs to fourteen pages.

The second debriefing report is much shorter. It is available on microfilm in the National Archives, file HS6/567. This 'interrogation' was conducted by C P Whittaker on 13 June 1945, and it supplements the first debriefing by concentrating on 'Source's experiences in France between "Arrival" and "Arrest".'

Also, in the surviving SOE files in the National Archive at Kew is the SOE War Diary: July–September 1942, which mentions Cesar's arrest but nothing else about him, and Buckmaster's 'History of F Section' which has several important pages about the early days of 1941/2 but does not mention Burney. There is a brief account of AUTOGIRO in 1941 but nothing about its collapse in 1942.

Chapter 3: Interrogation and Solitary Confinement

1 This quotation and nearly all others in this chapter come from Christopher Burney's book *Solitary Confinement*, published in 1952 and again in 1961, and from the three versions of his BBC radio talk with the same name given in 1946. Burney was entombed for eighteen months, so we have to rely on his word alone. The only other source is 'Letter from Buchenwald', his 'cri de cœur' written in January 1945. Here, his memories of SOE and Fresnes must reflect his state of mind.

What will become clear, I hope, is why his book became a classic of prison literature. His account of *Solitary Confinement* is perceptive, introspective, enveloping and vividly expressed; even more remarkable for a writer who finished his formal education at sixteen, kicked around for six years, went to war briefly and then was incarcerated for three years without access to books, paper, or pencil.

Several literary figures reviewed *Solitary Confinement* when it first came out. The poet Stephen Spender wrote in *The Spectator*:

> Christopher Burney's book is remarkable not only for the truth with which he describes his experiences which, though particular to him, yet seem deeply significant to others, but also for the attempt of the writer to understand and interpret his experience... As a writer I often feel how difficult it would be to create a fictitious personality as convincing as Mr Burney's self-portrait. As every writer knows, it is more difficult to make the real than the invented seem true. Yet Mr Burney actually achieves this.

The poet Christopher Fry went further. He wrote in his Introduction to *Solitary Confinement*, 'such is the quality of the writing that there are moments when the reader shares these experiences that he has never had'.

Incarcerated in a torture cell at S.S. headquarters or entombed in solitary confinement at Fresnes, Burney was on his own. There are no outside sources one may call on for witness to his suffering, except an S.S. torturer or a prison guard and they were most unlikely to leave a record.

So 'Interrogation and Solitary Confinement' is a chapter in Christopher Burney's words with my arrangement and interpretation.

Chapter 4: Buchenwald – Descent into Hell

1   The Royallieu-Compiègne internment and deportation camp has been preserved as a memorial to the 48,000, mostly political prisoners, who were housed in the former army barracks before being deported to Germany. Burney's train of cattle trucks carried about 1,500 men, well over one hundred in each wagon, with the doors nailed by planks from the outside and the ventilation almost boarded up. The journey lasted three days and nights, following the River Aisne and what is now the N31 road to the town of Soissons and then into Germany. The food ration was a portion of bread and sausage, replenished at one stop over the journey, but hardly any water. The sanitation was one bucket per truck. In January 1944, 6,500 men and women suffered this journey.

2   Primary Sources on Buchenwald Concentration Camp I consulted in writing this chapter:

I *The Buchenwald Report*, translated from the German by David Hackett and published by Westview Press in the USA in 1999, consists mostly of first-hand accounts collected immediately after the liberation in April 1945 by an intelligence team from the Psychological Warfare Division of the U.S. Army. Prisoners were still in camp when they were interviewed, unique in holocaust history, and over one hundred of them contributed 168 reports. These were given to a prisoner committee led by Eugen Kogon, and over the next few weeks they were translated into German, checked for accuracy and annotated with footnotes.

Representatives from the national committees at Buchenwald formed an over-arching body to vet the Main Report that preceded the individual accounts. The West Europeans, including in theory Christopher Burney, though he had already left for home, were chosen to offset the strong influence of the German and Austrian Communists. In fact, the Information Bureau of the Communists in Buchenwald published their own first hand reports but seventy per cent of these were duplicated in Kogon's collection.

Kogan said that the first draft of the 125-page Main Report, a history of Buchenwald with references to the theory of concentration camps, was written by himself and read to the fifteen-member supervising committee in early May. They agreed that it was 'relevant and objective'. To this were added the 150 statements from individual prisoners in the collection of Individual Reports.

That was the genesis of *The Buchenwald Report*, described by a reviewer as 'one of the most momentous documents in holocaust history'. So what happened to it? Extracts from it were used as supporting evidence in the Dachau and Nuremberg Military Tribunals but then the original copies of the manuscript were lost or buried in U.S. Government archives. However, in 1987, the U.S. Army officer who had headed the interrogation team in 1945, Captain Albert Rosenberg, found a duplicate set of carbon copies and gave it to the author David Hackett. The rest is history.

II *The Theory and Practice of Hell*. The main beneficiary of *The Buchenwald Report* was Eugen Kogon because Richard Crossman, later a well-known Labour politician but in 1945 a civilian member of the British Psychological Warfare Division, persuaded him to turn out a German-language book based on the report. This he did, adopting, he said, a tone of 'calm objectivity' and thoroughly reworking the original Report. The result was *Der S.S. Staat*, first published in 1946. In 1950 the first English-language version appeared with the new title, *The Theory and Practice of Hell*. It has been republished many times since, translated into eight languages and sold approaching one million copies. It is regarded as an unsurpassed first-hand account of life in concentration camps, predominantly Buchenwald.

III *Dungeon Democracy.* I have written enough about Christopher Burney's first-hand account of Buchenwald, except to speculate on its relationship with *The Theory and Practice of Hell.* Burney wrote his account in 1945, so he would not have seen *Der S.S. Staat* but he would have known about *The Buchenwald Report.* As a member of the supervising committee, he should have read Kogon's Main Report in 1945 before it was approved. In any event, Burney's concluding part, called 'Curtain', on the liberation of the camp is very similar to Kogon's 'The Dramatic End of the Camp' in the main report. They had been accomplices, of course, so this is to be expected, but it provides weighty evidence against the Communist version that it was the Communist underground in Buchenwald that liberated the camp on its own.

IV *Buchenwald Concentration Camp 1937–1945: A Guide to the Permanent Historical Exhibition*, is a factual and thorough history (at 320 illustrated pages) of Buchenwald. It is a German publication translated into English and published by Wallstein Verlag in 2004. Unlike histories of the camp in the GDR period, which were Communist propaganda (see later), this guide is without bias. It had access to 1,500 documents in order to tell the story as far as possible as it happened.

V www.arolsen-archives.org (The International Centre on Nazi Persecution)

This is a comprehensive on-line archive on the victims and survivors of Nazi persecution. It is fairly simple to operate but a lot easier if you speak German. I found Burney's file and got the details of his registration (see text) but I needed the help of Stefanie Dellemann in the Buchenwald Archive Department to find out more. First there was the question of what work he did in Little Camp and later (see text), so this required locating his *Arbeitseinsatzkarte.* Then, following up the code, there was more information available on-line. This turned out to be an interview Burney gave to the *London Evening Standard* on 18 April 1945, translated into German.

I praise German thoroughness and thank Stefanie and others who helped me in the library and archive for their help.

3   Buchenwald Concentration Camp Today

Big Camp and Little Camp have mostly been raised to the ground, and on the sites of the blocks are innumerable memorials – Block 17, a memorial to the murdered Resistance agents; Block 15, a memorial to Soviet POWs; Block 22, a Jewish memorial; Block 14, a memorial to the Sinta and Roma victims, and so on. But the various chambers of horrors remain; the crematorium and the execution room below with the butcher's hooks just below ceiling level, the two connected by a lift for the transportation of bodies. Next to Commander Koch's riding arena is the stable where Soviet prisoners of war were executed by an ingenious device for shooting in the neck, a model of which has been constructed.

The Disinfection Station and the Effects Depot are now the homes of permanent exhibitions. The aim of 'Buchenwald; Ostracism and Violence' is to show how ordinary citizens of Weimar, and by implication anywhere else in Germany, were gradually converted to, accepting if not following, Nazism, the evils of which have been preserved at Buchenwald. Obedient files of over-twelve-aged school children are shown round by carefully trained guides.

After the war the Soviet Union took over the concentration camp and converted it into Soviet Special Camp No. 2 (1945–50). Here over 28,000, mostly low-level Nazis, were interned without trial or limit of duration and, hard to believe, over 7,000 died from the inhumane conditions. They were buried in mass graves in the beech wood below Little Camp or behind the railway station, only the outline of which remains today. In 1950, when the GDR took over from the Soviet Union, the Special Camp was quickly dissolved and destroyed. *Steles* (steel poles) were stuck in the ground to mark these mass graves, and a huge memorial erected to commemorate the concentration camp. The *National Mahn – und Gedenskatte* is the biggest concentration camp memorial in Germany, and in the early 1990s it was incorporated into the Buchenwald and

Mittelbau-Dora (an adjacent concentration camp) Memorials Foundation which is financed by the Federal Republic and the State of Thuringia.

Visiting Buchenwald in November 2021 was a depressing experience, worsened by a biting cold wind and the presence of the plague of Covid. However, it was mitigated by the staff in the library and archive. They were very helpful in my paper hunt for Christopher Burney (see later). Buchenwald is committed to public education about the evils of Nazism – there are four permanent exhibitions altogether, a Visitor Centre, Young People's Centre, guided tours and film shows – and this endeavour to turn evil into good is the lasting impression I took away. In contrast, my visit to the extermination camp at Auschwitz was overwhelmingly awful so that, like other visitors, I wanted to learn about the complete degradation of humanity and then leave as soon as possible.

Chapter 5: Buchenwald – Living Hell

1　There is a fraternity of researchers about the victims of Buchenwald, and one of them is Pat Vinycomb, the daughter of Stanley Booker. She put me in touch with her father and arranged the interview conducted by his ex-policeman carer. She also guided me to the Arolsen Archives.

2　She then introduced me to the Phil Lamason Trust, chaired by Mike Harold. He was very helpful too, particularly in steering me to the audio interview between Phil Lamason and Warren Barton in 1999 which includes the unforgettable scene (to me) of Lamason being body-shaved by Burney in the Disinfection Station and their whispered conversation.

3　Quoted in *Destination Buchenwald*, Colin Burgess, see below.

4　The gallantry and fame of 'Tommy' Yeo-Thomas
　In 1946 'Tommy' Yeo-Thomas was awarded the George Cross, 'the highest award for non-operational gallantry or gallantry not in the presence of the enemy', equivalent to the Victoria Cross, to add to his two Military Crosses. The French Government awarded him the Legion d'honneur and the Croix de Guerre

with palm. His 1952 biography, *The White Rabbit*, became a huge best seller, selling 50,000 copies in the first six months despite heavy editorialising by its author, Bruce Marshall.

5   Mike Harold passed me down the line to Frederick Martini, son of another of the captured airmen and author of *Betrayed*. He sent me several files of Burney interest, including the witness statement of Balachowsky at the Nuremberg trial of Goering, in which he stated that Luftwaffe cadets were often visiting Hut 50 in Buchenwald. This seems to me a likely explanation of how the letter about the false detention of 168 airmen eventually got to Goering. This file came from the National Archives at Kew, but unfortunately without a full reference number. He also sent me from the National Archives a copy of Burney's reporting of war crimes (see below).

6   Finally, I was encouraged to contact Colin Burgess, author of *Destination Buchenwald*. He was very helpful too and it was from his book that I based my account of the release of the airmen on 19 October 1944.

I am very grateful to the fraternity and hope that I may help them in any relevant way too.

Biographies of Buchenwald survivors with knowledge of Burney:

Bravest of the Brave: The True Story of Wing Commander 'Tommy' Yeo-Thomas, Mark Seaman, Michael O'Mara Books (1997).

Destination Buchenwald, Colin Burgess, Kangaroo Press (1996).

I Would Not Step Back: Squadron Leader Phil Lamason DFC and Bar, Hilary Pedersen, Mention the War Books (2018).

No Banners, The Story of Henry and Albert Newton, Jack Thomas, W.B.H. Allen (1955).

Spirit of Resistance: The Life of SOE Agent Harry Peulevé DSO MC, Nigel Perrin, Pen & Sword (2008).

'The Twins' The SOE's Brothers of Vengeance, Peter Jacobs, History Press (2020).

Chapter 6: Buchenwald – The Last Weeks

1 *The Sunday Times* article, 1 May 1966

The article is headlined 'BURNEY: How he was told of MC', and goes on to quote him as saying that the first time he heard of the award was when he read about it in Foot's book. This is clearly rubbish. The article startled sister Joan who wrote to Christopher for confirmation. He replied in one of his rare letters on 25 August 1966: 'The MC, as you guessed, was a silly mistake by the author. I was put in for it but it was changed for a Beatle' – he means the MBE, of course.

Presumably Burney had known about his award, since it was made in June 1945, twenty years before Foot's book which anyway does not mention it. There is no secret about military honours. The citations are published and listed in open files in the National Archive. Christopher Burney's citation ends, 'It is recommended that he is awarded the Military Cross' and the 'Recommended By' column, next to this, is signed by Colin Gubbins, Major General. In the next column, 'Honour or Reward', is written 'MC', crossed out and replaced by 'MBE', signed by an administrator. If Burney did not see this he was surely told what had happened by Gubbins, Buckmaster or the South Wales Borderers.

More significant in this *Sunday Times* article is the quote from Burney that his Gestapo interrogator 'rattled me by producing a copy of my official SOE identity photo'. This cannot be true. He does not refer to this in either of his detailed debriefings by SOE when he returned, nor in the thorough description of his interrogations in *Solitary Confinement*. Had this happened this would surely have been 'curtains', to use a Burney word. How could he have talked his way out of that? And had the Gestapo got hold of his 'official SOE identity photo', he would surely have created havoc with SOE when he got home?

As I wrote in the text, in one of his debriefings he makes the criticism that SOE gave him a spare identity photo with the words 'for Caesar' on the back, so presumably he did not take this with him. There is no mention that he did take it and that his interrogators produced it in Julia's memoir and Christopher made many criticisms of SOE to her.

2   Liberation from the Outside; Liberation from Within

As this tactful title from the *Guide to the Permanent Exhibition* makes clear, that is how Buchenwald was liberated. On 11 April 1945, the Third U.S. Army defeated S.S. troops in the area around the camp; then S.S. guards in Buchenwald fled from the approaching American tanks; then, when this became clear, the camp resistance opened the almost entirely unguarded camp, prevented chaos from breaking out among the inmates, and rounded up scattered remnants of the S.S. outside.

Under the German Democratic Republic, however, the liberation became a political issue. It began with this statement by the International Camp Committee at its first legal meeting on 12 April 1945: 'The strategy of the German inmates to delay, and not to rise up, proved right... The liberation of twenty-one thousand inmates [was due to] the Allied troops in collaboration with the anti-fascist inmate cadres.' As the Cold War set in, the Communists adopted the point of view that an independent act of self-liberation had been achieved by the inmates. It was even claimed that American troops did not reach the camp until 13 April. The issue of 'liberation' by American troops or 'self-liberation' by the inmates became a political symbol, a matter of political affiliation. Even to talk of 'liberation' meant to reveal anti-Communist sentiments.

The first exhibitions at Buchenwald in the 1950s had an overtly political purpose without any regard for the international composition of the camp. 'The patriotic character of the anti-fascist resistance' meant that the uprising had been conducted by German Communists for a new and better Germany, realised in the shape of the GDR. The non-Communist, Western memory of Buchenwald had no place.

So the historiography of Buchenwald fell into the hands of politicians, and it could be argued that the purpose of the permanent exhibitions now – to show the insidious and barbarous effects of Nazism – has political intent too; but no one should question the rightness of the cause.

Chapter 7: Homecoming

1 Burney's letter re the fate of Macalister and Pickersgill comes from *Unlikely Soldiers* by Jonathan Vance, published by Harper Collins (2008).

2 *Savage Continent: Europe in the Aftermath of World War Two* by Keith Lowe, published by Penguin Viking (2012).

3 War Crimes. More on this in National Archives. File WO 301/103.

4 Christopher Burney kept a file on his BBC correspondence. Also, I am grateful to Jeff Walden of the BBC Written Archives Centre for his research locating the Christopher Burney talks and his interview with Robert Reid for *War Report*. Interestingly, a transcript of this interview is also kept in the Buchenwald library. Once again in my writing, I praise the BBC Written Archives Centre for its efficiency and helpfulness.

5 Julia's memoir has provided most of the information about her wedding and living in America. I have also quoted from her letters and Christopher's letters to Dorothy that are kept by Joan's son-in-law, James MacKenzie.

Chapter 8: The Enduring Evil

1 I consulted two experts about PTSD. Dr Robert Oxlade, a former Consultant Psychiatrist now retired and living in Canada, was retained by the Royal Navy and London Fire Brigade as a consultant on stress. He read Julia's memoir and Christopher Burney's books and, after a Zoom meeting with me, sent me his conclusions. He wrote of *Descent from Ararat:*

> To me, this reads as the thinking of a man troubled by suicidal thoughts, or even considering suicide. The derealisation and depersonalisation [forgetting who he was] are usually attributed to major anxiety. It's an allegory about his mental health, fortitude, and suicidal thoughts. An imagined dialogue between self – who'd forgotten who he was – and a guide (another part of himself), lost with broken ankle on a mountain top, unable to walk unassisted, needing help to get down to the road for help, discussing thoughts about life, and suicide.

And this was Dr Oxdale's general conclusion:

> Based on the information you have sent me, and from what I
> have learned in my professional career, Christopher Burney was
> deeply distressed after his war experiences by Post-traumatic
> Stress Disorder, depressive illness, and later, alcoholism,
> accident proneness, several physical illnesses, sleep apnea and
> or other sleep disorder, and probably additional, unreported to
> me, conditions, such as tuberculosis, and perhaps lung cancer,
> and heart damage or disease. I have described briefly what the
> known (in the sense of reported) conditions were, and how they
> might have impacted on his social and relationship life.

I also consulted Richard Worthing-Davies, a neighbour and
friend, but more important a psycho-therapist specialising in
trauma. He also read Julia's memoir and Burney's books. He
introduced me to *The Body Keeps The Score: Mind, Brain and
Body in the Transformation of Trauma* by Professor Bessel van
der Kolk (Penguin, Books 2015) and pointed out significant
passages that explained Christopher's behaviour, such as the
severe panic attack that afflicted Christopher that Sunday
morning when reading a newspaper. My sincere thanks to both
of them.

2   The correspondence between Julia Burney and Benjamin
    Britten comes from the Britten-Pears Archive, The Red House,
    Aldeburgh.

3   The correspondence between Joan and Christopher in the 1960s
    and '70s was lent to me by Joan's son, the late Andrew Adams.

4   The very revealing study of 'KZ-Syndrome' by the Medical
    Academy in Kraków may be found on-line under that title.

Photographs

I am grateful to the Auguste Favier family for permission to use his
drawings. The copyright is owned by the Favier family.

Also, my thanks to Barry McGlashan for permission to reproduce
his painting, *Cromlins Quarrel*.

PART II

ROGER BURNEY

CONTENTS

CHAPTER 1

THE MAKING
OF A PACIFIST

Leaving School

IT WAS OVERCAST and damp that spring day when the great sprawl of Wellington College was emptying. Two small lorries overloaded with trunks moved cautiously along the back lane in the direction of Crowthorne railway station, and small groups of boys were exiting their college houses and converging on the station. At Picton, the nearest house to the grand façade of the College, a big black Armstrong Siddeley with muddied running boards stood near the entrance, its doors open, a stack of boxes and equipment on the ground. Roger Burney had wheedled his mother Dorothy into picking him up, and certainly the sum of his four years at Wellington otherwise would have been tricky to get home to Hay.

> I couldn't bring even half of all my things home in my trunk, playbox and suitcase. I've got thousands of books (nearly 100!!!) and my medicine ball too. There will be linen to fill up my trunk, so there will be no room for my squash racquet and hockey stick and violin and all my music, of which there is a lot. Also, there will be my eiderdown and rug.

Dorothy, having offered help, now stood by holding a small book and smiling patiently while her beloved youngest stopped his careful arrangements to shake hands with a few friends who would be staying on until the end of the academic year. She glanced at the book before passing it to him: *Letters from A Chinese Official: Being an Eastern View of Western Civilization*, Goldsworthy Lowes Dickinson, was not a name she recognised. There was a deal she didn't know about her son's interests and enthusiasms.

The decision for Roger to leave Wellington after Easter, a week after his eighteenth birthday, had been by mutual agreement. University was five months away. He was restive. For a boy with a reputation for winning ways, there was some concern about his mental state. R.G. Evans, his tutor since the beginning of Michaelmas term, clearly liked him: 'He's a delightful person with a very high sense of duty, very sensitive and a thinker of more than ordinary intensity.' What concerned Roy Evans was the way Roger seemed to run out of steam:

> Towards the end of each term, as he tires, he tends to become neurotic and unbalanced. He becomes antagonistic to all those who have previously been his friends and obsessed with an exaggerated sense of the injustice in the world. His 'escape' lies through pacifism and a scheme whereby he can preserve himself as an instrument of good when the horrors of a new war have passed.[1]

This pacifism first took concrete form when Roger, who had been Deputy Leader of the Wellington Officer Training Corps, resigned before Christmas. Two weeks before Easter, at Evans' instigation, Roger was sent to a consultant neurologist, Douglas McAlpine, in Harley Street. The report of that consultation to Dorothy is now lost, but whatever it contained determined her to seek a second opinion. In early April, she made an appointment for Roger with Dr Margaret Posthuma, a pioneering child psychiatrist with rooms in Harley Street. It would appear the main concern was that Roger's Kitchener scholarship for Cambridge was at stake since he had to be interviewed before final acceptance.[2]

128 Harley Street, London W1
13.04.1937
Dear Mrs Young
I rang Roger up and he came along & we had a short talk on the subject of the Kitchener scholarship. I don't think he is likely to make any mistakes in his interview. I should think he would make a good impression. We have been talking about the importance of a first-rate education plus experience of people & conditions generally before making up one's mind as to just how one is going to set to work to benefit humanity – I think he is realising this gradually but in many ways he is a young adolescent, even younger than his years and intelligence – I'm sure we must take this into account when listening to his views.

I am justified even at this early date in saying I have formed a high opinion of his essential stability and fundamental sanity of outlook. He has such a real integrity and goodness that I am sure he will be able to shed the impractical side of his idealism & be of real value to the world in his own way.

Roger, who had been parked for two weeks in the care of his stepfather's elderly sisters at 78 Onslow Gardens in South Kensington, wrote to his mother that:

Dr P says she doesn't think I should come home this weekend and anyway I think she has written about it. It is really for her to decide. She has been very good about finding out about cheap places I could go to and is altogether very nice and most helpful. We are still delving into my babyhood and will be I expect for some time.

Babyhood it transpired, had less to do with Roger's earliest days, those six years with his entire family in the North-West Frontier of India, and rather more to the return home to boarding school, whilst his parents returned to India. Dr P kept asking him, over and over, to describe his feelings during those early weeks at school, what he thought of, what he dreamed of. Was he upset when his first school closed, and he went to another? She asked him to remember when he was eleven. Daddy and Mummy were back, living near Salisbury. Happy holidays. Christmas, Easter. Not Easter? A point-to-point the first day home. Putting his cold hand in Daddy's warm one. It was icy. But they had laughed, and he was so happy they were all together. Then tea back at Larkhill. A fluffy wool chick hatching out of a tiny egg on top of the Simnel cake... a sudden scrape of chair legs, falling. His father up and falling across the cake and sandwiches... He had gone very white. He was gone... Devastating. Traumatic.

In late April, Roger took a break from Dr Posthuma and went to stay with the Achesons, the family of his dear friend James from Picton: 'I had a glorious weekend in Winchester and Anna says I look as if I have been three weeks by the sea. I certainly feel better and am brown. I also was thankful to discover a new cheap kind of exercise – climbing trees – we did it a lot and it was great fun!'

After returning to London, he attended his scholarship interview.

The Kitchener affair was uneventful – they wanted me to go into the army – but I didn't explode. Not v. nice men but I was v. quiet and so polite you would have taken me for a militarist. They say they will let us know their decision later – so, Mummy, if a letter arrives for me from them, open it!

Working in the East End

With that out of the way, at Margaret Posthuma's suggestion, he turned his attention to finding a short-term placement in one of the East End Settlements, something she felt would open him to experience the reality of everyday life. The settlements had been a late Victorian initiative, a reformist social movement to tackle poverty: through wealthy donors, 'settlement houses' were established in neighbourhood slums where volunteer middle-class 'settlement workers' would live, endeavouring to share knowledge and culture, and provide education and healthcare to improve the lives of the poor. Toynbee Hall in London's Whitechapel was the first. There were strong ties with some Oxford and Cambridge colleges, and students were encouraged to visit and volunteer during university holidays.

So it came about that Roger eventually found a place in Toynbee Hall. By 14 May, he moved into a room there, forsaking the elderly aunts in Onslow Gardens. 'When I left, they gave me £1. Wasn't that terrible! It's quite fun here and interesting.' He worked in the kitchens, accompanied community workers on visits to families in surrounding tenements, many of them Jewish and Irish immigrants. It was only eight months since the Battle of Cable Street, and Toynbee settlement workers were increasingly involved in campaigning against the rise of fascism.

Roger, when he wasn't working, signed up for art classes, a typewriting course, and attended talks staged for local people in the panelled lecture hall. If his mind drifted from the topic, his gaze would be drawn upwards to some remarkable frescoes around him depicting the Arts and Sciences. These were a labour of love returned, painted by Archibald Ziegler, a former Lithuanian refugee, who himself had been a beneficiary of Toynbee Hall's liberal education.

Occasionally, Dorothy would come up from Hay on brief visits, and in between wooed her son with flowers, tickets for concerts – he loved Samuel Coleridge-Taylor's trilogy of cantatas, *The Song of Hiawatha*, put on at the Albert Hall. What was it... Was she making amends? Had he burned his boats with her? Or she with him?

One Sunday he took the Piccadilly line out to the recently opened station at Cockfosters, in search of his first preparatory school, Heddon Court. It was under ten minutes on foot but it had evaporated. Roger stood silent, gazing around. Of that immense building, just one unrecognisable block remained: and the corrugated iron gym, now rusting and derelict. The great concrete road he walked up was a gash across the grounds.

He must have been six when he had first heard the words 'prep school'. In 1926, the Burney family had returned from India, spent a jolly summer with various grandparents, uncles, aunts, and cousins before Joan was sent off to the Royal School in Bath, and he and 'Chucha' came here. Their parents had returned to India on another tour of duty, this time in Dehradun. Roger had cried himself to sleep for most of a month. Slowly he adjusted, made friends, liked certain subjects – and Christopher was there. The school had gardens and woods that they loved; secret dens, playing fields, a bathing pool. All gone. Trees felled; gardens pulled to pieces. He had a moment of darkness: it was ten years ago, yet now suddenly he shook with homesickness for his mother, all over again. He had started to enjoy school then and wrote funny, misspelt accounts of it to 'My Darling Daddy and Mummy', ever so far away.

He walked back slowly along the new road he noticed was called Heddon Court Avenue, 'with 27/6d. villas everywhere'. At the station he looked in the phonebook for the one name he remembered in the neighbourhood: Dr Engleheart. But no one of that name was listed any more. He felt bleak.

Two days later he was in heaven. The Kitchener scholarship was his! One hundred pounds a year for three years. 'Isn't that wonderful? Won't it help!' Most certainly it would: in the late 1930s the annual costs for a student in residence at Cambridge averaged about £270 with £70 up front. The Kitchener scholarship for Roger also meant that going abroad that summer would be feasible. He started investigating ships to Sweden. 'At most it will cost £7/10/– return. But I am trying to get on a cargo boat and might do it for £4...' In between sessions with Dr P, and doing his voluntary work around Whitechapel, he was making progress towards a working holiday through the National Union of Students:

> I heard from Mrs Söderberg and she sent a photo of her husband, Hjalmar. He's a writer. I enclose it and her letter. It ought to be great fun. I have written to her saying I could arrive about the eighth by the *Patricia*, as that is the cheapest by £1.
>
> Last night I woke up with pain from a flea bite, and when I jumped up to search for him I found it was a fat louse. Horrible. I squashed it on the sheet and it was full of blood. I was nearly sick. I've seen all the squalor I need for some time.

Of course, London itself was full of charming distractions. There was *Studio 1* near Oxford Circus which showed esoteric foreign films. Music venues abounded: Roger returned from one of his regular sessions with Dr Posthuma to find an invitation to the Toscanini concert in the Queen's Hall. He got there just in time, and it was wonderful – 'wasn't it sweet of the person who asked me – an usher from college'. He invited Margaret Posthuma to an evening performance at Toynbee Hall by a Jewish male voice choir. And then there were milk bars, the latest places to hang out in the city with friends and drink exotic milk cocktails, though Roger's favourite was grape juice – 'tastes of raisins. Very good. 4d!'

> I'm snowed under with things to do and letters to write before I get home on Thursday week. I shall bring all my luggage home – I'm catching (I hope) the 4.15 or 4.20 train after I see

Dr P at 3. I arrive at Hereford at 8, I think – if you are not there, and I shall not expect you, I shall go on to Hay by the next train.

I don't know if I'm returning here or not but I am closing my account, otherwise I will have to pay for the weekend I am away! ... VBL Longing to see you.

Another last-minute invitation came to Roger on 15 June, when his old Picton chum Michael Patton-Bethune got him a cheap ticket for *Cosi fan Tutti* at Glyndebourne that evening. With a little calculation Roger found 9/– to fund the return train journey. A meeting at the opera would significantly change his life, as he later revealed to his mother.

Michael P-B has a great friend called Peter Pears I've heard so much about. At last, I've met him... the most lovely person, charming and so young, 26, very musical, sings for a living in Glyndebourne opera and with the English Singers. Really good. I sort of remember hearing him sing in concerts at Wellington last year. He's left wing, not fanatical, and he is going to share a flat with Benjamin Britten here in London. I don't remember meeting someone so strikingly compatible with my feelings – you'd like him so much I think. Anyway, I'm in for a lot of enlightenment now, because he knows all the great left-wing writers alive: T S Eliot, W H Auden, Stephen Spender, Christopher Isherwood, and so on and so on, & B Britten is one of the greatest composers and is only 24. I cannot ever really see myself as left wing, but contact with its better elements would give my Tory education a better shine.

Memories of Childhood

That Midsummer's Eve, Dorothy drove Roger and his sister along the Wye to Kenchester. It was time to let memories loose. They passed The Weir, the great rambling house on the river where the Burney grandparents, Arthur and Annetta, had raised their children and lived off and on with an extravagant

223

range of relatives right up to the 1920s. Dorothy slowed and slid her window open. Roger had no recollection of it: he had been a baby the last time Mummy and Daddy had taken them there. Joan had memories of it, of her grandparents, aunts, cousins. Dorothy took a small album from the door pocket and passed it to Jo. There were photographs of frilly little cousins in sunhats; huge perambulators – 'that's you, Roger!' – and Christopher, looking very Christopher, with a little squinty smile under his hat.

Dorothy drove on, turning left off the Hereford Road at a fingerpost marked Kenchester, up a rutted lane, passing a cluster of redbrick houses surrounded by fields. Turning left they parked before an ancient stone church in a neat churchyard. She got out and unstrapped the luggage rack. 'Come on!' She handed Roger a box of tools and Jo a hamper. They paused to read the legend under the roof of the lychgate:

To the Glory of God and in Loving Memory of
Arthur George Burney of The Weir in this parish, who passed
over Jan 20th, 1924, aged 75
and of his son Geoffrey Asteley who fell at the Battle of the
Somme, July 7th, 1916, aged 37

To the north of the church, in a shady place, overgrown, the Burney plot: so much family history buried in so few words. Lt Col Arthur Edward Cave (Jack) Burney DSO, MC, RA. Roger stood staring at the grave. Daddy. Six years. Mummy had her back to him, taking a long time to place a posy of pink and white rambling roses by the cross. She bowed her head. His thoughts dissolved. He was astonished to find tears running down his cheeks. Then he sensed Jo's eyes on him. He wiped his wrist across his face and turned away, bending to take garden shears from the box. When he straightened up Dorothy had moved to another grave, wetting the lichen, and rubbing it off with a flat piece of wood. He tilted his head sideways. Annetta Forbes Burney... Grandma.

Dorothy's mother-in-law. She had died when he was a very small boy in India.

They worked until the sun grew hot, then went to sit in the shadow of the church porch. Dorothy had brought a small picnic and a flask of lemonade. Roger raised his head and looked at her. 'Mummy, why did you marry Wilf?'

In the days following, Dorothy brought down an old leather suitcase not touched since she moved into Oakfield and wiped away the dust. Albums of photographs, many of them taken when the family were in India. The Raj bungalow where they had lived at 2 Peshawar Road, Rawalpindi. The pets, dogs and horses, more likely to be named than the people. The Battery. 'Us with Mr Martin [tutor], Daddy, General Hardie and Mummy.' 'Us in a mule cart'. 'Chucha' with a hockey stick. Polo matches and parades in Abbottabad. Visiting Dehradun. Villagers threshing dal. Running wild in Thandiana in the hot season. Then suddenly, the photographs are of English houses in 1927, of uncles, aunts, maids, the family warmly dressed for a country excursion. Daddy in a tweed shooting suit. 'Was that the day,' Roger hesitated, 'Daddy...' It turned out it wasn't. They sat quiet for a time on the morning room floor amid the debris. Joan spoke softly: 'You remember Roger, we all got back home to Larkhill Camp at the end of term. It was the first day of the holidays. We went to that point-to-point on the first of April.' The unspoken ending was that later that day, their beloved father had died. Right there, right then.

Roger reached for another album, but it was a sketchbook. He turned the pages, examining the fine pencil detail of an old forge, a chapel, a village climbing up a hillside from a shore, the study of a door at the corner of a house and an alleyway, a fortress overlooking the sea. Bormes-les-Mimosas. Joan and Roger looked enquiringly at their mother. Her face at that moment was... Roger thought afterwards 'luminescent'. Yes, she said, your father and I were there on holiday before Joan arrived. Before the war.

CHAPTER 2

CAMBRIDGE ON THE BRINK OF WAR

'Finding his feet'

ROGER WAS OF serious intent, though he had the capacity to hide it behind an amiable relaxed demeanour. Peterhouse, as befits the oldest college, had a considered and orthodox approach to learning that suited him. Cambridge itself did not. Nothing that he had experienced recently in London, nor on his Swedish working summer, prepared him for the alien world he would now have to negotiate. Some of his best friends from Wellington, those with whom he had been closest, whether in putting on plays, singing in the choir, playing music, debating, had gone elsewhere, up to Oxford, one deferring his place to go travelling, or, in one instance, going straight into business.

In common with the Freshers of today, he had to set out to find new friends, whether in his chosen field of study, European History, or among the plethora of societies and activities to engage his extra-curricular enthusiasms. Above all, in the late 1930s, fewer than twenty-five per cent of students at Cambridge were women and Peterhouse was an all-male college.

My darling Mummy,

There is an acting society, the ADC, but it is so expensive
– two guineas entrance and one guinea a term after, which
is a lot. Too much to risk in case I didn't like it. The majority
of societies here are fanatical politically or religiously. The
only cultural societies are the Art, the CUM and the Marlowe
– which only reads plays. The Art Society is worth exploring.
I know the members are mostly surrealists, but some will not
be – anyway, I can but try, and in that case, without great
expense. The majority of people here are grim: and Michael
Patton-Bethune says it is the same at Oxford. Conversations
concern wine and women almost entirely or those football
pools and sailing. And to think this is the cream of England.
Well, well, poor old England. I went to a thing called a
Footlights Smoking Concert – it was rather obscene – but
afterwards I and Wick Meyer went out into the streets, and
everywhere were drunk people. Some of them were certainly
very funny. If you told them, as we did, that they had no
trousers on, they believed you and altogether we had a most
amusing evening, but it wasn't really very funny. Still, it all
amuses me and then depresses me. I am not feeling desperate.
I only begin to look forward more and more to the day when I
shall find a real friend here. I wish Michael P-B were here.

Your lovingest Rog

In fact, it was a given that Roger would join the Cambridge
University Music Society, and within a short time was singing
bass in choral works. He eagerly invited his mother Dorothy,
and extended the invitation to his erstwhile psychiatrist Dr
Posthuma, for his first public performance in King's College
Chapel towards the end of November. It was a Recital of
Unaccompanied Motets, under the direction of Boris Ord.
Roger was in fine form to entertain them to tea in his rooms
in the Old Court at Peterhouse beforehand, and booked a late
supper table, glad they were staying overnight, long enough to
have a really good time together.

Roger had left Wellington College with a reputation for sensitivity and religiosity, an interest in people rather than things, and as one with strong views about the rights of the individual. Now at Peterhouse, he declared himself a conscientious objector. He floundered through much of his first term, despite studying hard and being fortunate in having some of the most celebrated historians of their day as lecturers and professors. His tutor was Bertrand Hallward – referred to in student circles as 'the Greek God', who, if he saw any of his students struggling mentally, prescribed outdoor physical activity. In Hallward's own case, that extended to a plunge in the River Cam most days.

Soon Roger was doing athletics at Jenner's running track and enthusiastically trying to better his high jump style under the direction of the coach. That cheered him up, though he was not yet jumping high. However, he was displeased with the company there: 'the kind of people who go to Jenners are very dull,' he reported, 'I'm trying to find a new ground where friends are more likely'.

It would seem that during this autumnal restlessness of Roger's, Hallward kept in touch with his former tutor at Wellington, Roy Evans, possibly because Evans had already written expressing his concern about Roger's 'tendency to tire and become neurotic towards the end of term'. The result was a warm invitation for Roger to spend a long weekend with the Evans family at Wellington at the beginning of December, an invitation Roger delightedly accepted.

There is no record of what transpired, yet it is clear that the weekend was beneficial and that the Lent term found him in a more positive frame of mind, something his professors remarked on: '… you took so long to find your feet, your real work now is only two months' old…'

Lent was also noteworthy for increasing activity in the Madrigals Society, where he was joined by three other Old Wellingtonians, Alastair Royalton Kisch, Jim Preedy and

Jim Pearson. The other joys to him were regular visits to the Cambridge Arts Theatre with its varied programme of offerings, and weekly classes at the Art Society where he found encouragement for his efforts painting landscapes, several of them begun as sketches of Hay and the riverine beauty of the Wye Valley during vacations home at Oakfield.

From then the only way was up and he finished his first year with a creditable body of work in every branch of History, and was moderately pleased to be told that if he maintained his form that he would be 'well up to the Peterhouse standards in History'. He was in very good form singing madrigals on the River Cam for the May Week celebrations.

That summer he was at home with Dorothy and the ageing Wilf, the stepfather to whom he now seemed reconciled, his older sister Jo, and the dog. Was Christopher there? Roger does not mention him. The old house was spacious enough, leading down to Hay in one direction and out to the River Wye, or up to the commons and into the Black Mountains in others. For Roger, the long vacation of 1938 was one of relative contentment.

Somehow, I find the atmosphere of this house surprisingly pleasant. For one thing, there are flowers and fields outside, not Cambridge streets. And I have a great affinity for bonds and Earth in general. Also, it is odd here if you are interrupted in what you are doing, while in Cambridge it is altogether odd if you are not. There is a good peace here and everything is miles away, and even if certain suburban attitudes of the family seem intruding, and quite consciously out of place, I think the people who say agriculture is the only real and lasting basis for any civilisation are right: though I can't be certain that isn't just a way of saying I cannot adapt myself to machinery and towns and so on. Society should be a human harmony, but how can you establish any harmony with a ferris concrete building or vast concrete roads and pavements. Is this the divine interval between the bareness of boyhood and the stuffiness of age that E M Forster talks of?

I'm going to a very upright lunch tomorrow to be 'matched off' with a damsel called Frisby. They won't expect my hair to be the length it is – I'll be tidy and, if I get a chance, gracious.

Whether Roger failed to have a haircut or simply didn't 'match' the lovely Frisby, nothing further was mentioned of the occasion.

To Fight or Not to Fight?

When he returned to his rooms in Old Court at Peterhouse at the start of October 1938, the Munich Agreement had just been signed and Cambridge was full of foreboding: news began to trickle through that German troops had already occupied parts of the Sudetenland. As a result of the crisis, the start of lectures was postponed. Members of the university were encouraged to place their qualifications and experience on the record and plans were drawn up for an emergency. Many colleges were equipping themselves with firefighting equipment and instructing students in fire fighting and ARP, Air Raid Precaution drills. Roger applied formally for exemption from military service as a conscientious objector.

He was full of plans for a reunion with his three closest friends, James, Peter, and Mike. The three had shared his deep love of drama and music at Wellington College, and most significantly, they had collectively espoused pacifism. Curiously, abhorrence of war had never come up as a subject in the Wellington Debating Society, of which they had been active members, but they had been strongly influenced by a debate in the Oxford Union in 1933: 'This House would not in any circumstances fight for King and Country', which made shocked headlines at the time and outraged Churchill. The Master of Wellington throughout Roger's time had been Frederick B Malim: in many ways rigorously 'old school', he held remarkably liberal views and was quite clear that boys who attended Wellington should not be regarded automatically as 'the future army'. That so many OWs did enter the army had more to do with following in father's footsteps. Not Roger. Now temporarily exempted from military service, he was keen to discover his friends' current thoughts. James Acheson, who had been outspokenly against armaments and uniforms, had spent a year in India, where his father was a colonial administrator, before entering Christ Church, Oxford. Peter McClintock, who at school had argued fiercely against the idea of war, had opted for a career in the City and lived with his family in Belgravia. Michael Patton-Bethune, fired by a strain of divine discontent and addicted to driving fast cars, was in his second year at Exeter College, Oxford; he failed to appear.

Roger reported to Dorothy:

> Weekends seem to be more furious socially than weeks and this one has been especially. Peter and James came to stay on Saturday night. Michael P-B was to have come but he couldn't miss an engagement he'd fixed. I haven't seen James for almost a year! But he's just the same and so is Peter. We all are really, fundamentally. We have only just acquired new knowledge.

Friendship with Peter Pears

Later that month, Roger had a first-class excuse for luring Michael Patton-Bethune over to Cambridge: the Arts Theatre was staging the premiere of a new Isherwood/Auden anti-war collaboration, *On the Frontier: A Melodrama*, and Peter Pears was to sing in it. Roger felt that as a play, it didn't work, though he went a second time and preferred that 'almost to seventy-six per cent'. But he had arranged a late supper for them and, when Mike still did not put in an appearance, Roger listened to Peter Pears describing his frustration about Patton-Bethune, a relationship going nowhere. Did it stem from the fact that

Pears and Benjamin Britten had become close after the death of a mutual friend? That they were about to start sharing a flat together? Roger and Peter Pears continued their analysis of Michael's strange aloofness next morning on a walk along the river, and then to talk earnestly about the threat of war; about pacifism, the Quakers, and the Peace Pledge Union... Soon Peter turned to describing the vibrant arts scene he had encountered in New York while he had been on tour with the New English Singers two years earlier. By the time Peter left to return to London, Roger's head was buzzing with new ideas, and the possibility of continuing his studies in some form after Cambridge, in the United States.

In his second year, Roger became so much more involved in the social round, and it told on his pocket. Early in Michaelmas term he had been profligate with his budget: he had hired his own piano and often of an evening it engendered impromptu singing parties and strong friendships: Peter Godden, for one, thought Roger the best friend imaginable.[1] Roger was very sociable, issuing many invitations to tea – an investment, he felt, as he got more and more reciprocal invitations to lunch, and indeed to stay with family of his new friends at weekends. Money, and the value of things worried him: the beautiful seven guinea grey-blue overcoat he had had tailored by Rimmel & Allsop in London only eighteen months earlier was beginning to wear at the elbows, and he was dejected to find the lining starting to fray – 'they should have guessed that I, at Cambridge, would wear it very hard. I shall have to get it repaired. Anyway, I have learned something.' He explored the idea of getting a job in the Christmas holidays: he placed an advertisement in the *Times* and was annoyed that he was not permitted to just say 'do anything, go anywhere', but had to add the word 'work' so that it cost him a full fifteen shillings, but reasoned that if he got any useful answers then it would have been worth it. Someone in Mayfair responded, but that fell through. Professor Hutton in Cambridge was seeking a minder for his three children for the whole of the Christmas vacation but did not offer any accommodation with the job. He had one firm offer of a job 'au pair' at the Dufour College in Glasgow. He thought it not very tempting; he reasoned he would have earned nothing and would have been 'so weary after a week'. He complained to friends that he couldn't manage the capitalist system very well at all.

An inveterate letter writer, Roger would spend hours dashing off letters to friends, to Dorothy, occasionally to his sister Jo, even more occasionally to his brother Christopher, in much the same way that emails and texts are exchanged today. It is extraordinary to see how last-minute arrangements could be made, in the confidence that the mail would arrive next day and be answered immediately.

His enthusiasm for his historical studies was clear in letters to Dorothy:

> ... it's terrible to be really interested but to have to break up work for lunches and teas and things. I have taken a good deal of exercise lately – yesterday, Water Polo, a little time ago Squash, and lots of tree climbing. More and more people are doing it now and soon there won't be a vacant spinney for miles around the Town.
>
> I must stop now and get to work on a late essay, I've only half-written that and there is a second I haven't yet thought out... Everything is so rushed – I feel next term must be less intense. It certainly couldn't be more. It's all very good for me I expect, to meet such crowds of people and all very different.

He also confessed to Dorothy to being dissatisfied with some aspects of university life. When his first-year tutor, 'the Greek god' Bertrand Hallward and his wife invited him to a dance at the end of November, he decided not to go:

> Such a horrid collection of people are going; all the foulest undergraduates from this college, with the most unpleasant

females from Girton and Newnham. I've been pining all this week to come across some pleasant ordinary female to relieve rather a mass of male life, but it's no good, they are all either silly or intellectual and neither mood becomes a woman. I wish Peggy Sheppard was here still.

One prospect brightened Roger's immediate future. He had become friends with a fellow student of Peterhouse called Michael Brockway. They were developing their sketching and painting techniques at Art Society sessions and had spent a few days the previous summer roaming the Black Mountains, doing just that from home at Oakfield. Now Roger was urged to spend the night of 5 December with Michael and his mother to discuss a skiing holiday. A far cry from his threadbare student existence.

Rolls Royces, Bentleys, peeping from enormous garages – swimming pools, squash courts – Scotch Gardens. Dower Houses and great log fires you warm by as tall as yourself. Elegant neighbours, the Sidney Webbs and the Dolmetseches quite close – a great fairyland of extravagances.

[The Brockways] are people of considerable means and of an interesting circle of people and being so charming themselves it was impossible to refuse [to go skiing]. Of course, now I am faced with the grey prospect of vast expenses amounting to more than what I would spend on my own in France during five or six weeks. All the same I do think it will be worthwhile and I am certain I shall enjoy it. But I must most firmly search for some job in the Easter break. By then my creditors will surely be in tears over my silence.

More concerning was the situation at home in Hay. Wilf was frail, Dorothy was acting nurse, giving him daily injections, milking two cows, separating the cream, churning butter, feeding hens, and now suddenly her domestic staff were deserting that big house. She did not complain but hinted in letters that she was suffering dizzy spells and headaches.

Roger wrote immediately to tell his mother of his impending return:

> I will not be extra trouble I assure you – I may even be able to lighten what you have to do without me. I am sorry you are in such a way. I've done quite a good painting – rough – of a sketch I did of Hay some time ago. If it's dry and finished, I'll bring it home.

Peter Pears had sent Roger a copy of André Maurois' *Three Letters on the English* and a china cat, enclosing his new address with Britten at 67 Hallam Street and a pressing invitation to come and stay on his way home to Hay at the end of term.

> My dear Peter,
> In great haste I write to thank you very much for your invitation for Monday and Tuesday nights. If you are certain that will mean no special trouble for you, I would like to come very much. About lunch on Tuesday: I would very much like to meet both your cousin and the infamous pop.
> There is terrific chaos at my home… my stepfather ill, my mother worn out, my sister (almost certainly) nagging, no maids and worst of all a worthless son inviting enormous expense in Switzerland.
> I am looking forward to Monday.
> Love Roger[2]

Term ended in a discussion with his second-year tutor, Brian Wormald, a polished lecturer on seventeenth-century English History and a young don noted for questioning his own interpretations of history. Not much older than Roger himself, the two had hit it off and Wormald's quiet analysis of Roger's body of term work, delivered through ceaseless clouds of nicotine, was encouraging. As he packed up to leave

Old Court, Roger dashed off a note to Dorothy that exuded pleasure:

> How I'll long to be back here. Work is only really possible
> here. I've got to develop my style now – Brian says I am better
> and better but for that. You have one child with a curiously
> inventive mind in some directions which seems to please some
> people here.

By Wednesday, Roger had returned by train to Hay, his mind in an exhausted whirl. His time with Peter and Benjamin had been stimulating beyond belief and the idea of turning around and going straight out to a social event with his family that evening was too much. Instead, he stayed in his room, studying a canvas he had begun before leaving Cambridge at the end of term: it was a landscape, quite promising, he thought, begun as an experiment with colour. He observed 'a curious twist of houses on a hill and trees and a chimney' – another landscape of Hay perhaps?

He began writing his thanks to Peter and Ben, expressing his pleasure in their company:

> I think you do know how much I enjoyed it and how
> remarkably it has affected me – the more I live the more I feel
> immature, and the more I want to live. I find myself now with
> three main things I'm really interested in: music, painting and
> writing.
>
> Your kind of life appeals to me more than anything. I can
> imagine that far more than a painter's or a writer's life. It
> holds everything I value in one hand – and only my own over-
> intimate knowledge of my own inadequacy stops me from
> setting out at once on your kind of road.
>
> Anyway, it's no good to dally altogether. I must do what I
> can to learn with my violin – I understand so little about the
> theory of music. Are there books which can help me over that?
> Are [Sir Donald] Tovey's *Musical Analyses* good? I do hope

this interest in music is deep. I hope I shall not get back from Switzerland believing dancing to be the only valuable art – but I hardly think that's likely – it's all a contest between these three now I'm sure – and although I'm nervous, I hope music wins.

Clearly, while Roger was with Peter Pears (and Benjamin Britten) in London, the vexed question of why their mutual friend Michael Patton-Bethune had broken off responding to either of them came up. Several times in their subsequent exchange of letters, the anguish surfaces.

Dear Peter, I wish I could help you about Michael. If ever there is anything you would like me to do, please ask me, and write as much as you like about it when you are worried, and I shall always answer. I really do understand what you feel because only lately I've been tormented by just the same brutality and heartlessness. I cannot believe that Michael's present view of feelings will live very long.

Life here is very bleak. Everyone on the verge of illnesses (various). I cannot invite the one pleasant person in the neighbourhood here because we have no maids, and my offers of work are laughed at – it is rather depressing at times. I shall indeed be glad to be away from it all with people who are alive and at least a bit progressive... I've done another painting. Quite a large one and reasonably pleasing I think, but I can't really understand it enough. I understand sheer colour and sheer design but not both together properly. I must be quick, or I shall miss the post tonight. Floods everywhere here and an aeroplane crashed a mile away from here down in the valley on a hump. It's been taken away now but I could see it from here. The man half blind I'm afraid.

Love to you and Benjamin.

From Roger.

If Hay in winter felt bleak, Switzerland provided the antidote. In the 1930s, Klosters was the go-to ski resort for old monied families. With some of the world's earliest ski lifts in operation, it was an exhilarating experience for those who could stay upright to discover downhill skiing. After an early panic about what to wear, Roger threw himself into the business of mastering elementary braking, the snow plough, pole planting and stem christies at the expense in the first few days of a painfully sprained right thumb, which necessitated a visit to the doctor, and a few bruises. Soon he was managing the occasional adrenalin charged run down through the woods. He loved it all. Klosters was a spartan alpine village lying close under the icy spell of the great Silvretta glacier; horse-drawn sleighs transported baggage from the station; smells of woodsmoke and hay and livestock wintered indoors. Even the top place to stay, the seventy-year-old Hotel Silvretta, was family-run and unpretentious.

However, there were the usual impoverished student worries. Roger had underestimated what he needed to wear, the penetrating cold and the weight of snow on the heavy woollen trousers Peter Pears had insisted he borrow – 'your trousers are much admired here'. Eventually Roger was forced to buy proper ski pants. 'So now I've got the smartest trousers imaginable – ones which all the best skiers wear! I have a new reputation to live up to having given up yours.'

Doubts About Sex
He had another concern, which he confided in correspondence with Peter Pears:

> This place is rather odd – life is terribly bourgeois and love making looks boring and rather one-sided. I have seen nobody who really looks interesting for a long while. The most lovely girl is here with her brother who I know but she's a model for the front page of *Vogue* and her face is well shaded with blue – it's a shame because stripped of all her daubing and frills she'd be very like the only kind of person (girl) I could

feel much for. This is an embarrassing abnormality, I find. It doesn't worry me a bit not feeling like everyone else but to feel so mightily and un-ideally attracted to my own kind rather annoys me. I can't decide whether it should. When I was idealistic about it, it was as good as any kind could be, and as desirable, and I can't say anyone's criticisms worried me – but as I am now, I feel all wrong. I'm unhappy and undecided over that at present and it's especially disturbing because there's someone here who causes all this reflection and I'm afraid some definite result will be forced on me soon. But still the difficulty of deciding on that is covered during the daytime by the excitement of skiing.

Just after New Year 1939, Roger had further thoughts to share with Peter on the issue:

I'm waiting for another of these incessant drinking evenings. They really are without end and so upsetting because I cannot arouse a scrap of delight in them. Only ten more days now left. It has never been really natural, and I shall be glad to be at Cambridge again with people I appreciate and care for more. My rather ludicrous problem seems to be dissolving now. I had felt so sure that I could love in an ideal fashion and that was just a silly reaction. I'm sorry to have landed you with my troubles so suddenly.

There is a sense of unfinished business in his words, carried over from those many years in ninety-nine per cent male company in boarding school: that febrile adolescent atmosphere, the company of one or two openly gay masters, the usual crushes and pashes that tend to accompany male development in cloistered public schools. Peter Pears, by expressing his own anxieties and concerns over his increasingly fraught relationship with Michael Patton-Bethune, sexual or not, had offered Roger an opportunity to share his own doubts and confusion about his sexual inclinations.

In his next letter Roger raised again a discussion with Peter and Ben about the prospect of the three of them travelling in Scandinavia the following Easter: 'I do hope Sweden or Norway will materialise because I've written to my Baroness in Göteborg and have said I hope to see her soon – I forget whether she is interested in Music but no doubt she will be.' Another plan under discussion involved Britten coming to rehearse the CUMS Madrigals group. 'Please make sure that Ben doesn't answer my letter – I cannot book the rooms until next term – I know quite well how busy he is – I only write now to stake an early claim on him, and, if you will be there too then, on you too.'

Roger returned to Cambridge at the beginning of the Lent term to find a letter from Ben saying he would come to hold the first class three days later. He responded hurriedly, saying he was booking rooms and a space to rehearse and, so far, had six voices for the classes.

Peter and Ben invited him to join them on 17 January in their London flat for their farewell party for Christopher Isherwood and W H Auden, on the eve of departure for the United States. Roger's debts had rocketed: he couldn't buy yet another train ticket to London. Besides, the singing class was to be two days later, and he was nursing a sore throat.

He buckled down to having the 'quiet term' he had promised himself, submitted his essays on time and enjoyed singing in the CUMS and experimenting with landscapes. Any optimism he had nursed for an escapist Easter in Scandinavia with Pears and Britten evaporated. Encouraged by Auden to join him in North America, they had started planning a professional tour to Canada and the USA soon after Easter that might last for months.

Roger returned that Easter to Oakfield in a melancholy frame of mind to find his mother overwrought. Wilf, frailer than ever, and Dorothy, carrying the burden of the house and gardens, was suffering from high blood pressure and complained her knees were giving her hell. The issue of domestic help had been resolved by the increasing flow of refugees out of Europe. Roger overheard Lotte, the new Austrian housemaid, telling Emeney, the Czech parlour maid she thought he would do for her. 'Do for her!' he snorted to his sister, 'what fun by Jove. I really think I hardly would.'

Roger spent as much time out of the house as possible, roaming the hills with his sketchbook, or with Jo and her Labrador. Jo told him about a rich young man living nearby who was known to be queer: 'absolutely devoted', she told him, to an Italian – much younger than he was – and living almost naked. Roger received this news gleefully and shared it with Peter Pears:

> I was delighted to hear about Randolph Trafford and the Italian boy; I never knew that would happen in Herefordshire. Surely an example for me to follow. This bed business is bad. Here I am getting old, and nothing done. Next term I'll see to it. I've got too much to get past in Roger.
>
> Then I ended a painting. I thought it was good and perhaps will tomorrow again, but the *Pathétique Symphony* ended a few minutes ago and I liked it so much; I ought to cry a good deal more often. I feel so much better. You see, I've done a smattering of work and have enjoyed it lately and it seems to have justified my feeling of liberation now. Why can I do more with painting than with music? Hell. I wish I was more musical or something or I could employ myself in more music.

The main topic of conversation around the dinner table that Easter was the increasing threat of war: the news out of Europe was not good. Christopher rarely put in an appearance. At Oakfield preparations were in hand to ensure adequate stores were laid in should the worst happen. Dorothy coerced Roger and Jo to go with her to a poultry farm up-country and they returned with eighty dozen eggs to be preserved:

… laid by chickens which were in boxes all sloping floors and
when they laid their eggs they rolled out into a basket – and
there they sat for a whole year without moving – poor devils,
it seems wicked – they're only hens of course but I'm just the
same – no room to move. No eggs laid either, unfortunately
– not my sex at fault but just cooped up. Why have I been
lucky enough to realise it. I haven't escaped, of course not, but
I realise it. This country is a very stubborn, silly place. Why
can't I just get away from it all to declare my feelings, not love
but just everything. Just ordinary delight even.

Roger was nothing if not forthright. He could express his
innermost feelings on paper: and his feelings swung from
angst to teasing self-mockery. 'Now I'm broken down – tired
– headachy – fed up – literally.' He weighed himself naked on
the bathroom scales.

Everyone ought to be naked in the whole world for a whole
day (and night). It would be terrific/ Couldn't we start a
campaign. Would Keynes finance it? Would you [Peter] help?
A sort of armistice day and you could give concerts in aid of it
& Ben could compose a Naked Day song or a Naked Concerto
for two violins. My mother says she likes the name Bohemia.
I've had enough. I must go to bed. They're packing eggs.

CHAPTER 3

THE UNMAKING OF A PACIFIST

1939: Preparing for War

ROGER'S EASTER LETTER to Peter and Ben ended with, 'Let me know when you are coming'. Were they hoping to meet his family at Oakfield? If so, the visit never took place.

On 29 April, Pears and Britten embarked from Tilbury on the Cunard liner *Ausonia* for Quebec and Montreal. Roger wasn't there to wave them off. He was back in Cambridge. It was a time of some significance: choral rehearsals were taking up more and more time. They would sing at the May Ball. The Joint Recruiting Board was out and about, assigning undergraduates to duties in the Forces: Roger needed to renew his temporary exemption from military service.

He made concerted efforts to get the gang of four OW friends together to plan a summer escape. Peter McClintock alone responded and spent a weekend with Roger in June. He explained that though he remained utterly opposed to war, he felt that if the time came, he would join the Air Force. Roger was dismayed. James, meanwhile, said he was enjoying 'playing with aeroplanes' and was going to spend the summer putting in the flying hours needed to gain his pilot's licence.

And Michael? So passionately pacifist? Michael Patton-Bethune had been in the Oxford University Air Squadron all along and had just signed up to join the RAF at the end of his second year.

The summer of 1939 opened into a void. Would it be better to be alone, in Spain? Portugal? France? A third-year medical student called Colin suggested Roger should drive with him to Palestine in his car and then bring it back and keep it if it still worked. In the end, he went to western Finland, Lake Hirsjarvi, whether alone or with friends there is little trace other than that he was writing long letters: Peter McClintock, by then in pilot training with the Auxiliary Air Force in East Anglia, sent him a delighted postcard in response.

Reality set in fast, propelling Roger back from Finnish waters to Wales two days after Hitler invaded Poland, and on the day Britain and France declared war on Germany. He found his maiden Great-Aunt Emily [Burney] from Putney, newly installed at Oakfield, more confused than he remembered her. Dorothy had acquired her third Jewish refugee, Hermine Wagner, to help with the cooking for her growing household. Roger's post contained two pieces of news: James, his dear friend, had lost no time dropping his studies to join the RAF. Michael P-B had followed. Both were now at Flying School, bound up to serve the cause of war.

Roger went up to London, offering his assistance to the Society of Friends and to the International Red Cross, training in first aid and working as a stretcher bearer with the Joint War Organisation. He was keen to join a volunteer ambulance unit but those that existed then were fully staffed. With the capital experiencing a watchful calm, he prepared to return to Cambridge and complete his studies.

He found Peterhouse transformed. His early expressed wish for 'pleasant and ordinary females to relieve rather a mass of male life' had been granted unexpectedly. The governing body of the college had agreed to host 120 full-time women students and seventy-five male students from the London School of Economics, at a charge of three guineas a week for board residence. LSE academic staff, men and women, were to have high table privileges. Adjacent to Peterhouse on Trumpington Street, Grove Lodge was rented to provide LSE common rooms, a library and facilities for classes, and there was to be some combined teaching with Cambridge University.

Did this have much impact on Roger socially? Hard to say. The masculine culture was undoubtedly diluted. The tradition of afternoon tea and sherry parties dwindled [butter and sugar were rationed from the beginning of the following term]. His block in Old Court had been given over to LSE members and so he retreated to 11 Tennis Court Road, a terraced house where Mrs S Gadsby reserved rooms for Peterhouse students and provided 'bed and board'. While he still had to show up for formal nights in Hall, he seems to have enjoyed the low-key atmosphere of Mrs Gadsby's home and willingly helped his landlady with domestic chores. 'My Mr Burney was so thoughtful, good and kind. He made our home so happy.' She clearly relished student company and he was welcome to entertain friends at weekends, filling the house with laughter and singing. But there was an increasingly dark side to life too, when Roger wasn't labouring over a history essay upstairs in his room or researching in the library. On the very day war with Germany had been declared, a U-boat had torpedoed and sunk the British passenger liner *Athenia*, en route from Belfast to Montreal. No warning. Many lives lost, including Jewish refugees. For all his conscientious objection, Roger was anguished and enraged. It was a subject of much earnest debate throughout Michaelmas term, and it weighed heavily, for in November, he was called finally before the tribunal to determine his standing.

'War is against the Spirit of our Lord'

His submission was unambiguous:

> War is against the spirit and teaching of our Lord; and to prepare to fight evil with Force is an inadequate recognition of the immaturity of man's Spirit which was revealed by our Lord. War is part only of a diseased society, and its disease may only be overcome by digging down to the moral and spiritual foundations of human existence and by reviving the moral ideas that govern the true social body. Upon this basis I submit my refusal to join any of the military Forces for ensuring the conduct of war.

When he stood for examination before the Local Tribunal on 15 November, it was noted on the record that Roger planned to extend his studies at an American university; that he was C of E and had been attending Society of Friends' meetings; that he rejected the possibility of joining the Royal Army Medical Corps on the grounds that it was part of the machinery of war, but was willing to undertake educational or social work, having done some at Toynbee Hall. Nor would he object to civilian ARP work. Three days later the morning post brought confirmation that he, Roger J G Burney, had been added without conditions to the Register of Conscientious Objectors.

The patriotic fervour that had engulfed Cambridge at the outbreak of the First World War was not to be repeated. Memories of that conflict were too recent, too terrible. The recruitment of students organised by the military authorities was undertaken in a much more respectful, considered way. Roger was not censured for his position. And yet... having attained exemption, he began at once to question it. As he had written in a separate context seven months earlier: 'I've got too much to get past in Roger.'

Christmas at Oakfield that year was a different matter.

He sensed unspoken reproach: Wilf, Dorothy, sister Joan, on leave from the WRNS and dreaming of her wedding, only a month away; Great-Aunt Emily, now permanently resident at Oakfield (she would die there in 1944).

Wilf and the women piled into the car and drove down into Hay for Midnight Mass at St Mary's. Roger went ahead on foot, muffled in one of Jo's big scarves and his blue-grey overcoat against several degrees of frost. The church was packed with families, many of whom already had sons, husbands and fathers volunteer or conscripted into military service. The vicar had special prayers for those defending our country. Roger never lifted his head. He sensed from Dorothy's resolute stillness on her aching knees that she was invoking Jack, his father, her husband, lost to war, or at least, as its consequence.

Afterwards, the family drove home while he walked up through the blacked-out town until he stood in the square below the ancient castle. At that moment an almost full moon slid from behind cloud to illuminate the gaunt and ruined Jacobean addition. Burned. Derelict. Like a stage set for war. He took out his pocket sketchpad and leaned at the corner of the old cheese market.

The next day Christopher appeared unexpectedly, arriving in his South Wales Borderers uniform. 'Last-minute leave,' he said. He had jumped on a train at Barnard Castle; countless trains, who knows? But there he was, grinning, and the family around the festive table was more complete than it had been in years.

Roger went back to Cambridge in the first week of January. One evening, he found Mrs Gatsby's family huddled around the kitchen fire listening to the wireless: Finnish forces were battling Stalin's army on their common frontier. Immediately, his thoughts turned to the friends he had made on Lake Hirsjarvi in western Finland the previous summer. He was troubled, found himself tossing and turning in his sleep. In that dark and frozen season, he became more introspective. He knew he must 'get past Roger'. He began to go more regularly to chapel. His elegant tutor, Brian Wormald, himself preparing for ordination, encouraged him to question received wisdom about historical events and analyse them for himself. This forced him to confront his ideals, to recognise what was real and desirable and what was illusion. Was he so bound up in the preservation of self that he could see no way to set aside beliefs that he had acquired in peacetime to defend humanity against fascism? The laughter and companionship of friends in Mrs Gatsby's parlour diminished. The government had introduced rationing at New Year: Mrs Gatsby said she could no longer put bacon on the breakfast table. Coal was less easily afforded too, the very month that produced the lowest temperatures since 1895. Indeed, around Hay, Dorothy reported that it was minus four degrees Fahrenheit [–20°C] overnight on 23 January, and colder still further west. There were reports of the sea freezing at Folkestone, along the south coast and up the Solent. The Cam froze and Roger's first-year tutor Bertrand Hallward was reputedly doing the 'Skaters' Waltz' with his wife on the river. Roger huddled in his room under layers of clothes and the thin eiderdown off his bed and tried to study. He took refuge in candlelit evensong in the college chapel and questioned his pacifism. The temperature began to rise, sufficient to bring blizzards in across East Anglia.

Roger 'Prepares to Fight Evil with Force'

Towards the end of the Lent term he went in search of Charles Burkill. Burkill was not someone with whom Roger was naturally aligned, given that he was an analytical mathematician, but he was a Fellow whom he occasionally encountered in Hall or in chapel; Burkill and his German wife were respected for their tireless work of several years helping rescue and settle several hundred refugee children from Germany. Now Roger sought him out for another reason: Burkill was in the Territorial Army as an acting Major and in the university Officer Training Corps. The don was not to be found, having contracted German Measles – no irony there. Roger made an appointment to visit Admiral Sir Herbert Richmond, the Master of Downing College. He had attended Richmond's enlightened naval lectures. He requested Richmond's help to get a commission in the Navy, skipping basic training – 'a waste of three months, but probably a political necessity', Richmond had growled. But he did suggest contacting the Tottenham Committee, seemingly being set up to examine Special Entry applications for the Navy. Young Burney was not content to leave it there; he pursued every avenue, writing a few days later to Richmond saying no-one knew of the Tottenham Committee but that 'Mr Slater suggested that the Admiral write a letter to the Admiralty, who could give the best information'. It is uncertain that Richmond answered on this occasion. What is certain is that Herbert Richmond was sufficiently impressed by the intelligent and charismatic Roger Burney, with his eloquent European languages, to commend him twelve months later to his old friend Admiral Dickens.

A few days before Easter, Roger took the train back to Hay in sombre mood, not minded to paint, nor enter into jolly discourse. Christopher was off somewhere on manoeuvres. Joan was off somewhere with her new husband, Henry Adams. He sat in his window, looking out over the great oaks in the pasture beyond the gardens.

> Oakfield,
> Hay.
>
> 19 March 1940
>
> Dear Dr Burkill,
> I was very sorry not to see you at the end of term; I hope you are quite recovered. I particularly wanted to see you because I found that the conditions under which I refused military service so altered, and my own opinions so thoroughly revised after the exercise of much thought and the benefit of a little

experience, that I no longer wish to accept the decision of the Tribunal; and I am in fact now negotiating my entrance into the Navy for June or July of this year…

I have sailed a bit off the west coast of Sweden, off Tynemouth and round Sidmouth. Three years ago, I anticipated three weeks on a trawler with some study of Navigation which however I never actually used. My purely military record is scant, amounting only to a Cert A, but I was second head of the Wellington OTC until I left as a pacifist…

I am in the category of Reserved Occupations and therefore I have to volunteer for the RNVR [Royal Naval Volunteer Reserve]. It is evidently of great help if Naval blood can be produced – the enclosed tree I found amongst some papers here; it is of doubtful value perhaps… although we have here the letters of Admiral James Burney who was on the *Discovery* with Captain Cook, and therefore I suspect this is not entirely irrelevant. My mother's family claims one admiral in the last fifty years. I am trying to investigate the exact relation of Admiral Sir Arthur Moore who died about 1930 – I believe he was a cousin – so much for that!

I hope to hear soon from Admiral Richmond. I'll let you know all developments and progress.

Yours very sincerely,

Roger Burney[1]

Charles Burkill certainly helped Roger in his ambitions and gave him a good reference at the beginning of summer term. So, in addition to sitting his finals, Roger had to present himself before the Cambridge University Joint Recruiting Board: a letter dated 22 May recommended he be trained as an Officer in the Royal Navy. Twelve days earlier, Winston Churchill had replaced Neville Chamberlain as Prime Minister.

Roger Burney got a decent degree but is missing from the Peterhouse graduation photograph taken outside the chapel in June; he had moved on. A further brief letter to Burkill sent from Oakfield on 11 June complains that he is still in the dark about his call-up date. 'Life here seems to be the epitome of peace – my studies in navigation and signalling are proceeding slowly and I am looking forward to using them.'

His call-up papers arrived at the end of June and on 6 July he attended a medical board in Worcester, where Arthur Dale pronounced him Grade I with the identification of MAN, Age 21 yrs. Height 5ft 10½ ins. Blue eyes. Brown hair. Appendix scar.

He may have been recommended for officer entry, but rather as Admiral Richmond had predicted, given his track record, Roger had to do 'the politically necessary training'. He signed on in the Royal Naval Volunteer Reserve to be instructed in the finer points of crewing a warship.

CHAPTER 4

ORDINARY SEAMAN BURNEY

On His Majesty's Service

ON THE LINCOLNSHIRE coast behind a beautiful sandy beach north of the fishing community of Skegness, Billy Butlin opened his first holiday camp for working families in 1936. It housed 1,000 people in brightly coloured cabins, had 250 shared bathrooms and was set in landscaped gardens with a theatre, gymnasium, swimming pool with cascades, a boating lake and all manner of other entertainment. People could spend a week there at the height of summer for three pounds all found. It was an instant success and the accommodation had to be doubled that same year.

It was to Butlins Roger was directed in July 1940, at what should have been the height of the holiday season; instead, the British were dealing with the enormity of defeat in France and the herculean evacuation of their retreating army, and the many French soldiers, from Dunkirk. The Battle of Britain was about to begin. Requisitioned by the Royal Navy, Butlins Camp Ingoldmells had been transformed into HMS *Royal Arthur*, a shore establishment for the training of 'Hostilities Only' (for the duration of the war only) communications branch ratings and officers (signalmen, telegraphists, coders, and wireless operators). The beer garden had become a sick bay, the Viennese Dance Hall the armoury. The rose gardens were 'rearranged' to allow the construction of air raid shelters, and all buildings were repainted in camouflage. It must have been quite a squeeze, Roger and 3,999 other trainees housed in accommodation which at best was designed for 2,000 holidaymakers, adults and children. Morning parades in the familiar 'duck suit' with its stripey squared-off collar – itchy as hell he reported; lectures, tests of stamina such as running a six-minute mile and running cross-country. Now that was exhilarating – he was fit.

We next find Roger at HMS *Ganges*, yet another 'stone frigate', further south at Shotley, close to Ipswich and no more than rows of hastily erected Nissen huts. He signed in for a few days of instruction: boat drill, including lowering boats down into the River Irwell, use of oars, swinging the lead on the foreshore, and using sailing dinghies to master the art of tacking. He was challenged to shin up a main mast he thought could have graced the *Victory* at Trafalgar – he came down smirking, grateful for all the tree climbs he had done. His section, the Signal School for HO ratings, was outsourced that summer to Highnam Court, a rather fine seventeenth-century manor west of Gloucester – and useful for short visits to Oakfield.

The Deaths of Close Friends

In late August, he was home for two days and found a letter from James Acheson to share the news that their friend, Michael Patton-Bethune, was no more. Indeed, three months had elapsed since Pilot Officer Patton-Bethune, flying with three other crew, had crashed in heavy fog in Devon. They had been on a surveillance training flight: all were killed.

Roger took Prince, the family Labrador, up the track onto Pen-y-Common and sat for a long time staring down across the Wye Valley. Then he went back and wrote a long letter to Peter Pears, telling him of the tragic death of their mutual friend. Peter and Benjamin had been travelling and working in Canada and North America for fifteen months and now gave an address, c/o Mayer, Amityville, Long Island.

James Acheson wrote again in September telling Roger that he had properly earned his wings and been promoted to Flying Officer. He was stationed near King's Lynn with 206 Squadron and proposed a reunion when Roger returned to East Anglia. That cheered him up to the extent he went with some of his fellow trainee signallers 'to the flicks' in Gloucester. The newsreel before the feature film showed General Charles de Gaulle and Admiral Émile Muselier inspecting units of the Free French Navy 'which are cooperating with the British Navy in its relentless fight against Nazism,' including boarding 'the famous submarine *Surcouf* which has joined the Free French Navy'. It was a brief piece of film in an undisclosed location.

Signal School finished in the first week in October when the trainees returned to Shotley. A little way north, on 10 October, Roger's dear friend James took off on a reconnaissance flight with two sergeants and one other flying officer; they failed to return.

On 11 October, according to naval records, Roger was posted to his final training assignment, on a modern light cruiser, HMS *Birmingham*, which had had a dramatic spring in Norway, culminating in her part in the evacuation of 1,500 troops from Åndalsnes. However, *Birmingham* was undergoing an extensive refit in Liverpool. Roger's letters home express bewilderment, disclosing that he had been sent to sort mail in a hut in the naval base in Portsmouth for weeks and was pretty fed up with it, being 'under a foul and assertive wretch – a fat Leading Seaman like Charles Laughton. I do by far the most work in the office and he does by far the least. Today he did none at all! He actually threatened to take me up for punishment today; he doesn't realise what a formidable opponent he has.'

Three weeks later, he is still writing from 4CC Mess, Portsmouth.

My darling Mummy,
Thank you so much for your letter which came today. How sad about the apples which would have been very welcome. I cannot discover my fate with any degree of certainty at all. Then today I was told I would be drafted to a new aircraft carrier next week – thus destroying my chances of leave unless I get it from the ship. Anyway, I think it still wisest to keep any mail there may be for me until I have a more settled prospect, which should be soon – this week... People already drafted to this ship I am told I may go to, have drawn warm clothes and tropical kit, so I've no idea where I shall be going. I do so hope I can get home, but it seems rather unlikely now. And if this ship goes where I think she's going, it will be a long time before I get home. My commission seems to be so extremely far off. I must start new and more vigorous intrigues. Jo gave me the telephone number of a friend of theirs [Joan had married her naval lieutenant, Henry Adams, in January] – I will ring up tomorrow, I think.

If you see depots of Portsmouth bombed by German planes, don't worry – yesterday there were two slight raids reported by Germany as heavy, and no damage was done at all. I saw one plane crash and there were lots of our silver fighters all over the sky.

Please give my love to Wilf,
VBL from your lovingest Rog

The Consolations of Home

By November, Roger was in Liverpool living in gloomy old barracks, awaiting completion of his ship's refit. It was deeply depressing, the hanging about, although he could go on board and familiarise himself with the ship. Just then he got a few days' leave and was able to reach Hay, and Dorothy. He was home. Home to a good log fire in the drawing room. They

255

had walks, visited friends, ate an early plum pudding – and Dorothy gave him presents of a winter coat and lined boots; she drove him back to Hereford station and they made each other laugh on the way. On the platform she pressed into his hand what Roger later described as 'a grotesque amount of money'. In those straited times it was, eleven pounds. He sat and scribbled heartfelt thanks in the station buffet at Chester, waiting for his connecting train back to Liverpool:

> Such a heavenly weekend. On Friday I don't think I could have been more depressed and now I'm just as fortified as I could be. I've just finished tea. It's ten to six and an old man has come in to sit and read. I put on my chamois coat here and my boots and I'll be quite warm now. I feel a terrific glow; I can hardly believe I'm returning to that dungeon. Still, I'm leaving it soon and then it will be better. Anyway, I'll write to you from Scapa and tell you all about our Christmas celebrations.

With this letter he enclosed an elaborate code – like every young recruit to the armed services, he schemed to reveal more in code than would otherwise get past the censor.

On 22 December, the Hay postman delivered a small brown envelope to 'Mrs Burney, Oakfield, Breconshire'. Inside was a formal card bearing the insignia of HMS *Birmingham* and wishing the recipient 'Every Good Wish for Christmas and the Happiness You Desire in The New Year'. It was signed by Leading Seaman Hampton. Dorothy was a bit surprised it was not from Roger, and was in two minds whether to be worried or amused.

Scapa Flow and Troubles on the Lower Deck

Following her refit sea trials, *Birmingham* sailed for Scapa Flow with Ordinary Seaman Roger Burney on the lower deck and under Captain Henry Berwick Crane. For the novice in those early days, it was 'Eyes Only' or 'Safety Training'. *Birmingham* arrived off the Orkney Islands on Christmas Eve in cloudless windless conditions. What a scene: the Home Fleet at anchor with the vast flagship HMS *Hood* in quiet waters among the islands, defended by a circle of barrage balloons tethered to fishing trawlers on the sea and to great concrete anchors on land. This then was Scapa Flow.

Christmas Day, rain thrummed through morning service, and Captain Crane barely managed to make himself heard. At half past one the RAF base on Orkney relayed a message to the fleet: 'a Christmas present for all of us; one enemy aircraft brought down over Orkney Mainland'. The day ended with a singsong. One would hope Roger's rather good bass swelled the choir.

In his rest time, such as it was, Roger sketched the Orcadian hills, calm under fresh snow – and the barrage balloons. Two weeks after he first saluted his captain, Henry B Crane wrote into record that Seaman Burney was of 'Very Good Character' and satisfactory in efficiency. It was New Year's Eve. 'The ship's bell was tolled on the stroke of midnight and the crew drank a toast to 1941: "Peace and Victory!" and sang "Auld Lang Syne".'

For the first half of January, HMS *Birmingham* patrolled the NW Approaches, to intercept enemy commerce raiders or vessels carrying contraband. On 24 January, with three Fleet destroyers, she was underway to the Swedish port of Gothenburg, familiar to Roger from his working summer before going up to Cambridge. What a long time ago that seemed. How exposed and perilous were those waters now, with U-boats on the hunt and the Luftwaffe expected to appear at any moment. They escorted three merchant ships carrying essential supplies back to safety in Orkney, at Kirkwall.

By early February *Birmingham* was preparing for a voyage lasting three months, part of the escort for troop convoy WS6A on the first stages of its journey to the Middle East via the Cape. She met the convoy in the Clyde on 9 February. At that moment, a huge submarine was undergoing sea trials on the Clyde. Would it be too fanciful to think that Roger Burney might have had a glimpse of FFS *Surcouf*, that extraordinary vessel he was fated to join later in the year? Perhaps. Perhaps not. The convoy sailed on, its escort augmented the following week by several more warships and the impressive aircraft carrier HMS *Ark Royal* to get them through the U-boat infested waters of the eastern Atlantic. They arrived without mishap in Freetown on 1 March where they remained for five days waiting to be joined by convoy WS6B.

HMS Birmingham

4 March 1941

Darling Mummy

There is very little to say except that I am safe and well. I've heard nothing from you since early February but please don't trouble to write as I expect I shall see you before any letter you may write reaches me – with luck in May or June, very probably later but that is as uncertain as the end of the war itself, so don't count on anything – I have thoroughly learned to set no store by promises until I can re-enter the paths I am used to, so it will not be exactly unforeseen whatever happens. Not only do I have no news of you, but I have no contact with the world, for News is rare and particularly hard to come by on the lower deck as indeed are most comforts at present.

Just lately I have been overtaken by the most terrible depression occasioned by the discovery of just how undependable men are – if the two axioms of a civilised society can be said to be the displaying of appreciation and of consideration, I have been lucky enough to have enjoyed both, more or less always – but now both seem to be particularly scarce – indeed I shall have a lot to say both to you and to others about this all. I have never appreciated my training (or education or whatever it was) so much as now and I have never before believed it possible that any educated people could seem to lack all facility for coherent thought, planning, and understanding. Three years of fairly clear and ordered thinking make me feel like a foreigner here. Still, it must end sometime one way or another, and I hope indeed it will be soon – in a way it must be far worse for older people although they are at least blessed with minimal comforts and some facilities for carrying on their work. I find that on the lower deck both in one's relations to one's messmates and in relation to officers, these most elementary human faculties hardly can be exercised let alone any faculties which have been diligently and expensively trained.

Haste,

VBL from Rog

The envelope was stamped PASSED BY THE CENSOR, 7 March 1941.

There is no question, anyone who grew up in privileged circumstances would have found living conditions, especially for ratings, on board ship in wartime aggravating. Although HMS *Birmingham* was a modern vessel, she was carrying more crew than had been allowed for in her design, due to additional radar and weapons systems. Personal space and sleeping facilities were cramped and the quality of food served up below decks left a lot to be desired.

On 6 March the amalgamated Convoy WS6 set course for Capetown. Ordinary Seaman Burney was put to work on the bridge, learning the finer points of navigation as he took the helm, altering course or keeping a steady-as-she-goes under instruction by the officer of the watch – 'Port 15, steer North'. At times while accompanying the troop convoy its escort would practice foiling U-boats by maintaining a zigzag course, so if Burney was at the helm of HMS *Birmingham*, he would have to alter course at the correct time to throw off potential attackers.

As he honed his skills, so he found purpose and, it seems, began to feel less 'foreign' in the company of his shipmates, the ordinary seamen, discovering himself to be more empathetic towards them. Increasingly, the idea of joining the officer class dominated private conversations with other 'Hostilities only' RNVR colleagues on board, making them uneasy. Roger said that had he been in the wardroom on *Birmingham*, he would have been 'raving mad' by now.

On 21 March they arrived in Cape Town where the *Birmingham* tied up and most of the crew had an afternoon and evening at leisure ashore. Queues of local people were at the port gates to welcome them with warm invitations to drive up Table Mountain and view the sights. Some sailors did go but Roger, mindful of the wartime rationing affecting his family in Hay on Wye, went shopping; a 5lb chest of tea, 4lb sugar and 8lb of Cape gooseberry and plum jam in tins; the maximum he could import into Britain. By the time he staggered on board with his purchases, the ship was being readied for trade defence duties in the South Atlantic with the 18th Cruiser Squadron. She sailed that night.

At the beginning of April HMS *Birmingham* was recalled to the Home Fleet, on the way joining in escorting merchant convoy SL70 out of Freetown heading north for Britain. She arrived at Scapa Flow on 22 April. Three weeks later, she would be involved with six other Fleet destroyers in a dramatic operation to intercept the German Weather Ship *München* and seize an Enigma Coding machine from on board. By then Roger, and two other RNVR colleagues, Mark and Guy, were long since disembarked and had headed through London to Portsmouth.

O/Seaman RJG Burney
P/JX 211302
C W Candidate
Leigh Park
Havant Nr Portsmouth
3rd May 1941

My Darling Mummy,

I do hope you got my [postcard] and had your mind put at rest by it.

I left the ship at Scapa on May 1st and got some butter and jam at Thurso which was lucky. I'll send the various things I have as soon as I can. I hope they will arrive safely.

London was not a quarter as damaged as I expected. Portsmouth is fairly bad – parts of the main street, Commercial St, are actually flat but may have been demolished. A great many disgusting buildings have been destroyed, which is all to the good – people say Southsea is fairly bad too. You do get older areas shattered with floors and windows and roofs blown through in a great many houses, but by far the majority of buildings are intact, windows, glass and all. Barracks have been badly damaged. Various schools have been hit, but the outlines of the buildings are very much as they were six months ago. Don't worry about me being here. It isn't as dangerous as all that or the Admiralty wouldn't have us here.

Leaving the ship was terrible. Six months on board living with those people gave me the most complete sympathy possible with them and, while before December I couldn't understand Mark's liking for the lower deck, discomfort and all, I can understand it now perfectly. The position of a Naval officer is fundamentally awkward and the sort of people who are Naval officers nowadays are unbelievable. This sounds a silly argument at the moment for not taking a commission and I have by no means decided to do this; but there are very good reasons behind Mark's attitude which I'd like to talk about when I come home. I am going to try to see Brian Wormald [Roger's tutor at Peterhouse] as soon as possible and discuss it all with him. I trust his judgement very much and knowing me better than most people I think he could help me get out of the muddle I admit I am now in.

Liaison Officer Burney

I stay here until my Admiralty Board in about two weeks. Then I may get seven days leave or I may go straight to the training place at Hove for three months there. Leave is not being given too generously now. I am longing to be home again and see you.

Please give my love to all.

VBL from your lovingest Rog

He sailed through his Board, aided by a high commendation of his character and skill from his former commanding officer, Captain Crane. At this point he went straight to HMS *King Alfred* at Hove marina. This sparkling new leisure centre had been constructed just before war broke out and was immediately requisitioned by the Navy to train 'Hostilities Only' officers commissioned into the RNVR. Its vast underground car park was converted to simulate different parts of 'the ship', including instructional areas and dormitory accommodation. Instructor Commander David Howell RN noted 'his many qualities. He is outstanding amongst the people who've passed through [the course]. The sincerity of his mind is a virtue rarely met with these days. He has a brilliant future ahead of him.'

By 7 August Roger was a Temporary Sub-Lieutenant headed for life as a Liaison Officer and under specialised training, though he took some leave at home in Hay. All was not well at Oakfield: Wilf was again poorly; his mother was stressed. But it was summer, the Black Mountains called, he had a few games of tennis at home with local friends. Dorothy and he paid another visit to Kenchester. A floral tribute, cleaning lichen off the family graves, a serious conversation in the sun. What next, Dorothy wanted to know. Roger was hesitant. Liaison, on a Dutch ship. 'Joan is pregnant,' Dorothy said, 'so I know she'll be here. But you two... I shall worry about you until you come back.' 'If I am captured you may like to know that prisoners are treated very well in both Germany and Italy. If I am killed…' 'No,' Dorothy said determinedly, 'you will not go before your time – DV'.

After he returned to his studies, Roger wrote finally:

I am being sent to a Dutch submarine. I didn't tell you this because I saw no reason to increase your worries; and the submarine service is by no means as suicidal as people imagine. I left [you] an informative, if bad, book on Subs behind the old books by my bed. I accepted this job, not out of recklessness, but because I was offered it, and have no objections that I yet know of about submarines (you get danger in anything). I felt that I could not refuse it and at the same time conform to the reasons I have for fighting at all. Dutch submarines have a particularly high reputation for efficiency among our own submarine men, so if I am lost, you will know it is not through carelessness. I get the best companions in the world on submarines, so I am told. As I said to you, I am simply a British Liaison Officer and I think I'll have a very good time.

In time of war all manner of plans are subject to change. The Dutch submarine had been in the Mediterranean for long battling months and at that moment was undergoing a major refit in Dundee. Instead, Roger was assigned to a vessel about to join the uniquely international 9th Submarine Flotilla operating out of Dundee: this was an old USN S-class submarine on loan to the Royal Navy which had passed her on to the Poles, who renamed her ORP *Jastrzab*. Despite the archives suggesting otherwise, Roger Burney never set foot on the *Jastrzab*.

Back in Cambridge in 1940, when Roger had sought advice from Admiral Richmond, such was the impression he had made that when the Principal Liaison Officer to the Allied Navies, Admiral Sir Gerald Dickens, urgently requested Richmond's help in identifying someone to fill a particularly tricky role,

Richmond thought of Roger Burney: the intellectual flower of his year, fluent in French, passable in German, and with a modicum of Italian.

Roger's naval records were amended on 10 September 1941. HMS *Victory* (his accounting base) was scored out and in its place was inserted HMS *Malabar*, the Admiralty's Command Base for America and West Indies. Temporary Sub-Lieutenant Burney was being summoned for a tougher assignment than he could have imagined.

CHAPTER 5

SURCOUF – THE MONSTER SUBMARINE

Boarding the Monster

PORTSMOUTH NAVY YARD, New Hampshire. Autumn 1941. A slim man in the uniform of a British Naval Lieutenant with a large canvas kitbag over one shoulder and a leather suitcase in the other hand picked his way alongside a narrow-gauge track. The October sun was warm on his face as he moved towards drydock No. 2 and gazed up at the immensity of the vessel under refit. 'Golly! who dreamed you up?' Roger Burney was confronted by the largest submarine in existence, half as long again as any submarine he had yet encountered. At HMS *Malabar*, Rear-Admiral Powell had merely said *Surcouf* was 'unusual', a 'big boat'. Roger snorted. Typical British understatement.

Out of the water, she was a monster. Roger pushed back the peak of his hat to look up at the bridge; two riveters up there seemed half-grown – she must be at least four storeys high. And those guns... formidable eight-inch cruiser guns. He took in the hangar on deck – he had heard she carried a reconnaissance seaplane, but the hangar appeared empty. This vast experimental submarine was something of a French imperial vanity project: devised in the 1920s to 'show the flag', she had a range of 10,000 miles and carried fuel and stores for ninety days. In wartime, her primary purpose was as a submersible commerce raider, with twenty-two torpedo tubes as well as arrays of anti-aircraft and general-purpose machine guns. Roger slowly inhaled and his lips moved... For... mi...dable... So, this was it, the alien whale that, for better or worse, would swallow Jonah, bearing him to who knows what adventure. The words he had written to allay his mother's fears came back to him: 'I think I'll have a very good time.'

At that moment someone on the bridge hailed him and pointed to the gangway to come aboard. The two British lieutenants saluted each other and shook hands as they introduced themselves. Frank Boyer. Roger Burney sized him up. Slightly on the short side, a strained look, he thought, maybe three or four years older than Roger. They quickly went below to Boyer's cabin. He explained that most of the crew were ashore enjoying the hospitality of local families and the two communications ratings who made up the British Navy liaison team were off exploring. The captain, Ortoli, had left for a posting in de Gaulle's War Cabinet in London two weeks earlier. Boyer explained that Ortoli's second-in-command, Louis Blaison, was taking over. 'Ortoli was a "head case",' Boyer commented. In Bermuda, Roger had been told much the same about Boyer, the man he was relieving. 'Lost his bottle' was the official line.

The two men did not exactly hit it off. Boyer certainly had been at the end of his tether by the time *Surcouf* had arrived in Portsmouth Navy Yard for her overhaul at the end of July. Called up from the Merchant Navy into the Royal Naval Reserve as an acting sub-lieutenant in 1939, Boyer trained on battleships and submarines. In April 1941 he was upgraded to lieutenant to join *Surcouf* as her British Naval Liaison Officer. There is little in his background to suggest he was fitted for the role.

From early in the war, the Admiralty had appointed British Naval Liaison Officers, speedily reduced to the acronym BNLO, to smooth relations on board any Free French, Free Polish, Free Dutch, and Free Belgian naval vessels that had escaped the German occupation of their countries. Their task was vital, to act as go-between between the Admiralty and the foreign entity now signed over to the Allies: to explain how the British Navy expected them to act, to interpret policy, translate commands, signals, and expectations. For this, it quickly became apparent, a working understanding of the on-board language was necessary. In the case of *Surcouf*, language, dialect, patois, led to misunderstandings and even quarrels among the crew, therefore any BNLO appointed to her needed to be something of a diplomat – and sensitive to the far more delicate situation for his liaison ratings, accommodated on the lower deck and often mocked for their lack of language skills.

The British Navy Siezes *Surcouf*

Surcouf had had a dreadful start to her career with the British after the fall of France in June 1940. She had escaped from Brest part-way through a refit only just in time to evade capture by the Germans. Her captain and crew had reached Devonport full of misgiving. Four days later the signing of the Franco-German Armistice required their country to direct a cessation of fighting against the German Reich in France, in French possessions, colonies, protectorates, and on the seas. Specifically, the French war fleet was to be collected in designated ports under German/Italian control and demobilised. This put the Admiralty in a desperate situation: Hitler could significantly increase his limited naval assets if he took over the French fleet. The British issued an ultimatum: come to Britain, place your ships outside Nazi reach in foreign ports, scuttle them or be destroyed. It was a terrible day for Franco-British naval relations when, on 3 July, they attacked a French squadron lying at anchor at its Mers-el-Kébir base off the north coast of Algeria. In fifteen minutes, 1,297 French naval personnel had been killed and nine battleships and destroyers sunk or severely damaged.

At dawn that same day, Royal Naval boarding parties were sent to seize all French vessels in British ports, peaceably. In Devonport, several French ships were taken over. Commander Dennis Sprague, at the head of thirty Royal Marines and thirty of his own submariners, boarded *Surcouf*. Ultimately, tempers flared on both sides, there was an exchange of gunfire and three Britons, including Sprague, and one Frenchman died. The consequences were immediate: all but two officers and fourteen of *Surcouf*'s crew of 140 refused to fight on the British side. It would be months before *Surcouf* was made seaworthy again and before she had sufficient crew to get back to war, now as a symbol for the Free French, under orders from the Royal Navy.

FFS *Surcouf* – A Ship of Troubles

That winter, *Surcouf* proved an unwieldy instrument in the turbulent North Atlantic escorting convoys. Before her second convoy duty was completed, she was detached and recalled to Devonport, where her first British Naval Liaison Officer was unceremoniously dumped ashore. His communications team, who had been on *Surcouf* since her commission into the Royal Navy in September 1940, survived the putsch to enjoy several weeks' leave with their families before returning to meet their new BNLO Francis Boyer. Leading Telegraphist Bernard Gough and Leading Signalman Harold Warner had been boy apprentices in what was known during the Great War as the Royal Fleet Reserve until they qualified for the Navy at eighteen. They had served in submarines for a decade and taken specialist courses in signalling. Gough was well-qualified in radio transmitters and could get by in French: he had left the service in 1938 to become a furniture salesman but rejoined through the RNVR when war broke out. They made a good team.[1]

In May *Surcouf* was sent to the South Atlantic, assigned 'as an independent command to be borne on the books of HMS *Malabar* in Bermuda', shore base of the Commander-in-Chief America and West Indies (C-in-C AWI). Lt Boyer's initial experiences were discouraging. *Surcouf*'s orders were to patrol a sector north of the Azores where German vessels were blockading Allied merchant shipping: the Admiralty warned of the possible presence of *Prinz Eugene*, a massive heavy cruiser, equipped with guns similar in size and range to *Surcouf*'s own. The encounter never materialised: possibly she was handicapped by the loss of her reconnaissance seaplane, damaged in an air raid on Devonport and left behind for repair. Indeed, on her first patrol of the sector, *Surcouf* came across only a cluster of American destroyers around USS *Wasp*, a small aircraft carrier. According to Boyer, he reported to C-in-C AWI and to Flag Officer Submarines in London, and now repeated to Roger, that Captain Ortoli had used the presence of these vessels as an opportunity to rehearse his crew in the art of underwater attack. Ortoli may not have planned an actual attack, but the incident had induced suspicion between Boyer and Ortoli.

Paul Ortoli was an experienced submariner, but as Captain of *Surcouf* he displayed his fiery Corsican disposition to the full; he had inherited few seasoned submariners. The remaining crew had been recruited in England: Breton fishermen, farmers even, who had escaped across the Channel in small boats, but the majority from French merchant ships. The ratings tended to be left-wing, in some cases communist, the officers right-wing, even fascist. Ortoli had spent six months attempting to transform this disparate bunch into an informed and skilled crew. He would write of the difficulties, even hinting in his monthly reports that he did not entirely trust a handful of his raw recruits, since they were self-selected.

Indeed, so great was his mistrust that he issued orders that none of his crew should go ashore when in foreign ports; that did nothing for morale. Nor did Ortoli much trust the British Admiralty, deeply resentful that they took precedence over his boss, the Free French Admiral Émile Muselier, and he found the orders the British dished out hard to interpret. He had kicked out Boyer's predecessor for his failure to translate Admiralty orders to Ortoli's satisfaction – one might wonder whether he even spoke French. The captain's troubles were compounded by *Surcouf* being such a complex vessel without enough specialist engineers.

In June, FFS *Surcouf* reached Bermuda to reprovision after thirty days at sea, before continuing to patrol for the German raiders plaguing Allied shipping routes. Handicapped by the lack of her spotter plane, again she found nothing. During three further weeks at sea, she suffered three major electrical failures and a fire in the engine room. On a practice dive she went spectacularly out of control down to a depth of thirty-five metres: a deck hatch not fully secured had allowed seawater to pour into the control room and onto her batteries, causing them to corrode, releasing chlorine gas. The incident could have led to the loss of the vessel with all hands. The steering system broke down twice, necessitating improvised repairs. Ortoli realised that the pride of the Free French Navy needed a major overhaul. She limped back to the naval dockyard in Bermuda on 20 July. Several crewmen were admitted to hospital with burns. Others showed signs of mental trauma. Urgent negotiations started between the Admiralty and the Americans to get *Surcouf* repaired in drydock – a fiendishly tricky piece of diplomacy, since the US was at the time technically a neutral country.

Frank Boyer and his two communications ratings were shocked by these events, if not terrified. Boyer described sleeping with his pistol under his pillow. He claimed to have hatched a plan with Gough and Warner that at the first sign of a fight on board, they would lock themselves in the wireless room with their personal weapons and send out a distress signal. All this and more he reported to the Admiralty. All this and more he told Roger.

Thirty-nine years later, he would write to an American researcher claiming that Lieutenant Burney had appeared sceptical, even contemptuous – and he was happy to repeat it in a drama-documentary for Television South-West in 1987.

At the time of their preliminary meeting in Portsmouth, New Hampshire, with the submarine slated to remain in dry dock for a further three weeks, neither BNLO was required on board. Boyer left to spend time with his hastily married American bride. Burney headed for New York.

Time Out with Peter Pears and Benjamin Britten

As the train pulled in, his eyes searched the blur of people hurrying, crisscrossing the station concourse, then above all the heads, a placard waving gently: 'R BURNEY RN'; underneath, Peter and Ben grinning.

They were staying out at Amityville but had decided to return to the place in Brooklyn where they had lived for several months, to introduce Roger to the freedoms of 1940s New York. Number 7 Middagh Street in Brooklyn was a quirky 'tudoresque' brownstone that sheltered many creatives and refugees from Europe. Burney, Britten and Pears sat down that first evening to a cramped meal with the fiction editor of *Harper's Bazaar*, George Davis, in his third-floor rooms. Roger was intrigued to be confronted by a life-size saucy cardboard cut-out of Gypsy Rose Lee and to learn that the burlesque artist had been co-resident with Ben and Peter, W H Auden, Louis MacNeice, Carson McCullers, two adult children of Thomas Mann, and several more. Gypsy wrote a detective thriller, *The G-String Murders*, under George Davis's tutelage. Now it was out to sensational reviews and women were queuing round the block all hours to buy copies. Roger was disappointed Gypsy was not around. They climbed to the top floor, where Ben and Peter had shared a suite of rooms for a while until the house had become a little too foetid and extreme for their taste – yes, fun, a sort of live-in club for hotshot literati and visiting fellow composers like Aaron Copland – not though, Ben said wryly, conducive to composition. In fact, in that brief hush after war in Europe began, the house acquired the reputation as the greatest artistic salon of the era – a year-long fevered party, but in daytime a place of study, devotion to writing, composing, painting. That was then. This was now.

From the top floor windows, there was a clear view of the East River down across Brooklyn Navy Yard. Though it was late, the yard was full of lights and a rhythmic metallic hammering and clanking: recently it started to operate around the clock. They walked down to the bars and dives along Sands Street – known locally as Hell's Half Acre. No longer were those seedy joints frequented by sailors and burly mechanics in search of booze, brawls and brothels, so much as by serious female shipfitters and welders. Roger had never seen women in this context, but men registered for the draft were getting their call-up papers and women were upskilling.

The scale of New York blew him away. One hundred and two storeys! Roger spent days wandering among pushcart men selling everything from fish to shirts; he frequented the ubiquitous milk bars he had first enjoyed when one opened in London in 1937; walked the Hudson River gardens; selected sister Jo a fabulous lipstick in the Coty boutique. With a returned ticket for the Metropolitan Opera, he watched Ballet Russe perform *Labyrinth* from the third tier of the vast horseshoe auditorium. Discussing the ballet afterwards it was the immersive minotaur stage sets created by Salvador Dalí that impressed him. Surrealism was challenging. Another night he went with Peter to Carnegie Hall for a thrilling performance of *Tristan and Isolde*.

One morning, Roger went in search of MoMA's recently acquired van Gogh and had to wait patiently for the crowd to thin out. A vibrant canvas, full of movement and points of light... a village, a waving tree, a crescent moon. He leaned forward and read the label: '*The Starry Night, Saint Rémy* – Vincent van Gogh, June 1889.' He stood for a long time, marvelling. He thought of the stars over Oakfield, over Hay, with the roofs gleamed by moonlight. He tried to uncover the artist's meaning: those swirling waves in the sky...

By the time he met Ben at Boosey & Hawkes on West 23rd Street, Roger was breathless: he had had to push through a press of people around a newspaper vendor at the subway. The papers were filling up with horror stories: besieged citizens of Leningrad going hungry; summary executions of young Jews trying to flee the ghettoes of Warsaw and Kraków. A tall striking woman with dark hair curling to her shoulders was with Ben. 'Beata, meet Roger. Roger, this is Beata Mayer. She works here.' 'Hi Roger. You're going to stay with my mother next week out at Amityville.' 'I am?' Roger looked enquiringly at Ben, who smiled quietly, 'You'll enjoy.'

The following Tuesday Beata came to lunch again: this time there was Peter but no Ben. He was flying up to Boston for a first rehearsal of his *Sinfonia da Requiem*, commissioned, ironically, by the Japanese government to commemorate the 2,600th anniversary of its ruling dynasty. Ben declared he had made it as anti-war as possible.

A fourth chair at the table was taken shortly by a plump grey-haired woman with the sweetest smile. Beata said, 'Roger Burney, my mother, Elizabeth Mayer'. She apologised for being late: a morning meeting with Klaus Mann, editor of the anti-fascist *Decision Magazine*, had gone on longer than intended. Ah... the woman who moves mountains: 'one of those grand people essential for the production of art; really sympathetic and enthusiastic,' Ben had said. Roger felt constrained to do a handshake, though his emotions were of finding his family after a long absence. And so, they became friends.

Elizabeth drove them out to Long Island to a cottage in the grounds of the Amityville mental hospital where her family lived. William Mayer, her husband, fled Munich in 1935 when the Nazis removed his licence to practice psychiatry. Here he was medical director of the hospital. Roger was aware Ben and Peter had lived here off and on for a year, and marvelled that so many people could squeeze into the small house, but Beata said she now lived with her fiancé in the Mayers' apartment in downtown New York and her three siblings squeezed into whatever other accommodation happened to be free in the hospital grounds when visitors came. Before dinner, they walked on the beach and dipped their toes in the water and talked incessantly. After dinner, and all next day, they played on the Bechstein grand piano, listened to records, discussed Stokowski's symphonic synthesis of *Tristan and Isolde* and much besides. Such a pleasurable interlude, culture, intellectual debate in the company of friends. When Roger got all the way north to Portsmouth navy yard again, he was glowing with wellbeing and full of plans for when the war came to an end, as it surely would.

Captain Louis Blaison 'Seeks Out The Enemy'

Surcouf finally left dry dock at the end of October – two months late. Her new captain, Louis Blaison, spent ten days meticulously checking every detail to satisfy himself that the smallest defects had been corrected before signing off on the American repairs.

During the many weeks of inactivity, *Surcouf*'s crew, for the first time, had been at liberty ashore. Louis Blaison was a gentle and religious man with a more sympathetic approach to handling personnel and, where his predecessor Ortoli prevented social contact between the crew and local families, Blaison encouraged it: some of the men had even ventured north into Canada. The newspapers and radio carried a great deal of news about the progress of the war in Europe, and not a few of the crew were exposed to the Vichy sympathies of many Americans. Those who had visited Quebec found themselves in a circle of French Canadians who especially favoured Maréchal Pétain, the head of the Vichy government. Warner and Gough were also hospitably received ashore in New Hampshire and found their American hosts remarkably oblivious to class and rank.

BNLO Boyer formally handed over to his successor on 5 November and returned to England under a cloud – spending the rest of the war in and out of hospital, or in training, and sometimes delivering a vessel wherever it was to be handed over to an ally.

Admiral Gerald Charles Dickens, Principal Liaison Officer to the Allied Navies had needed someone of strong constitution and a real understanding of French to replace Boyer. When he turned to his friend Admiral Richmond in Cambridge for ideas, Richmond had immediately recollected that engaging young man Burney with his fluency in French, German, and a modicum of Italian.

'Ici Londres! Les français parlent aux français!' Sometime towards the end of *Surcouf*'s stay in Portsmouth Navy Yard, her capitaine de vaisseau, Louis Blaison, gave an interview to Radio Londres on *Les français parlent aux français*. The programme was operated by the Free French and used regularly to send coded messages to the French Resistance, to appeal for uprisings, and for all men of duty to support the Free French.

> As long as there is an enemy on the soil of my country, I have a duty to fight to drive him out, alongside whoever is my friend and ally. One only becomes a slave when, out of weariness, one admits the possibility. Never admit defeat. However, one must avoid rushing to judgment. I am quite certain that in France, just as here among our men, there is every bit as much

devotion to duty. I know that plenty of people have returned to France out of a high sense of duty.

Blaison was an impressive operator for the Free French cause. A few days later he gave another interview, on this occasion to *TIME* magazine:

> The heaviest submarine in the world is ready to go back into action. Captain Louis Blaison told his countrymen by shortwave radio last week that his vessel would soon again 'seek out the enemy'. His vessel is the huge *Surcouf* which has been in Portsmouth NH, for repairs... so big that she carries a seaplane in a hangar aft of her turret. Most of *Surcouf*'s crew left her after France fell, choosing to return home to their families. Captain Blaison told how she was put back in service. 'With a small nucleus of veteran submarine men, we built up a crew. We transformed fishermen into gunners, peasants and college boys into electricians, and firemen and soldiers into mechanics...'

Louis Blaison was good on PR, but behind those brave words, he still lacked skilled submarine engineers; and of course, *Surcouf*'s seaplane hangar remained empty.

Early in November, the British Foreign Office relayed an urgent request from General de Gaulle to several overseas missions: 'Free French Navy is especially interested in French volunteers, minimum age seventeen, good education for the following specialities: radio, signals, ASDIC (a sonar system for submarine detection), engineers, air pilots, electricians.'

Meanwhile, BNLO Burney was getting to know his small communications staff, Harold Warner and Bernard Gough, seasoned submariners in their late thirties. Roger found them supportive and would soon write about them as 'ratings who have proved themselves to be of the best sort and under the most difficult circumstances possible...'

Surcouf was still attracting media coverage when she

sailed south into New London, Connecticut on 12 November, flying the Free French flag, and tied up at State Pier. The local newspapers implied she was on a goodwill visit. Her officers were invited to speak to Bulkeley School's class of 1923 reunion; some were entertained by a French catholic church group at a private home on Post Hill. Five French submariners, after an unscripted night out, crashed their car returning to the sub. Several miles inland, the French Club of Norwich welcomed the captain and his crew to a lavish dinner, laying on coaches to transport them.

Roger heard nothing of this until later. Once again, he had grabbed a few days' leave and headed for the bright lights of New York and the friendly intellectual Mayer household.

On 14 November, Roger pocketed his sketchpad and returned to the Museum of Modern Art. He spent the morning examining a Matisse, marvelling at how a squeeze from a tube of paint could be employed to such remarkable effect. How he ached for the possibility to paint again.

By 17 November, he was glad to escape the city and take the suburban train out to Amityville. He brought modest presents for the Mayers, books for Ben and Peter. He wrote a long letter to his mother enclosing a book token. These were a happy few days. On 19 November, Elizabeth drove 'her boys', as she thought of them, into New York. She and 'the geniuses' – her term for Ben and Peter – were on their way to Chicago and Grand Rapids for a series of concerts. Roger was returning to his submarine, with a pressing invitation from Elizabeth to celebrate Christmas with them. At that moment, anything seemed possible.

New London was the US Navy's principal submarine base on the Atlantic seaboard, with deep waters off Long Island Sound. *Surcouf* was there essentially to be put through her paces and test the efficacy of her refit. BNLO Burney was back on duty for her several days of test manoeuvres, carried out in tandem with an American submarine. Other observers had a

277

vested interest on the outcome: Admiral Richard S Edwards, Commander, USN Submarines Atlantic Fleet, and Admiral Émile Muselier, Commander of the Free French Navy. On 23 November the two submarines managed to collide. Who was at fault is not entirely clear, but it was not fatal, despite *Surcouf* suffering leaks in two bilge tanks. Muselier was not happy.

Surcouf returned to HMS *Malabar* on 29 November. She was scheduled to be at Ireland's Island dockyard in Bermuda for several days, preparing for a new role. The Admiralty in London had reached the conclusion that *Surcouf* would best be employed defending French overseas territories, and after some debate with de Gaulle's HQ in Carlton Gardens, the pride of the Free French Navy was being sent to the Indian Ocean to harry German merchantmen supplying enemy raiders around Madagascar; a crucial strategic element in the future of the Allied war effort, currently in the hands of the Vichy régime.

Bermuda's new Governor, Lord Knollys, paid a courtesy call on *Surcouf* and her crew. Roger was pleased to discover that a contemporary from Wellington College, Frank Giles, was Aide-De-Camp to Knollys. To his delight, they invited him to stay at Government House while *Surcouf* was in dock and entertained him royally. At dinner one evening, Frank introduced Roger to two lively daughters of Commander Guy Ridgway, Chief of Naval Intelligence in Bermuda. Next evening, they went dancing, and by all accounts the older girl Mary and Roger got on so well that they agreed to meet up again.

Surcouf again received new orders from the Admiralty. Instead of sailing directly for South Africa, she departed Bermuda on 7 December for Halifax, Nova Scotia, to rendezvous with Admiral Muselier. On this day, the Japanese bombed Pearl Harbor, the largest US Naval Base in the Pacific. Someone had messed up and failed to forward a warning to the appropriate authorities in time: America was in the war.

Next day, 550 nautical miles south of Halifax, FFS *Surcouf* encountered the Norwegian tanker *Atlantic*. It was ten o'clock in the morning and BNLO Burney was on the bridge with Captain Blaison, the first officer, and a Canadian naval lieutenant hitching a ride back to Nova Scotia. Blaison stared intently through his binoculars, lowered them and asked Roger, 'What is the British protocol for stopping and questioning a foreign ship? Can we stop her or not?' He raised his binoculars again. The *Atlantic* was starting to zigzag. 'Perhaps we should show more than the Free French flag? Would it be in order to raise the British Ensign?' While this was under discussion, the tanker sent out a distress signal that she was under attack. Blaison was concerned: he wanted to know if it would cool things down if *Surcouf* altered course. 'Which way should we turn?' Roger was appalled. But should it have been a surprise? Blaison was for the first time in charge of *Surcouf* on a war footing, under orders from the Admiralty. If his predecessor Ortoli had resented taking orders from the British, Blaison, that decent man, accepted them and expected Roger, as the British representative on board, to help him out.

Reporting the incident later to Admiral Sir Max Horton, Flag Officer Submarines in London, Roger described how not once had *Surcouf* tried 'to get into a suitable position for attack or defence; during the most critical part of the investigation, she was beam on to the stern of the tanker whose gun... was trained on us; none of our guns was manned'.

Atlantic's log recorded: '10 am. Chased by large submarine wearing French flag. We had to steer all points of the compass to avoid her. She then disappeared in NNW direction.'

The event would later fuel speculation about *Surcouf*'s loyalty to the Allies.

BNLO Burney Reports 'Very Great Hostility' on Board

Surcouf glided into Halifax on 10 December. Burney prepared his first report to Admiral Horton, his Flag Officer. His initial weeks on board had tempered his enthusiasm for the French. If he found a captain confused by British rules of engagement, Burney's general analysis was of a crew riven by Vichy versus Free French differences:

> ... very great hostility between the petty officers and the men...
> who at their best moment have no hostile feelings against the
> Allies, but who frequently question the validity and services
> being rendered by the Free French forces, especially in
> operations against the French themselves. Because the issues
> are not clear, the majority are open to any strong influences
> either one way or the other; and it is hardly necessary to
> say that most of the influences are against the Free French
> movement and take their toll on the actual operation of the
> vessel.

In this respect, *Surcouf* was no different from other Free French vessels and this is confirmed in reports from other BNLOs: Sub-Lieutenant Ruari McLean described the atmosphere aboard another submarine, engaged in mine-laying off France and Norway:

> Patriotism and loyalty is not to de Gaulle (who, however, they
> admire) but to France and is as strong as an Englishman's
> to England... if they are captured by Germans, they may not
> be shot but, if they are captured by Vichy Frenchmen, they
> certainly will be... they are fighting Germany for France, not
> for Britain.[2]

No-one was more aware of this than Captain Blaison himself. From the moment he took over command and made that broadcast from Portsmouth, New Hampshire, he was in the sights of the propagandists. The good man was bombarded with fake news about his family in Vichy France: his wife was having an affair; his daughter had been confined to a sanatorium with TB; his wife had advanced cancer. One evening, over a quiet meal with BNLO Burney and Louis Audette, a Canadian naval liaison officer of his acquaintance, Blaison unburdened himself. It was in the mail he received, it was in muttered threats in French in the docks, along the streets. Burney reasoned that if it was happening to the captain, it was happening to his crew.

Roger noted a certain tension, but he recalled that, at the time of his appointment, the Admiralty had put emphasis on praising and encouraging the Free French because of their difficult personal circumstances in having volunteered to join the Allies:

> The Frenchmen who have joined the de Gaulle movement comprise a very small minority of their countrymen and, in taking this step they have invited much harsh and hostile criticism from many other Frenchmen. They are, moreover, fully aware that the line of action which they have taken may lead to the victimisation of their families in France.

Admiral Muselier duly reached Halifax on 12 December to inspect *Surcouf*, and three Free French corvettes, *Mimosa*, *Alysse* and *Aconit*, based in Nova Scotia as escorts for the North Atlantic convoys. It can be assumed that the admiral was aware of the political divisions in his crews, for he hastened aboard *Surcouf* to look around, making a speech praising everyone for their diligence and for the immaculate state of the engine room, the galley and wardroom. In the brief hour and a half Muselier spent on board the submarine, BNLO Burney noted a face of strong character with deep-set kindly eyes.

Next day, Muselier was off, leaving *Surcouf* and the corvettes idle. He said he needed to confer with the Canadians – and Americans – in Ottawa on urgent matters. In the wireless room on board *Surcouf*, suddenly Signalman Warner and Telegraphist Gough were busy with incoming coded communications: MOST SECRET – further instructions from Admiral Stuart Kennedy-Purvis, C-in-C Americas & West Indies:

REQUEST YOU WILL SAIL SURCOUF FROM HALIFAX ON 16TH DECEMBER FOR POSITION 21°N, 40°W.

This location in the South Atlantic was to be the start of a journey routing her to Simonstown Dockyard in Capetown. *Surcouf* was further informed that specially engineered pistons, shells, and torpedoes were being loaded onto a Greek vessel, *Marika Protopapa*, to reach Simonstown ahead of her scheduled arrival.

On 16 December, Muselier had not returned.

On 18 December, Roger wrote belatedly to Elizabeth Mayer:

F S *SURCOUF*

c/o GPO LONDON

My Dear Mrs Mayer,

Please forgive my inglorious silence after such hospitality. At least it isn't the measure of my gratitude or of my memory of Amityville and I hope you will put it down, as you really may, to the many preoccupations that have hedged me in ever since I saw you away that morning in New York. How exhausting it has been. Sometimes I feel as if I have sold my soul to this job. You know how uninteresting French bourgeois can be. They are my only companions – talking all day about their wenches, and especially about certain places in ports they know and affording me the least companionship possible. I don't think I have ever felt so lonely.

Well please forgive my mood, which is extremely unsuitable for writing to you. Thank you again very much for your hospitality which made me long to return and indeed I hope my luck will not be so bad as to keep me away for too long. I feel terribly homesick for America, and I miss being amongst people who are physically pleasing too. There's just a chance of seeing you about Christmas or afterwards, but very slight indeed.

Please give my love to all your family. I hope you have a good Christmas.

With best love from Roger.

While Roger Burney fretted on board *Surcouf*, elsewhere, a sequence of events was falling into place that would literally take him out of his depth.

FFS *Surcouf* Captures Vichy Islands and Causes Diplomatic Crisis

Somewhere back in June, disquiet had been growing among the British, Canadians and Americans about the apparent ease with which U-boats were picking off vessels sailing in convoy between Halifax and the Western Approaches. On a tiny cluster of French-owned islands just south-west of Newfoundland, there was a vital wireless relay station through which a large proportion of transatlantic communications were routed. Since the fall of France, the islands had been under Vichy governance. The suspicion was someone in St Pierre was intercepting signals about Allied convoys and relaying them to Vichy France and Germany: in effect assisting the enemy. Admiral Muselier had been restive, wanting to intervene, but five months passed while the Allies dithered: hundreds of extant pages detailing meetings, committees, telegrams show the diplomatic sensitivities. After the fall of France, both Canada and the United States had recognised the Vichy French government under Marshal Pétain.

However, the government in Ottawa was considering sending military wireless specialists to the islands to censor outgoing communications and was prepared to take further action if the Vichy governor resisted. De Gaulle was appalled.

On 12 December, the Chiefs of Staff meeting in Whitehall finally addressed the issue under pressure from Churchill, who sent them a clear message: 'I must have a definite recommendation from the COS. I like it personally if only done by the Free French.' The COS agreed there were strong arguments on military grounds for authorising Admiral Muselier to rally St Pierre and Miquelon to the Free French as soon as practicable.[3] De Gaulle urged speed for, with the Americans now firmly in the war, Washington had concluded an agreement with Vichy France to neutralise the French Caribbean fleet based in Martinique; he was adamant that they should not extend that neutrality to St Pierre and Miquelon.

No-one comes out of this very well. Admiral Muselier had tried to persuade the Canadians and Americans to agree to it being a Free French operation but ended up assuring both governments he would cancel it, something he had no intention of doing. The Foreign Office sought to support the Free French by a telegram, urging the Americans to endorse the urgency for action and expressing confidence that the plan would not in any way embarrass the US Government. Washington dug its heels in.

By Friday 19 December, word came from *Mimosa* that the admiral had returned and a meeting of the four captains would take place next day. Twenty-four hours passed. Silence. Roger received some Christmas mail, including a heart-warming letter from the Mayer family.

BNLO Burney wrote an account of what he knew:

After [Admiral Muselier's] return I was given no information at all. But at 10.15 on 21st December, I overheard our chief engineer confirming a report that he had evidently received earlier for another officer, namely that we were sailing at 11.00 that day with the three French corvettes *Alyse*, *Aconit* and *Mimosa*, to proceed, not to the occupation of St Pierre et Miquelon, but simply to carry out exercises. Neither the captain nor the first lieutenant was on board at the time, so I went to the Halifax Operations Room to get the details of our programme. The Chief of Operations [COAC, Commander Harry DeWolf RCN] knew as little as I did, said he had no word at all of our sailing, and it was only when I went on board again and found the captain that I was told officially that we were to proceed for exercises with the corvettes and, afterwards, we were to sail directly to St Johns, Newfoundland. We left Halifax at 11.55 that forenoon and carried out the exercises as arranged.

Late on the evening of 22 December, the Admiralty received a cypher message from Commander DeWolf:

IMPORTANT
FREE FRENCH SUBMARINE SURCOUF AND FNFL ARMED
MERCHANT VESSELS MIMOSA, ACONIT, ALYSE SAILED
1600Z/22nd FOR ST JOHNS N.F. UNDER ORDERS OF
ADMIRAL MUSELIER IN MIMOSA.
SHIPS WILL CARRY OUT EXERCISES OFF HALIFAX
THEN PROCEED BY MOST DIRECT ROUTE. ESTIMATED
SPEED 11 KNOTS. ROYAL CANADIAN AIR FORCE BOMBING
RESTRICTIONS LIGHTENED.

This discrepancy between BNLO Burney's retrospective report of the Free French flotilla's departure and the Chief of Operations' version of events might raise eyebrows – but then, Muselier already had a bad conscience about his empty assurance to the Americans and Canadians that he would drop his planned takeover of the islands: perhaps he did file sailing intentions that would give him a twenty-eight-hour start to achieve his objective.

After a series of inconsequential exercises, *Surcouf* and the three corvettes had set course for Newfoundland. Burney was on the bridge with Captain Blaison when a line-gun was fired from the deck of *Mimosa* and a rating went scuttling along the deck of *Surcouf* to retrieve the canister; it contained a note for Blaison to alter course for St Pierre. Blaison remarked that this surely meant that they were going to remove the Vichy administration.

Burney rose from sleep early on Christmas Eve to find the Free French entering port at St Pierre. It was dark and very cold. The three corvettes docked in harbour, *Surcouf* hovered outside in a defensive role, sending parties of men ashore in small boats. The British Naval Liaison Officer's report was factual:

> All the best-known supporters of the [Vichy] regime were imprisoned immediately; otherwise, there were no incidents of any kind, and within half an hour, the Free French Ensign was hoisted over the Town Hall.
>
> The ensuing difficulties with the Canadian and American governments were not at all clear here; from Admiral Muselier's point of view the quarrel was between the US Government and France as represented by General de Gaulle, and not at all between the Vichy Government and the Free French. At all events, it was only on the 29th December that Admiral Muselier told me the Admiralty was satisfied with the operation.
>
> During the nights of 27th and 28th *Surcouf* patrolled the entrance to the harbour of St Pierre... we had formal instructions from the admiral to fire on any ships we should see in our waters with the exceptions of British ships. 'And if they're American,' said the captain of *Surcouf*, 'it will be just too bad'.

Just before midnight on 24 December, Christmas Eve, Admiral Muselier sent a cypher message of his own to the Chief of Naval Staff Canada; Admiralty; NSHQ Ottawa; COAC Halifax; CONF St Johns, Newfoundland.

I HAVE THE HONOUR TO INFORM YOU THAT IN
COMPLIANCE WITH ORDERS QUITE RECENTLY RECEIVED
FROM GENERAL DE GAULLE AND AT THE REQUEST OF
INHABITANTS I HAVE PROCEEDED TO ISLAND ST PIERRE
AND RALLIED PEOPLE TO FREE FRANCE AND ALLIED
CAUSE WITH ENTHUSIASTIC RECEPTION.

Washington, in the shape of Secretary of State Cordell Hull, was outraged: he it was who had concluded the agreement with the Vichy Government to ensure the neutrality of French possessions in the Western hemisphere. He threatened to resign if Roosevelt did not demand the restoration of the status quo in the islands. And Churchill, recently arrived by sea on HMS *Duke of York* to spend Christmas in urgent strategic talks with President Roosevelt, must have had a frosty reception in the White House.

The Canadians were having second thoughts, probably under pressure from Washington, about leaving the Free French in continued occupation of the islands. They let it be known that they were sending their own ships. While Burney was not privy to messages received by Muselier, he reported a signal sent on 28 December from the admiral's flagship to both the Commander of the Canadian Navy and the Head of Operations in Halifax. Clearly things were very tense:

OF COURSE, I WILL BE HAPPY TO RECEIVE YOUR SHIPS
AT ST PIERRE, BUT THE CURRENT POLITICAL SITUATION
OBLIGES ME TO REQUEST THAT YOU WARN ME OF THEIR
ARRIVAL... THE WIRELESS TRANSMITTER IS UP AND
RUNNING AGAIN. I AM PLEASED TO BE ABLE TO RESTORE
IT TO YOU FOR THE COMMON WAR EFFORT.

Roosevelt's Assistant Secretary of State in charge of Intelligence was Adolf Augustus Berle. His diary for 29 December 1941 records:

... the infernal affair of St Pierre and Miquelon. We told
the Free French they had no business filibustering on our
shores; and a string of propaganda has been circulating in the
newspapers, chiefly, I suspect, of English origin, indicating
that by not signing for the Free French we are playing the
game of Vichy, therefore the game of Berlin. For the life of me
I can't make any sense out of it...

Churchill is pushing the President to whitewash and
sanctify de Gaulle, and the President is caught in a cleft
stick. What Churchill is not telling him of course is that he,
Churchill, secretly authorized the de Gaulle filibustering
expedition...[4]

At close quarters, Roger Burney admired Émile Muselier's
resilience and courage. Ashore on the islands, watching how
the admiral interacted with the local community, he sensed a
warm-hearted generous man. However, he was disquieted by
the extent to which Muselier had taken the initiative and said
so:

Since arriving here, I have said both to the Admiral and to
Captain of *Surcouf* that I am attached to *Surcouf* to help her in
any operations she may undertake, particularly by maintaining
communications with the Admiralty... Throughout the whole
operation the Free French Naval Authorities have given
both me and the other Liaison Officers concerned [those
attached to *Mimosa, Aconit* and *Alysse*] the least possible help
and confidence. Also, they have made a great point of their
independence in this operation and will not, I think, allow this
precedent to be overlooked. So far as I know, we have not yet
received any direct Admiralty approval for the operation.

Burney, observing the crew's reaction to the rallying of the
islands, reasoned that there remained that constant tension
between anxiety at the possibility of finding themselves in
action against their own countrymen and the execution of

orders from the Admiralty: '... because there was no bloodshed and because we were welcomed by ninety per cent of the islanders, the operation has acted as a tonic on the morale of the crew.'

On one trip ashore, Roger acquired late Christmas cards for family and friends with little unfocused photographs looking down over St Pierre pasted inside. When he went to purchase postage stamps, he discovered they had been overprinted with 'Noël 1941, FRANCE LIBRE FNFL' and promptly bought several sheets of them and mailed them home to Oakfield:

> Dear Jo, these stamps are worth an enormous amount already so do keep them, even duplicate sets. There are only about 100 sets of 'Noël 1941' in the world!
> Please forgive haste.
> I hope they reach you alright.
> VBL Rog

Surcouf remained on patrol around the islands for two weeks, during which groups of crewmen were given leave to go ashore. On not a few nights, this led to wild scenes and a scramble to return to the submarine. On New Year's Day a large unidentified vessel seen approaching from the north at 21.40, necessitated *Surcouf* weighing anchor to investigate. Ten men ashore heard she was preparing to move. They commandeered the local fishermen's pinnace, making very unsteady progress towards the submarine, sailing right under the bow just as she weighed anchor. Burney reported ten drunk crew and the torpedo officer 'so drunk that he spent the night talking complete nonsense or else sleeping'. Perhaps fortunately, *Surcouf* found no ship.

It was not without irony that Burney ended his report to Flag Officer Submarines by repeating Captain Louis Blaison's remark to him that day: ... '[he] hoped that the Admiralty would insist upon the return of *Surcouf* to its original purpose, and under Admiralty control.'

On 7 January, a Royal Navy submarine, *L-27* was engaged in trials off Newfoundland to test new ASDIC equipment. On board were twenty-eight-year-old Telegraphist John Green who had briefly served in FFS *Rubis*, and twenty-year-old Signalman Lawrence Stannard, conscripted a few months earlier. They were ordered over to St Pierre to relieve Warner and Gough, who had been on board *Surcouf* for fourteen months and were heartily sick of her. They said their farewells and hitched a ride back to Halifax to await passage to England.

John Green was appalled by conditions on the lower deck and young Stannard was frankly frightened. He had no French at all and found the crew intimidating in the extreme. He appealed to Burney to get him off and told him he was desperate enough 'to do something silly'. Much later in life Stannard was grateful that he had found in Burney a sympathetic listener who promised to find replacements and would say his new team were too inexperienced. In fact, he signalled ahead to Halifax, requesting urgent replacements, and if Warner and Gough had not yet left for home they should return on board temporarily.[5]

On 11 January, *Surcouf* left St Pierre to return to Halifax and immediately ran into gale force winds and massive seas that caused her to roll forty degrees to port, then forty degrees to starboard. One giant wave bore down on her, breaking part of the bridge. The turret quickly coated with ice rendering her guns, weighted down by huge icicles, inoperable. The rangefinder was frosted, the lenses needed replacing.

That three-day voyage into Halifax was the worst Burney had experienced and Green and Stannard were petrified. This was like no other submarine.

CHAPTER 6

THE MYSTERIOUS DISAPPEARANCE OF THE FFS *SURCOUF*

Burney Reports *Surcouf* Unfit for Purpose, and Personnel Problems

Surcouf went straight to the Navy Yard on her return to Halifax. Repairs would take at least two weeks to get her in any state for her next journey. Warner and Gough had indeed been hanging around and were ordered back on board. Such was the bad feeling when the four ratings came face to face, that Warner refused to speak to Stannard and Green, and Gough chose to express his anger with his fists. There is nothing in the official record to identify precisely what transpired: Gough may have been kept in custody until he cooled off, and possibly was never charged. Of course, Green and Stallard departed in short order. Leading Signalman Harold Warner took himself off to Boston to find solace. Soon afterwards he wrote to his wife Lilian: 'It's an astounding fact that being so fundamentally and essentially British, I realise my best friends on whom I could count in *any* situation are American, which rather shakes me, but it is true.'[1]

How Lt R J G Burney handled this highly sensitive personnel matter is not clear. The attitude of naval ratings towards 'Hostilities Only' officers, often with striking disparities in education and social backgrounds, was a well-known cause of friction during the war: grudges over poor conditions or lack of leave undoubtedly exacerbated the situation. In this instance, Burney spent a considerable portion of his time trying to sort things out. Increasingly worried about his ratings' morale, he addressed himself to writing another difficult report to Admiral Max Horton, Flag Officer Submarines:

> Memorandum:
> ... My O431Z/10 requesting the temporary retention of the two original liaison ratings was sent, not because of any lack of technical ability on the part of the two reliefs, but because the position of the two liaison ratings in *Surcouf* is fraught with difficulties which demand not only years and character, but also great patience, experience, and independence. These qualities are naturally rare in combination at any time and in war time especially; but the delicacy as foreign sailors, whose presence is always resented however necessary they are for the safety of the boat, the enormous difference in the standard of living in which they have to acquiesce, and the great responsibilities in which they are involved, make it necessary to have on board ratings with enough character and seniority to compensate for the degree of inefficiency in their respective departments and to resist the exhaustion of their perpetual battle.
>
> As she is run at present, I do not think *Surcouf* could possibly be judged by an experienced Naval officer to be a unit of any direct Naval use to the Allied cause, beyond her symbolic use to the Free French Navy; and as a result of recent experience, I would respectfully submit the following observations for your consideration:
>
> Lookouts are on watch for a period of two or four hours at a stretch; they are not the least acquainted with Morse; at

no time have I seen them employ their glasses for more than one minute in twenty... [On 9 January] the Canadian corvette *Algoma* arrived at St Pierre, sighted *Surcouf*, and signalled to her; it was fifteen minutes before she received an answer to her signal. I have repeatedly discussed the extreme importance of lookouts with the captain, but whatever he may say to them, he gets no results...

A detailed record of our almost daily crises would not give a very much clearer picture of our state, because all my assessments are based on very little submarine experience. I would respectfully submit, therefore, that if it were possible for a senior submarine officer to spend some time in *Surcouf* at sea, her naval value might be assessed in a positive way rather than negatively as I necessarily have to.

I would like to repeat my request for reliefs for the two original liaison ratings; and I would like to express the hope again that they may be rewarded for their extreme patience and exemplary loyalty with more responsible appointments.[2]

It is very clear from the careful and diplomatic manner in which Burney phrased his report, that he was rattled and would this time expect some positive action from the Admiralty. What transpired was that Admiral Max Horton, his Flag Officer, stamped it as read on 30 January – two weeks later – and passed it on to the War Office with a comment that of course the BNLO was inexperienced.

Nor was it a simple matter to describe the state of *Surcouf* to the Canadian Head of Operations in Halifax, Commander DeWolf. He and Lt Burney mulled over the issues in an intensely private discussion. DeWolf had no authority over *Surcouf*, that was an Admiralty matter, but he had observed *Surcouf* on her visits to his operational patch and saw a vessel with such major defects that he thought her of decreasing value in the rapidly escalating global war.

Respite in New York

Eventually, while *Surcouf*'s latest damages were being repaired, Roger tried to put aside his troubles and concentrate on what for him was real, friends, the cultured life. He returned to the bosom of the Mayer family at Amityville, Long Island, and spent days walking the seafront, or sat huddled in his warm chamois coat, writing letters and notes to several friends and, as always, attentive to his mother Dorothy and sister Joan. Peter Pears and Benjamin Britten were back in residence, rather low in spirit for, having determined it was their duty to return home to England, there were weeks of waiting for berths on an uncertain voyage in a North Atlantic convoy. Ben was closeted in Elizabeth's music room much of the time, preoccupied with a setting for three poems by his friend Wystan Hugh Auden that would become 'Hymn to St Cecilia'.

Amityville,

18th January

My dear Peter [Godden],
You would not believe what your friend Rog has got himself into. How I wish we were both back making music in Cambridge. I am staying with Elizabeth Mayer and her husband William, who is psychiatrist-in-charge here. They got out of Germany with their four children when the Nazis stopped William practicing. Mrs Mayer is formidable and wonderful: she had hoped to be a concert pianist but here she translates great European literature for the Americans. Peter and Ben are here too, though Ben is in a bate. We arrived off the same local train, me from the airport, Ben from Philadelphia, where he had attended the premiere of a piece commissioned by a one-armed pianist called Paul Wittgenstein. Ben is full of recriminations over some changes to the score. Anyway, now Ben and Peter are waiting to get back to England. Hey ho. Everyone is trying to get home. The sky has darkened after Pearl Harbour. New Yorkers scurry

along the streets as though Japanese planes might appear overhead at any moment.

Amityville,

20th January

My Dear Jo,

Just a scribble to send you some late Christmas stockings which I hope reach you alright. I hope you are hearing from Henry regularly and that he hears from you. I am longing to catch up with all the mail I have owing. I think I'll send you some valves for your radio if I can get them in New York tomorrow. I'm longing for the time to write to you again. By the way, did you see *Surcouf* was in the seizing of those islands off Newfoundland?

Best love,

Roger

When will this war ever end?

As good as his word, Roger next day found radio valves for Joan so that she could listen to the seven and eight o'clock news, which she had missed dreadfully. As for the stockings, she was over the moon and wrote back on 11 March telling him all the local and family news and to say 'Ma' was buoyed up at receiving a long letter from him from Bermuda enclosing press cuttings about the adventures of *Surcouf*. A bureaucratic delay: Roger's letters and presents for his sister were held by HM Customs in Liverpool for weeks while they determined what charges should be imposed on such luxuries.

On his last evening with the Mayers, Roger spent two hours closeted with Elizabeth after supper, pouring his heart out. In the short time since he came into her family, she had not known him like this. The memories of their profound exchange were to haunt her for years to come. She rose sleepless the following day. He was gone.

Premonition of Doom in Bermuda

On 1 February, *Surcouf* left Halifax for Bermuda, unusually, escorted by a Canadian corvette, HMCS *Weyburn*, captained by Lt Commander Thomas Golby. This is thought to have been ordered because a surge of U-boat activity down the Atlantic seaboard post-New Year exposed *Surcouf* to considerable risk, having neither ASDIC nor radar on board. She reached Bermuda unscathed on the fourth day and the two British ratings went back to Benker House to stay with their kindly hosts of previous visits, Ruth Baker and her husband. The Bakers later said they were mystified by the state of Gough and Warner, usually full of smiles and banter but now with scarcely a word to say to anybody.

On Thursday, 5 February, Lt Burney was summoned to an urgent meeting with the C-in-C, Vice-Admiral Charles Kennedy-Purvis, taking with him copies of his liaison reports to Flag Officer Submarines in London. As Kennedy-Purvis read through these long and detailed accounts of the previous two and a half months, he occasionally looked directly at Burney and asked him to elaborate on the vessel's defects and vulnerabilities, his analyses of the culture wars within the crew and the inability of officers to have their orders obeyed. After a while he summoned his Chief of Naval Intelligence in Bermuda, Commander Guy Ridgway, to sit in on what became two hours of probing interrogation as much as clarification. Ridgway went aboard the submarine that afternoon while Burney made himself scarce.

Kennedy-Purvis's report was on Flag Officer Max Horton's desk in London when he arrived at eight o'clock next morning. It was to the point and, as usual, MOST SECRET:

05FEB42 C in C America & West Indies to Flag Officer
Submarines + the Admiralty

BNLO *Surcouf* has given me copies of his reports dated 17th
December 1st January and 16th January. After discussion
with BNLO and from my experience of *Surcouf*, I am

convinced that this most unsatisfactory state-of-affairs is not in the least exaggerated.

2) The two main troubles are lack of interest and incompetency (the Engine Room however is moderately clean and efficient, and the machinery is in fair order), discipline is bad, and the Officers have little control. I have no suggestions to make which are likely to assist in eliminating those defects which I am afraid are inherent.

3) *Surcouf* is a large complicated and indifferently designed submarine and in my opinion could only be of operational value if manned by an exceptionally well-trained crew. Even her size places severe limitations on her sphere of usefulness. At present she is of no operational value and is little short of a menace.

4) *Surcouf* will leave Bermuda on 7th February to Tahiti via Panama Canal unless otherwise ordered. For political reasons it may be desirable to keep her in commission; but my view is she should proceed to UK and pay off. Request very early decision on this.[3]

Vice-Admiral Horton's response was immediate, the tone brusque:

MOST SECRET
I am sure Commander, Free French Forces, Southwest Pacific, can make use of *Surcouf* in an active warzone.

In defence of the soil, I consider *Surcouf* may be of considerable use. *Surcouf* occupies a peculiar position in the French mentality and the Free French would hate to pay her off.

In any case her care and maintenance would be a nuisance in the UK, therefore I strongly recommend *Surcouf* proceeding as already ordered.

Despite the diesel engine room being in order, *Surcouf* was in no position to leave Ireland Dockyard on 7 February after all. Captain Blaison reported to Max Horton on 5 February that the starboard electric motor needed replacing. Two electric motors were essential for underwater manoeuvres, but Blaison was reluctant to wait three months for a replacement engine as it would impact on the morale of his crew. Temporary repairs sufficient to get her across the Caribbean would take one week and allow her to dive on one motor in an emergency.

Roger considered his options. Frank Giles might still be in Government House, but he hadn't heard from him. The one free spirit he had met in Bermuda might be available. Mary Ridgway met him with her sister's bicycle for him, and they spent hours riding along dazzling crushed coral roads with the wind in their hair and the smell of the sea. Writing to his mother a few days later, he said it was 'a carefree moment, like it used to be when we were children careening about the lanes and tracks by the Wye'.

Once, Mary took him down a long steep set of concrete steps into a vast cave. He couldn't see far with the crude lighting but what he did see made him catch his breath. A wide clear lake reflected sparkling iridescent stalactites, white, pinks, browns and all the colours in between. Mary leaned on the safety rail. 'Is this what it's like on your big boat?' she asked. Roger turned and looked coolly at her. 'Would you like to see what it's like? I'll show you.'

Roger's mind was elsewhere. He was perturbed the Admiralty still appeared to have made no arrangements for his sorely tested liaison team to be relieved, despite his specific request four weeks before. He asked for a second meeting with Kennedy-Purvis, a conscientious man he felt would listen. The Vice-Admiral had a lot on his own plate, not least increasing U-boat activity close to the Bermuda archipelago. There was a delay before he invited Burney in. The BNLO produced a copy of his Memorandum to Max Horton asking for experienced replacements; and he drew Sir Charles's attention to the end of his liaison report of 16 January:

I would like to repeat my request for reliefs for the two
original liaison ratings; and I would like to express the hope
again that they may be rewarded for their extreme patience
and exemplary loyalty with more responsible appointments.

Kennedy-Purvis made little comment. Perhaps encouraging
noises from an admiral to a sub-lieutenant when he had no
power to act in the matter was diplomatic. Even an assurance
he would take it up with the Admiralty might have helped
Burney's distressed frame of mind.

A day or two later, Roger kept his promise to show Mary
Ridgway over *Surcouf*, but it was not the cheerful Roger who
had biked around the island days earlier. He took her up to the
bridge, introduced her to Captain Blaison. He showed her the
hangar where the spotter plane should have been, the wireless
room, the wardroom. According to an interview she gave half
a century later to the author James Rusbridger:

> He was the saddest man I ever met and longed to get off
> *Surcouf*. He told me the crew were absolute stinkers and he
> was scared stiff. When we said our last goodbye, he said,
> 'When we sail, I'll never come back. They will throw me
> overboard.' It was like shaking hands with a man already
> standing on the edge of his grave.[4]

It is always difficult to be sure that such detailed memories
recounted so long after the event are reliable. I have seen too
many anecdotes involving similar words from other sources,
and myths beget myths, but there is no question in my mind
that Roger Burney felt he had let down Warner and Gough,
and he was being let down by the inaction of the Admiralty,
especially his Flag Officer.

On Tuesday, 10 February 1942, Roger wrote another liaison
report to Max Horton:

In the course of conversation on submarine warfare the captain, who claims considerable submarine experience, made the following remark to me: 'I often wonder how it is possible to identify a friendly ship from a hostile ship simply by seeing her through a periscope lens.' Since coming out of dry dock she has carried out one crash dive only and that for the benefit of her refit supervisors. Throughout the latest voyage to Bermuda, she did not even so much as make a trim dive, although the captain has told me that in the event of meeting a U-boat... he would dive immediately. Just before leaving Halifax, I discovered that of our sixteen listening microphones [hydrophones], only seven were showing any signs of life and even these could not be relied upon.

Roger Burney's official reports were frank. No funk. Factual. Objective. What he was describing were the weaknesses of a vessel on which his life depended.

On Eternal Patrol

Despite C-in-C A&WI's pleasant and cooperative attitude towards Burney, he was preoccupied. Since the beginning of January, U-boats heading for the eastern seaboard of America had caused a full-scale alert and, days before *Surcouf* reached Bermuda, the Admiralty had issued orders that all British and Allied shipping under HMS *Malabar*'s control from the Caribbean and the Gulf of Mexico headed north for Halifax was to be routed to either side, but not within one hundred miles of Bermuda. Diverting shipping in the area was complicated: it could not be made from London due to the time delay in receiving intelligence on U-boat movements and sending convoy information to Bermuda. Responsibility had been devolved to Admiral Kennedy-Purvis to divert shipping as far south as Jamaica. Possibly this complex situation, added to the normal tasks of keeping *Malabar*'s complement of warships on patrol and supplied with intelligence, may account for the fact that C-in-C A&WI had issued *Surcouf* with orders to sail on 12 February before he finally addressed himself to BNLO Burney's anxieties:

MOST SECRET 977.

From C in C America and West Indies

Addressed Admiralty Repeated FOS [Max Horton]

YOUR 2121A/25 DECEMBER, NOT TO FOS, DIRECTED THAT ON ARRIVAL IN TAHITI SURCOUF WOULD COME UNDER COMMAND OF C IN C EASTERN FLEET. IT IS PRESUMED THAT, AS A RESULT OF THE RECENT REORGANISATION OF COMMANDS, THIS NO LONGER APPLIES AND IT IS CONSIDERED MOST DESIRABLE THAT SURCOUF SHOULD BE QUITE CLEAR UNDER WHOSE ORDERS SHE IS TO BE...

(2) THE QUESTION OF THE BNLO AND RATINGS ALSO CAUSES ME CONCERN AND IT IS SUGGESTED THAT IF AS SEEMS LIKELY SURCOUF IS TO BE UNDER US ORDERS, BRITISH LIAISON PERSONNEL SHOULD BE RELIEVED BY US PERSONNEL.

IF SURCOUF IS TO BE EMPLOYED ON LOCAL DEFENCE OF FREE FRENCH TERRITORY, CONSIDER LIAISON PERSONNEL BE WITHDRAWN WITHOUT RELIEF. LIAISON PERSONNEL HAVE CARRIED OUT A VERY DIFFICULT AND MOST DISHEARTENING TASK IN A MOST PRAISEWORTHY MANNER AND ARE DESERVING OF CONSIDERATION. TRANSMITTED 16.02/12 FEBRUARY.

[FFS *Surcouf* had departed from Ireland island an hour earlier.]

If Admiral Horton took two weeks to read his liaison officers' reports, this missive from Kennedy-Purvis addressed directly to the First Sea Lord, Sir Dudley Pound, and twenty other individuals, only copied to Horton, put a firework under him. Horton instantly responded, not to Kennedy-Purvis, who was not even copied in, but to the First Sea Lord *et al*:

ENTIRELY AGREE WITH PROPOSAL THAT BRITISH
LIAISON PERSONNEL BE WITHDRAWN AND SUGGEST THIS
BEING DONE AT BERMUDA OR PANAMA.

It was accepted: the British Naval Liaison team, Roger
Burney, Harold Warner, Bernard Gough would not be needed
and should be taken off at the first opportunity. But the
messages that would determine their future, their fate, were
all too late.

Surcouf laboured south on her designated route, heading
for Tahiti via Panama Canal under direction from C-in-C
A&WI:

ROUTE TO COLON [Panama] VIA CAICOS PASSAGE AND
WINDWARD PASSAGE. ADJUST SPEED TO ARRIVE COLON
AT 08.00R ON 19TH FEBRUARY.
    ROUTE TO TAHITI VIA GREAT CIRCLE, SUBJECT TO
MODIFICATIONS DESIRED BY OPNAV.
EXPECTED ARRIVAL TIME TAHITI TO BE REPORTED TO
ALL ADDRESSES.
    OPNAV [Office of Chief of US Naval Operations]
REQUESTED TO ARRANGE FOR BOMBING RESTRICTIONS
ON ROUTE, AND FOR FUEL AT BALBAO.

From Bermuda to the Port of Cristóbal in Colón, at the
mouth of the Panama Canal is a voyage of 1,660 miles which
it was calculated *Surcouf* would cover in 160 hours, arriving
between eight and nine o'clock in the morning at Cristóbal
Docks in the Bay of Colón. Bombing restrictions were imposed
along the route and the detail relayed through OPNAV to all
services: an exclusion zone of fifteen miles either side of the
giant submarine cruiser and 120 miles ahead and astern for
her protection.

Day after day, *Surcouf* reported her position to HMS
Malabar. At noon on 16 February, she crossed the sixty-
fifth meridian, now heading south-west towards the Caicos

Passage where she reported her position. Next, she navigated the Windward Passage between Cuba and Haiti into the Caribbean, where there were some reports of U-boat activity.

At noon on 18 February, *Surcouf* sent her regular message to HMS *Malabar*, reporting that she was now south-west of Jamaica on a course of 210° at a speed of ten knots. Four hours later, the Admiralty Diary[5] plotted her position as 11°N 79°W; that suggests that she was on course, and slightly behind her appointed schedule to cover the remaining 122 nautical miles into the Bay of Colón, the mouth of the Panama Canal. She was expected next morning. Instead... she vanished.

CHAPTER 7

LOST! WHAT SANK THE *SURCOUF*?

'THE SURCOUF CONSPIRACY', 'MYSTERIOUS DISAPPEARANCE OF GIANT SUBMARINE', 'WHO SANK SURCOUF?' 'DID THE ALLIES SINK THE SURCOUF?' – this last a headline from the *Sunday Times* in 1984. These questions, writ large, have been central to my search for what happened to that brilliant young man, Roger Burney, like so many of his generation, lost to war, lost to the world. In the eighty years since the extraordinary vast French submarine disappeared, there have been many books in many languages, hundreds of articles, and several films. Conspiracy theorists continue to feed off each other to this day. Many people claimed to have solved the mystery. After two years of research, I have proved what did NOT sink *Surcouf*, and probably what did, though due to lack of access to a crucial archive in the USA, this is still not proof positive.

Surcouf 'Not Arrived'

Admiral Kennedy-Purvis was about to leave his office for lunch on 19 February, when a telegram arrived from the British Consular Shipping Adviser in Colón:

FRENCH CRUISER-SUB SURCOUF NOT REPETITION NOT ARRIVED.[1]

The Admiralty's MOST SECRET reply to Kennedy-Purvis came that same afternoon, a week after he had requested that the liaison team aboard *Surcouf* should be relieved:

THE WHOLE QUESTION OF LIAISON PERSONNEL IN FREE FRENCH VESSELS OPERATING IN THE PACIFIC IS AT PRESENT UNDER DISCUSSION WITH DE GAULLE.
DECISION CANNOT BE MADE IN TIME TO PERMIT RELIEF OF BRITISH PERSONNEL IN SURCOUF DURING STAY IN CANAL ZONE.

By seven o'clock the previous evening, the brief Caribbean twilight had given way to utter darkness, the waxing moon obscured by thick cloud. Sea conditions in the approaches to the Panama Canal were deteriorating rapidly, making *Surcouf*'s progress slower and more laboured. Based on her previous radioed coordinates, the Admiralty calculated that her position would be further south along the line of longitude 79°W. *Surcouf*, in common with all submarines of that era, spent most of her time on the surface, even at night; diving was a last resort and depended on her electric motors and her doubtful batteries. *Surcouf* had form though: in heavy seas she would wallow, and her heavy superstructure would cause her to lurch from port to starboard and back again. A factor often overlooked was that French naval vessels made a point of never entering foreign ports during the hours of darkness so, after sending her midday coordinates, Captain Louis Blaison would have reduced speed to eight or nine knots to reach the docks at Cristobál no earlier than eight o'clock the following morning.

The darkness and the heavy running seas were beginning to impede the progress of a convoy that had left the Bay of Colón at 16.40 that afternoon, escorted by two US destroyers;

this was heading in the opposite direction to *Surcouf*, bound for the Windward Passage. America's war was eleven weeks old but already Allied merchant vessels in the Caribbean had been sunk by U-Boats. Sailing at night, all exterior lights had to be extinguished, and radio silence observed. One cargo vessel, *Thompson Lykes*, on charter to the US Army, received a cypher message at nine o'clock to detach from the convoy and set course instead for Cienfuegos, in Cuba. Rather than pass east of Jamaica, she would pass to the west, among the Cayman Islands. The master, Henry Johnston, Junior Third Mate Andrew Thompson, and one or two others, were seasoned seamen. By contrast, the crew were mostly conscripts from the US Army 58th Coast Artillery Transport Detachment; many had never been to sea before.

Collision? The Wrongly Blamed *Thompson Lykes* Cargo Vessel

An hour and a half later, *Thompson Lykes* struck something forcibly. Crew rushed forward to look over the side. Some were convinced they saw the bow of a vessel rear up before sinking into the deep. Others described a cigar shaped object sliding along the side of the *Thompson Lykes*. Some believed they'd sunk a U-boat. There was a sudden underwater explosion and flames shot into the air. The *Thompson Lykes* continued for some time in the heavy seas before circling back to the point of collision (Lat 10°28.05'N: Long 79°02'W), searching for survivors or wreckage. She broke radio silence to report the incident and stayed in the area for some hours, where she was joined by two US destroyers. All that was discovered was a quantity of diesel oil, but that, it was later concluded, was from one of *Thompson Lykes*'s own fuel tanks, ruptured in the accident. The damage was slight enough for her to return to Cristobál Docks without assistance. The Consular Shipping Advisor included this news at the end of his telegram to the Admiralty, adding:

PRELIMINARY ENQUIRIES POINT TO LIKELIHOOD OF
SUNKEN VESSEL BEING AN ARMED LAUNCH.

And he had more to say:

USA 15TH NAVAL DISTRICT APPARENTLY NOT INFORMED
OF ROUTE OR SPEED OF FRENCH CRUISER-SUB SURCOUF
FROM WHICH TO ESTIMATE POSITION.[2]

So there, in one message, is the origin of the presumption
of a collision between a US Army cargo ship and the
disappearance of *Surcouf*, 127 Frenchmen, Lieutenant Roger
Burney RNVR and his two Royal Navy liaison ratings.

In the absence of accurate and trustworthy information,
tragedies happen; rumours thrive.

On 21 February, the Consular Shipping Advisor in Colón sent
a second report to the Admiralty: local US Naval Intelligence
had given him access to statements from two military gunners
who had been on watch on the cargo ship *Thompson Lykes*
at the time of the collision: 'Consider statements either taken
badly through inexperience or considerably condensed and
important evidence either not solicited or not recorded.' He
used 'allegedly' several times.

On 25 February, surveyors from the American Bureau of
Shipping examined the *Thompson Lykes* and lodged a report
noting that the only damage involved several forward frames
and plates that had been distorted and a bottom fuel tank
holed. Yet, on 11 March, a hastily convened board of inquiry
organised by the US Coastguard in New Orleans appeared
to point to the *Thompson Lykes* having accidentally rammed
and sunk a huge submarine? Surely not. Surely *Surcouf* was
built of sterner stuff? Assuming the two vessels had been in
position to collide that night, *Surcouf*'s hull was constructed
of steel weighing 50kg per square metre and 22cms thick;
against the cargo boat's hull made of thinner steel weighing
6kg per square metre. Indeed, in the eighty years since, naval

researchers have pointed out that *Surcouf* had been carrying fifty-four tonnes of munitions: the explosion heard at the point of collision that night was minor by comparison with what would have happened had that detonated. In any case, where was *Thompson Lykes* in relation to *Surcouf* at half-past ten that stormy night? The late Claude Huan, a submariner, a distinguished naval historian, and Fellow of the French Naval Academy, spent several years delving into archives to discover the answer to that question. At worst, he calculated, *Surcouf* could have been fifty-five nautical miles from the scene of the collision: at best, he believed she would have been further back along Longitude 79°W, behind schedule and potentially eighty-five nautical miles away, leaving some 112 to 120 nautical miles to cover in ten hours.

It was all too convenient to accept the findings of that three-day Board of Inquiry – unimpressively, they had thought they were dealing with an accident in the Gulf of Mexico. It was conducted without representatives from either the US Navy or the Panama Canal Company. The Free French were not invited to attend, nor indeed were aware of the inquiry until much later. The Admiralty sent an observer, Commander Robert Cecil Somers Garwood, then on the staff of the British Admiralty Repair Mission (Submarines) in Washington. He was invited to submit questions. He did not. The official report described the collision between *Thompson Lykes* and 'Vessel A – an unidentified vessel of unknown nationality, resulting in the total loss of the vessel and her crew'. Garwood's submission of the Board's findings to his masters at the Admiralty was accompanied by his own surprising and misleading conclusion – 'It is evident that it was the bridge of the *Surcouf* that had been struck and the submarine sunk by the transport...' He assumed the authorities responsible for each vessel had neglected to inform the other of the precise routes being followed. Indeed, many years later, it was discovered that two photographs of considerable damage to the bow of the *Thompson Lykes* attached to the filed report of the inquiry referred, not to the incident on 18/19 February 1942 at all, but to a grounding suffered by the vessel near Lewes, Delaware, ten months later, on 5 December 1942.[3]

The Search for Wreckage

To return to the events of February 1942. At Coco Solo, the US submarine base at the Caribbean end of the Panama Canal, considerable concern was expressed for the missing Free French submarine, and after two weeks Charlie Peters, a salvage diver with the US Navy Construction Battalion, got to hear talk that she had been bombed by the US Army Air Corps. He had no idea whether it had been an accident, or deliberate. Three years later, after demob, Peters was taken on as an engineer to maintain a Pan-Am radio beacon on San Blas Point, some eighty miles east along the coast from Colón Bay. He became curious about an informal cemetery occupying part of the hillside, and the local Guna Indians told him that ships were sometimes wrecked off the extensive San Blas archipelago and drowned foreigners would wash ashore. They would give the dead respect by burying them. Some Guna men described how early in the war, they had heard bombing out at sea one morning; later, uniformed bodies began drifting in on the tide to San Blas Point. Charlie Peters urged them to tell him everything. And what they remembered fitted the description of a large stricken submarine drifting helplessly in the current, until it sank off Isla Chichime, in the San Blas Archipelago. Peters seemed convinced it was *Surcouf*. Did he don his diving gear and go have a look?

The late James Rusbridger flew to Panama to investigate the end of *Surcouf* in 1990, but he did not get to speak to Charles Peters: he had died aged sixty-two in September 1982 and is buried in Corozál American Veterans' Cemetery on the fringe of Panama City. Rusbridger did however encounter John Mann, who had arrived in San Blas in the 1950s and became acquainted with Peters. Mann said he had a feeling that Peters had dived on the sunken submarine, knew what it was. That is all. There is authenticity in the story. *Surcouf*, if indeed it is her, would be lying at about latitude 9°35'N: longitude 78°53'W in relatively shallow waters, by now well colonised by corals and seaweeds and sea creatures. If that is *Surcouf* lying there, who carried out the bombing?

Bombing? Strong Likelihood of 'Friendly Fire' by the American Air Force

In the run-up to America's participation in the war, there had been much debate about how best to defend the Canal, indeed the whole of the Caribbean, strategically significant because of the Venezuelan oilfields to the east and the three largest oil refineries in the world: all crucial to the Allied war effort. The United States War Department had set up the Caribbean Defence Command (CDC) in 1941, a prototype combined command (Army, Navy and Air Force) to protect the Panama Canal and its access points, and deal with Axis threats throughout the region. The first year was hectic, creating a complex new organisation and figuring out the chains of command. By early 1942, U-boat activity was the greatest concern; heavy bomber squadrons were reinforced specifically for anti-submarine operations.

Notably, by 15 February 1942, four U-boats (U-67, U-156, U-161 and U-502) were in the eastern Caribbean and suddenly launched a series of attacks on shipping and vital installations from Aruba and Venezuela to St Lucia and Trinidad. Several Italian submarines joined in. Seventeen Allied tankers were sunk in two days and another eight ships were seriously damaged. The assault took the Allies by surprise. The U-502 in particular was a new breed of German submarine designed for long-range missions: less than a year old, she was fast – eighteen knots on the surface and, significantly, she was seventy-seven metres long and ten metres high, so large, though not quite on the scale of the 110m-long *Surcouf*.

James Rusbridger managed, with the help of researchers at the USAF archives at Maxwell Air Force Base in Alabama, to track down the logbook of the 3rd Bombardment (Heavy) Squadron containing sufficient factual detail to convince him that the answer was a matter of record.

On the evening of 18 February, before dusk, US Army bombers had been scrambled to attack a submarine observed by a civilian pilot off the coast a short distance from the Pacific end of the Panama Canal. At 7.13 on the morning of 19 February, the alarm sounded again at the US (Army Air Corps) 6th Bomber Group headquarters at Albrook Field, near the Pacific terminus of the Canal: Col. Henry Keppler Mooney was Commanding Officer. Rio Hato, sixty-five miles away, where two heavy bomber squadrons (6th and 3rd) were stationed, received a briefing from Mooney concerning a large submarine reported by an airline pilot flying over the Caribbean. He identified it in section R-13 (aviation speak), some fifty nautical miles from the Colón end of the Canal. At that moment *Surcouf* should have been visible thirty to fifty nautical miles from the Bay of Colón, according to her expected speed. Three bomber pilots, Lt Harold Staley, Lt John Pryor, and Lt Terry took off at 8am and flew north across the isthmus and out over the sea to the R-13 location. Staley arrived above a 'very large' submarine and dropped his entire bomb load on her; Pryor reached the location shortly afterwards and did likewise. Both claimed to have hit the vessel; Staley circled the area for ten minutes watching the submarine gradually submerge. By the time Lt Terry reached the location he could find nothing. The three aircraft had returned to Rio Hato by 9.35. They reported dropping 800 pounds of bombs on the submarine; their assumption was that it was German. Lt Wood relayed the result of their attack by teletype message at 11.47 to Colonel Mooney, at Albrook Field. The information was entered in the squadron logbook seen by James Rusbridger, confirmed by Harold Staley whom Rusbridger interviewed. Colonel Mooney's pre-sortie briefing had said nothing of an Allied submarine in the area.

Unfortunately, even the extremely helpful current archivists at Maxwell Air Force Base have not been able to identify that logbook, as the archives were closed for much of the pandemic period. While most Second World War records of the Army Air Corps have been digitised, they say logbooks were not, therefore the detail in the paragraph above draws in part on Rusbridger's researches in the late 1980s.

Despite her impressive specification, *Surcouf* suffered a major flaw: her trim was difficult to adjust during a dive, and she took over two minutes to dive to a depth of 12m (39ft), making her extremely vulnerable to aircraft attack. That fits the picture reported by pilots Staley, Pryor, and Terry. Whether the attack was sufficient to destroy *Surcouf* is impossible to say, but on previous performance her dive to avoid attack would have been slow, especially on her one electric engine; some of her hatches would have blown, seawater pouring in, though her watertight compartments should have limited that. One hundred and thirty men with no means of escape. Helpless.[5]

The Mourning for Roger Burney

Mrs W E Young,
Oakfield,
Hay

9 March 1942

Madam,

I am commanded by My Lords Commissioners of the Admiralty to inform you that they have learned, with great regret, that the vessel in which your son, Temporary Sub-Lieutenant Roger John Gilbert Burney RNVR, was serving has been lost, and your son has accordingly been reported missing and is presumed to have lost his life on active service on 19th February 1942...

In order that information be denied to the enemy, it is not at present possible to publish details of the circumstances in which your son lost his life and I am to ask, therefore, that you will refrain from disclosing it to those who do not already know the name of your son's ship, and to regard as confidential anything beyond the fact of your son's death on active service until an official announcement is made.

I am, Madam, your obedient servant,

H V MARKHAM

This devastating and conspiratorial news in its plain brown envelope came to Oakfield on 11 March, as Roger's sister Joan was preparing to post her effusive thank you letter to him after receiving her delayed Christmas stockings and radio valves. She placed the letter in her desk drawer and, sharing a long list of addresses with her mother Dorothy, began to relay their dreadful loss to all Roger's friends and associates.

By return, mailbags full of love, disbelief, and condolence began to arrive, some penned so rapidly that the authors would write again when they had shaken off the shock. Many of the Fellows of Peterhouse wrote, including the Dean. Brian Wormald, Roger's tutor, was so grieved his first letter was a 'scraping' that he wrote twice more: 'Roger meant a very great deal to me indeed and I have been desolated by his loss.' Six months later, he wrote 'He was such a charmer, and full of promise. We have lost 1 in 6 of his generation at the college.' Peterhouse also forwarded a letter addressed to Roger from George Washington University, offering him a place to pursue his studies after the war. Barbara Evans, wife of the head of Picton House in Roger's time, wrote from Wellington College: 'I have always dreaded this. Roger never gave me the feeling he would survive, and I prayed for him every night. There was always something ethereal and other-worldly about him. Of late he became the dear old affectionate Roger of the Picton, and I felt towards him the warm affection, deep love I would say, that I gave for my own boys. We went through so much together that the bond was very strong.'

In Amityville NY, the Mayer family became aware of Roger's loss when Elizabeth's last letter, posted in early April, came back stamped RETURN TO SENDER – SHIP OVERDUE

TOP SECRET: Loss of *Surcouf* Denied

28 March 1942: Telegram from the Under Secretary of State for Foreign Affairs in Washington to Viscount Halifax at the Foreign Office:

> HAVE DENIED CATEGORICALLY THE NEWS OF THE LOSS OF SURCOUF. ABSOLUTELY ESSENTIAL THAT NOTHING SHOULD BE PUBLISHED ON THAT MATTER.

The disappearance of FFS *Surcouf* was not readily shut down. The Free French had finally acquired their own copy of the US Board of Inquiry Report and were asking questions.

BBC: LONDON CALLING, April 18, 1942:

> The giant submarine *Surcouf*, the largest in the world, 'is considerably overdue and must be considered lost', Free French headquarters announced today. There was no indication of where the vessel went down, when it happened, or whether it was the result of enemy action or an accident.

Meetings were frequent between the US Naval authorities and M (Military Intelligence) Branch: more papers were gathered. By October, meetings of M Branch were still preoccupied with the fallout of the loss of *Surcouf*. By then, the Americans were willing to provide the Free French with a copy of 'the general warning broadcast to US ships in the zone concerned. Although it cannot be stated categorically that *Thompson Lykes* received this warning, she should have done so, assuming that normal procedure had been followed.' Admiral Geoffrey Dickens, Principal Naval Liaison Officer to the Free French, was to be the go-between, the Americans being anxious not to further antagonise de Gaulle and his new admiral. One thing they were not to receive, according to the minutes of M Branch on 2 October: 'report of BNLO *Surcouf* not to be supplied.'

General de Gaulle never took the matter up with Roosevelt. He had too much to lose. But it is telling that when the two eventually met in Washington in July 1944, de Gaulle presented the president with a working model of *Surcouf*: it could fire its guns, launch torpedoes, and submerge.

In 1947, Captain Louis Blaison and his First Officer were each awarded a posthumous Croix de Guerre avec Palme for their part in rallying the islands of St Pierre and Miquelon.

In 1945, Captain Paul Ortoli was made a Companion of Liberation, and in 1960 was an admiral.

In 1951, a war memorial to *Surcouf* and her crew was unveiled in Cherbourg harbour. An invitation for Roger's mother to attend was withheld by the Admiralty. She was shocked to receive the invitation after the event and to realise for the first time that two other Royal Navy men also lost their lives on *Surcouf*.

Surcouf was awarded the Resistance Medal with Rosette.

Ultimately, the French accepted that the pride of their Navy had been lost to 'friendly fire'. As well they might: twenty months later, the US submarine *Dorado* vanished without trace in the approaches to Colón Bay, en route to Panama and the Pacific. A US Navy Board of Inquiry accepted that she had been depth-charged in error by a Navy seaplane operating out of the Guantanamo base in Cuba.[6]

Do Not Disturb

Dorothy Burney had a feeling that one day Roger would come home, just as Christopher had. Life would resume. When Christopher and Joan brought their families to stay at Oakfield, one small child or other would occupy Roger's room, Roger's bed. Everything was as he left it, clothes in the wardrobe, papers in his desk, his beloved violin, his books, paintings, finished or unfinished. Please, Dorothy would beg, don't disturb anything.

Is it fanciful to think that Roger was one of those who washed up on the shore of San Blas Point to be laid reverently in earth by the Guna? The tribe knew nothing of the men they buried save that they came from the sea following a bombing. As the years pass, we may attempt to breathe life into men who, if we are lucky and can follow their traces, rise from the dead to become known to us. Roger Burney's death was a dreadful tragedy. A remarkably gifted and peace-loving young man, he signed up out of conscience. He was consigned to a doomed submarine, technically unfit for purpose, crewed by inexperienced men with divided loyalties. Duty done, he and his team were about to be relieved; his killing with 129 others was a massive blunder. His family was denied any knowledge of the circumstances of his death, suffering years of a kind of grieving mingled with hopeless hope.

Significantly, twenty years on, Benjamin Britten dedicated his profoundly anti-war *War Requiem* to Roger Burney, and to three other friends who enlisted – two did not survive the war, the third killed himself soon after.[7] Listen… understand the sacrifice and waste.

NOTES

WHEN I SET out to discover Roger Burney, I was not aware of any great trove of papers. The family is now scattered and have lived questioning – in some cases died disappointed – without discovering the truth about his death. I am all the more grateful to Juliette Paton, Christopher's daughter, who put up with us both for days, answering questions, pulling out papers, letters, and albums of photographs; to Professor Peter Burney who supplied Julia's memoir, and a number of articles and books relating to the mysterious disappearance of *Surcouf*; to James Munro Mackenzie, who married Joan's daughter Lucy, therefore a nephew by marriage, for his memories of Christopher and for producing a leather briefcase containing some sketchbooks and albums of Joan's, a printed First World War history of Colonel Arthur E C Burney, the father, but also, fundamental to my research, a large envelope of correspondence between Claude Huan, the French naval historian, and his researcher in the USA, relating to *Surcouf*, and a thinner, but important sheaf of correspondence between James Rusbridger and Joan. Most of all, my thanks to Andrew Adams and his wife Val. Andrew died, sadly, while we were preparing this book so he will never know how much their help mattered in resurrecting Uncle Roger. Andrew was born after Roger was lost. What he had were the family papers, handed down from Dorothy, his grandmother, to Joan, his mother. These remain with the Adams family; treasure trove in two coffers and a bureau. Roger's often detailed letters to his family were there and they more than anything revealed his thoughts and character. Interestingly, the heart-warming concern for Roger's wellbeing is revealed in correspondence between Wellington College and his mother Dorothy. There is also frank and sympathetic correspondence between Dorothy and Dr Margaret Posthuma, the psychiatrist who took Roger in hand for some months in 1937.

In places I have used letters, including descriptions drawn from Roger's friends' letters, as sources for scenes from his life. Docu-drama of a low-key kind.

To understand the detail of Roger's life and activities while he was at Wellington College, I thank the College archivist, Caroline Jones, for her assistance in giving me digital access during the time of pandemic.

I am indebted to Dr Nick Clark, Curator of the Britten and Pears archive at The Red House, Aldeburgh, for his patient help in directing me to a small cache of Roger's letters and letters from Elizabeth Mayer mentioning Roger.

Dr Roger Lovatt, the College Archivist at Peterhouse, Cambridge, was helpful in producing Roger's file, including correspondence between his tutors at Wellington College and at Peterhouse. This also yielded a 'narrow' family tree relating to his naval antecedents.

For the more extensive family history, photographs of their time at The Weir, and family tree, we offer our gratitude to Cynthia Comyn of the London College of Heralds, the cousin of Roger and Christopher.

Far beyond the scope of this book, for anyone with a deeper interest in the Burneys in the eighteenth and nineteenth centuries, there is an extraordinarily detailed family tree online at ORCA, Cardiff University.

Chapter 1: The Making of a Pacifist

1   Letter from R G Evans in Peterhouse archive.

2   Margaret Posthuma (1876–1961) was forty-nine by the time

she qualified as an MB from Bristol University. She did her psychiatry studies in the USA before establishing her pioneering practice in Child Psychiatry in London W1 in the early 1930s.

Chapter 2: Cambridge on the Brink of War

1   Letter from Peter Godden to Roger's mother.
2   Letter, part of a small collection, to Peter Pears in Britten-Pears Archive, The Red House, Aldeburgh.

Chapter 3: The Unmaking of a Pacifist

1   Letters from Roger to Dr Burkill in Peterhouse Archive, together with handwritten naval family tree.

Chapter 4: Ordinary Seaman Burney

Roger's medical card and his naval records of skills and suitability for further training, from the Burney family archive. R J G Burney Service record from Ministry of Defence, RN Disclosure Cell, Whale Island, Portsmouth. Details about the 'stone frigates' where he trained are drawn from a variety of sources; written archive, Wikipedia (see under names such as HMS *Royal Arthur*), augmented by reference to Roger's own letters; and from www.naval-history.net.

Chapter 5: *Surcouf* – The Monster Submarine

BNLO Burney's full reports from which all extracts are drawn are in the National Archives at Kew under ADM199/829. His reports were sufficiently alarming for the Admiralty to withhold some of his penetrating analyses when forwarding them to the Foreign Office, and especially when they were eventually sent to the Free French.

1   Gough and Warner's Service records; letters from Harold's son, Stanley Warner to Joan Adams. Additional information from Bernard Gough's son Glyn, on *memorial-national-des-marins.fr*.

For all of Roger's visits and encounters in New York, I have relied on his letters in the family archive; letters from the Britten-Pears and Mayer archive at the Red House, Aldeburgh. Additional information of Britten and Pears' life and work in 1941–42 came from Paul Kildea's biography, *Benjamin Britten: A Life in the Twentieth Century*. My grateful thanks to Dr Muki Wachstein Fairchild, a granddaughter of Elizabeth and William Mayer, who supplied the guestbook and calendar entries giving dates when Roger Burney stayed at Amityville, and outlining certain social events. For a description of 7 Middagh Street, Brooklyn, I have relied on *February House*, Sherrill Tippens, Simon & Schuster (2006).

2   National Archives at Kew FO 371 – on relations with Free French naval personnel, 27 January 1941, Commander G K Collett:

On 1st July 1940 there was nothing. Since then, all volunteers have been accepted who stated that they wished to fight for a Free France. Some volunteered purely for their own ends and in no way from a patriotic standpoint. The officers were those who volunteered, and no hand picking was possible. Apart from isolated cases the morale and discipline at the outset was of a high order.

The time taken to man the ships and put them into a state compatible with British fighting standards was necessarily long, and these extensive periods of enforced idleness began to tell on the morale of the men who wanted nothing more than to get to grips with the enemy...

Now that the Allied Forces Act is about to come into force, and in view of the prospects of active operations for the majority of FF ships, it is felt that the morale and discipline of the FFN[avy] will improve again, and this force will prove to be a valuable fighting unit.

3   National Archives, Kew, CAB 80/32. Memoranda Nos. 681–762, Chiefs of Staff 419th meeting held on Friday, 12 December 1941, at 3.30 pm.

4   *Navigating the Rapids, 1918–1971: From the Papers of Adolf A Berle*, Beatrice Bishop Berle, Travis Beal Jacobs (eds.). New York: Harcourt Brace Jovanovich (1973).

5 Based on an interview given by Lawrence Stannard in his Kent home to James Rusbridger, June 1990.

Chapter 6: The Mysterious Disappearance of FFS *Surcouf*

1 Copy of Harold Warner's letter to his wife, forwarded to Joan Adams by his son in 1984. Burney family papers.

2 BNLO Burney's penultimate report despatched on 16 January 1942 was stamped 'Admiral Submarines' two weeks later.

3 Pay off: meaning to scrap, take out of service.

4 Quoted by James Rusbridger in *Who Sank Surcouf?: The Truth about the Disappearance of the Pride of the French Navy*, Ebury Press, June 1991.

5 National Archives, Kew, ADM1/11348 War Diary. Also in BAD 401/42 in documents dated 18 May 1942.

Chapter 7: Lost! What Sank the *Surcouf*?

1 National Archives, Kew, ADM 199/829, p. 42, and further pages; also ADM 199/1858. Additional information in the Marine Archives, Vincennes, Paris.

2 National Archives, Kew; ADM 199/829, p. 44, from the British Admiralty delegation Washington to C-in-C A&WI, cc Admiralty and CSA Colón. 'I have seen copies of COMINCH's signal 1358 to Commander 15th [Naval District, Panama] in which he was informed of French Cruiser Sub *Surcouf*'s route, expected time of arrival and bombing restrictions.'

3 This was corroborated by a discussion in March 1996 of those photographs between the late Claude Huan and Commander David Brown, Head of the Naval Historical Branch at the Ministry of Defence in London. Brown concluded that:
   a) The bow is 'twisted' from port to starboard.
   b) The bow shows evidence of an earlier repair on starboard.
   c) The double bottom on the port side has a big hole.
   d) The bow has no streaking – usual after a ramming.
Commander Brown said, 'The damage is ridiculous and certainly not as a result of ramming *Surcouf*.'

4   In Rusbridger's book, *Who Sank Surcouf...*

5/6 Another submarine disappeared in the same location on 12 October 1943. USS *Dorado* was on her way from New London to the Coco Solo submarine base in the Bay of Colón. Lt Daniel T Felix Jr was flying a US Navy seaplane out of Guantanamo Bay, Cuba, when he spotted what he thought was a German U-Boat, attacked it and soon nothing was to be seen but bubbles and foam. Lt Felix had been aware of the safety zone around *Dorado* but had been given wrong information as to her location. A US Navy Board of Inquiry accepted that *Dorado* was destroyed by a depth charge fired by Lt Felix.

7   Benjamin Britten's *War Requiem* (1962) was dedicated to Lt Roger Burney RNVR, David Gill RN, Lt Michael Halliday RNZNVR; and to Piers Dunkerley RM.

INDEX

Also by the authors:

£9.99

Also from Y Lolfa:

£12.99

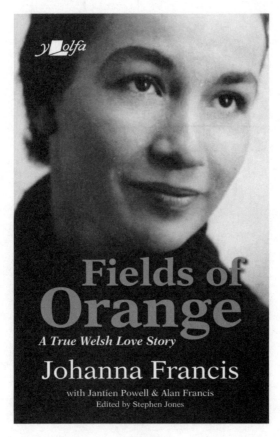

Fields of
Orange
A True Welsh Love Story

Johanna Francis

with Jantien Powell & Alan Francis
Edited by Stephen Jones

£9.99